My Samsung
Galaxy Note® 3

Craig James Johnston
Guy Hart-Davis

800 East 96th Street,
Indianapolis, Indiana 46240 USA

My Samsung Galaxy Note® 3

Copyright © 2014 by Pearson Education, Inc.

ISBN-13: 978-0-7897-5276-5
ISBN-10: 0-7897-5276-X

Library of Congress Control Number: 2013935190

Printed in the United States of America

First Printing: February 2014

Trademarks

All terms mentioned in this book that are known to be trademarks or service marks have been appropriately capitalized. Que Publishing cannot attest to the accuracy of this information. Use of a term in this book should not be regarded as affecting the validity of any trademark or service mark.

All Galaxy Note 3 images are provided by Samsung Electronics America.

Warning and Disclaimer

Special Sales

For information about buying this title in bulk quantities, or for special sales opportunities (which may include electronic versions; custom cover designs; and content particular to your business, training goals, marketing focus, or branding interests), please contact our corporate sales department at corpsales@pearsoned.com or (800) 382-3419.

For government sales inquiries, please contact governmentsales@pearsoned.com.

For questions about sales outside the U.S., please contact international@pearsoned.com.

Editor-in-Chief
Greg Wiegand

Acquisitions Editor
Michelle Newcomb

Development/Copy Editor
Charlotte Kughen,
The Wordsmithery LLC

Managing Editor
Kristy Hart

Project Editor
Lori Lyons

Indexer
Lisa Stumpf

Proofreader
Paula Lowell

Technical Editor
Christian Kenyeres

Editorial Assistant
Cindy Teeters

Cover Designer
Mark Shirar

Compositor
Bronkella Publishing LLC

Contents at a Glance

Table of Contents

3 Browsing the Web   109

4 Email   127

About the Authors

Craig James Johnston has been involved with technology since his high school days at Glenwood High in Durban, South Africa, when his school was given some Apple][Europluses. From that moment, technology captivated him, and he has owned, supported, evangelized, and written about it.

Craig has been involved in designing and supporting large-scale enterprise networks with integrated email and directory services since 1989. He has held many different IT-related positions in his career ranging from sales support engineer to mobile architect for a 40,000-smartphone infrastructure at a large bank.

In addition to designing and supporting mobile computing environments, Craig cohosts the CrackBerry.com podcast as well as guest hosting on other podcasts, including iPhone and iPad Live podcasts. You can see Craig's previously published work in his books *Professional BlackBerry*, and many books in the *My* series, including *My BlackBerry Curve*, *My Palm Pre*, *My Note II*, *My HTC One*, *My DROID* (first and second editions), *My Motorola Atrix 4G*, *My BlackBerry PlayBook,* and *My HTC EVO 3D*.

Craig also enjoys high-horsepower, high-speed vehicles and tries very hard to keep to the speed limit while driving them.

Originally from Durban, South Africa, Craig has lived in the United Kingdom, the San Francisco Bay Area, and New Jersey, where he now lives with his wife, Karen, and a couple of cats.

Craig would love to hear from you. Feel free to contact Craig about your experiences with *My Samsung Galaxy Note 3* at http://www.CraigsBooks.info.

All comments, suggestions, and feedback are welcome, including positive and negative.

Guy Hart-Davis is the author of approximately 100 computer books, including *Kindle Fire Geekery* and *How to Do Everything: Samsung Galaxy Tab*.

Dedication

"I love deadlines. I like the whooshing sound they make as they fly by."
—Douglas Adams

Acknowledgments

We would like to express our deepest gratitude to the following people on the *My Samsung Galaxy Note 3* team who all worked extremely hard on this book:

- Michelle Newcomb, our acquisitions editor, who worked with us to give this project an edge

- Christian Kenyeres, our technical editor, who double-checked our writing to ensure the technical accuracy of this book

- Charlotte Kughen, who edited the manuscript with a light touch

- Lori Lyons, who kept the book project on schedule

- Tricia Bronkella, who combined the text and art into colorful pages.

We Want to Hear from You!

As the reader of this book, *you* are our most important critic and commentator. We value your opinion and want to know what we're doing right, what we could do better, what areas you'd like to see us publish in, and any other words of wisdom you're willing to pass our way.

We welcome your comments. You can email or write to let us know what you did or didn't like about this book—as well as what we can do to make our books better.

Please note that we cannot help you with technical problems related to the topic of this book.

When you write, please be sure to include this book's title and author as well as your name and email address. We will carefully review your comments and share them with the author and editors who worked on the book.

Email: feedback@quepublishing.com

Mail: Que Publishing
            ATTN: Reader Feedback
            800 East 96th Street
            Indianapolis, IN 46240 USA

Reader Services

Visit our website and register this book at quepublishing.com/register for convenient access to any updates, downloads, or errata that might be available for this book.

In this chapter, you become familiar with the external features of the Galaxy Note 3 and the basics of getting started with the Android operating system. Topics include the following:

→ Getting to know your Galaxy Note 3's external features

→ Getting to know your Galaxy Note 3's S Pen (Stylus)

→ Learning the fundamentals of Android 4.3 (Jelly Bean) and TouchWiz

→ Setting up your Galaxy Note 3 for the first time

→ Installing desktop synchronization software

Getting to Know Your Samsung Galaxy Note 3

Let's start by getting to know more about your Galaxy Note 3 by examing the external features, device features, and how the Android 4.3 operating system works.

In addition to Android 4.3 (Jelly Bean), this chapter covers the Samsung TouchWiz interface, which is overlaid on top of Android to adjust the way things look and function.

Your Galaxy Note 3's External Features

Becoming familiar with the external features of your Galaxy Note 3 is a good place to start because you will be using them often. This section covers some of the technical specifications of your Galaxy Note 3, including the touchscreen, camera, and S Pen. There are many versions of the Samsung Galaxy Note 3, but no matter which one you own or which wireless carrier you use to connect it, the exterior, functionality, and look and feel of the interface is exactly the same.

Front

Earpiece   Proximity sensor

Indicator light

Front camera

Light sensor

Touchscreen

Home button

Menu button

Back button

- **Proximity sensor**—Detects when you place your Galaxy Note 3 against your head to talk, which causes it to turn off the screen so that your ear doesn't inadvertently activate things on the screen.

- **Light sensor**—Adjusts the brightness of your Galaxy Note 3's screen based on the brightness of the ambient light.

- **Earpiece**—The part you hold against your ear while on a call.

- **Indicator light**—Indicates new events (such as missed calls, new Facebook messages, or new emails).

- **Front camera**—2.0-megapixel front-facing camera that you use for video chat, taking self-portraits, and even unlocking your Galaxy Note 3 using your face.

- **Touchscreen**—The Galaxy Note 3 has a 5.7" 1080×1920-pixel Full HD Super AMOLED HD (Super Active-Matrix Organic Light-Emitting Diode) screen that incorporates capacitive touch.

- **Back button**—Touch to go back one screen when using an application or menu. This is a touch-sensitive button.

- **Menu button**—Touch to see a context-aware menu of options based on the screen or app you are using.

- **Home button**—Press to go to the Home screen. The application that you are using continues to run in the background. Press and hold to see a list of recently used apps and switch between them. This is a physical button.

Back

Rear camera

Back cover removal point

Volume up/down buttons

Power button

LED camera flash

- **Volume up/down buttons**—Enables you to control the audio volume on calls and while playing audio and video.

- **Power button**—Allows you to wake up your Galaxy Note 3 by pressing once. Press and hold for one second to reveal a menu of choices. The choices enable you to put your Galaxy Note 3 into Silent mode, Airplane mode, or power it off completely.

- **Rear camera**—13-megapixel camera with autofocus that takes clear pictures close-up or far away.

- **LED (light-emitting diode) camera flash**—Helps to illuminate the surroundings when taking pictures in low light.

- **Back cover removal point**—Allows you to remove the back cover. Insert your fingernail and pull to remove the back cover. After you have removed the back cover, you can install or swap SIM cards, and insert or swap the Micro-SD memory card.

Top

3.5mm headphone jack

Noise canceling microphone

- **3.5mm headphone jack**—Plug in your Galaxy Note 3 or third-party headsets to enjoy music and talk on the phone.

- **Noise canceling microphone**—Use in conjuction with the regular microphone on phone calls to reduce background noise. This microphone is also used when you record videos.

Bottom

Microphone

MHL 2.0-compliant Micro-USB 3 port

Speaker

S Pen (Stylus)

- **MHL 2.0-compliant Micro-USB 3 port**—You can use the Micro-USB 3 port to synchronize your Galaxy Note 3 to your desktop computer and charge it, but because it is Mobile High-definition Link (MHL) compliant, you can use it to play movies on your TV via high-definition multimedia interface (HDMI) using a special cable or dock.

- **Speaker**—Produces audio when you use the speakerphone or when you play audio.

- **Microphone**—You use the microphone when you are on a call and holding your Galaxy Note 3 to your ear.

- **S Pen (Stylus)**—Pull the S Pen out of its holder to draw on the screen and interact with apps. Read more about the S Pen in the next section.

S Pen

Your Samsung Galaxy Note 3 comes with a stylus, which Samsung calls the S Pen. The S Pen is stored in the Galaxy Note 3 on the right side and you pull it out from the lower right. This section covers some of the S Pen's features and functions.

Getting to Know the S Pen

Let's take a look at the S Pen itself and learn about its features.

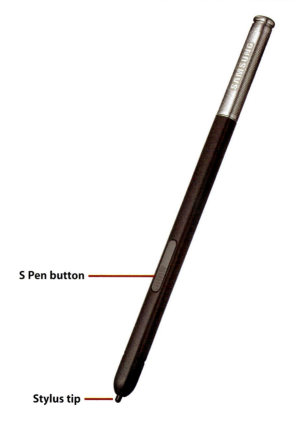

S Pen button —————

Stylus tip —————

- **Stylus tip**—The S Pen stylus tip is what makes contact with the screen as you write and draw. The stylus tip is pressure sensitive so it knows how hard or soft you are pressing. This is particularly useful for drawing as pressure translates into line thickness.

- **S Pen button**—The S Pen button adds extra functionality to the S Pen. When you press the button as you drag the pen on the screen, you can perform functions, such as moving between screens, taking screenshots, and even cutting out parts of any screen.

Air Command

When you remove your S Pen, Air Command is the first thing that pops up. Air Command gives you quick access to useful S Pen functionality.

- **Action Memo**—Write in a special note area and tell your Note 3 to take action on what you write. For example, write a phone number and tell Action Memo to dial that number.

- **Scrap Booker**—Capture a part of the screen by drawing around the area you want to capture. The captured images are saved to the Scrapbook app.

Scrap Booker   **Screen Write**   **S Finder**

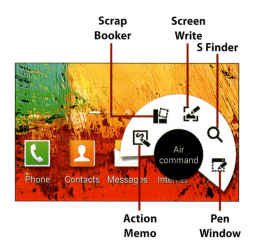

Action Memo   **Pen Window**

Write something first...   **...then touch here...**

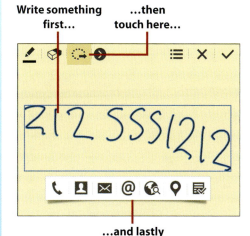

...and lastly choose an action

Draw around an area on the screen

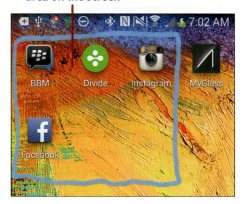

- **Screen Write**—Capture the entire screen and then write on the image of the captured screen. Your image is saved in the Gallery app in the Screenshots album.

Touch to save

Draw on the screen   Draw a box on the screen

- **S Finder**—Allows you to search your Note 3 for apps and other content, plus search the Internet.

- **Pen Window**—Allows you to draw a box of any size on the screen. You see a box with some app choices. Selecting an app launches it in a small window over whatever you are doing. You can use the app like you normally do even while it's in the small window.

Select an app to run

**Touch to make the   Touch to
app go full screen   close the app**

**App runs
in a small
window**

Air View

Air View is a feature that shows you a preview of information about an object and enables you to interact with it when you hover the S Pen or finger near the screen over an object that is Air View enabled. Make sure that Air View is turned on in Settings before you try to use it. Please refer to Chapter 2, "Customizing Your Galaxy Note 3," to see how to turn on Air View and customize how it works. This section shows you some examples of using Air View.

Hover over an album in the Gallery app

Touch a picture or video to open it

Album preview is shown

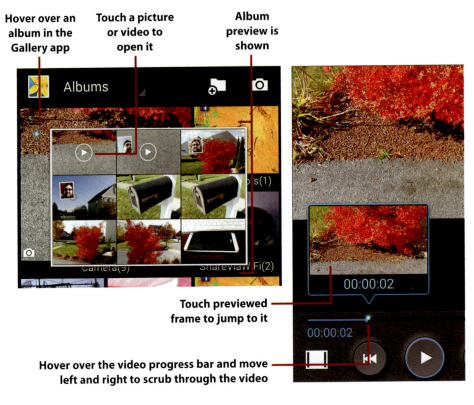

Touch previewed frame to jump to it

Hover over the video progress bar and move left and right to scrub through the video

Hover over a menu icon

Information about the menu icon is shown

It's Not All Good

Air View Is Not Always Available

Apps must be specifically written to support Air View, which means that as of the writing of this book there are not very many apps you can use with Air View. For example, although you can use Air View to preview emails in the Email app (which is written by Samsung), Air View does not work in Gmail. Air View is also a little buggy because it sometimes does not work. For example, Air View is supposed to work in the Contacts app to preview contact information, but it does not. By the time you read this book, some updates might have addressed the bugginess of Air View, and vendors like Google might have updated their apps to add support for Air View.

Gestures

While holding the S Pen button, you can draw symbols on the screen to take actions such as going back to the previous screen or bringing up the menu. Here are some examples.

Double-tap to create a new S Note

Press and hold to take a screenshot

Scrolling Using the S Pen

You can scroll up and down by hovering your S Pen at the top or bottom of an area of the screen that scrolls, such as a message list. For this gesture, you must not press the S Pen button—just hover at the top or bottom of the scroll area. You see an arrow indicating that the scrolling gesture has been recognized.

Hover to scroll up

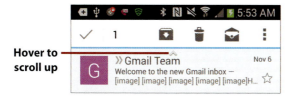

First-Time Setup

Before setting up your new Samsung Galaxy Note 3, you should have a Google account because your Galaxy Note 3 running Android is tightly integrated into Google. When you have a Google account, you can store your content in the Google cloud, including any books and music you buy or movies you rent. If you do not already have a Google account, go to https://accounts.google.com on your desktop computer and sign up for one.

1. Touch and hold the Power button until you see the animation start playing.

2. Touch to change your language if needed.

3. Touch Next.

4. Touch a Wi-Fi network to connect. If you'd rather not connect to a Wi-Fi network, touch Next and continue at step 8.

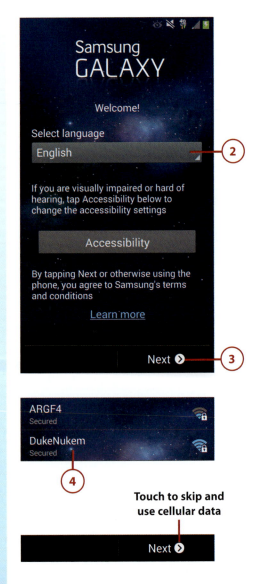

5. Enter the password for the Wi-Fi network using the onscreen keyboard.

6. Touch Connect. Your Galaxy Note 3 connects to the Wi-Fi network.

7. Touch Next.

8. Touch to sign in to your Samsung account, if you have one, or touch Skip and jump to step 17.

9. Touch to create a new Samsung account, if you don't have one, or touch Skip and jump to step 17.

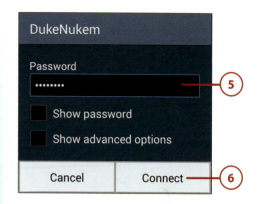

Wi-Fi networks

DukeNukem
Connected

Indicates that you are connected to the network

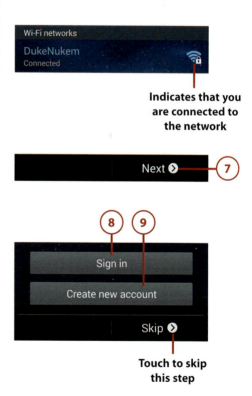

Next ➤

Touch to skip this step

>>>Go Further

DO I NEED A SAMSUNG ACCOUNT?

Android was designed to be used with a Google account. That Google account enables you access to the Google ecosystem of Android apps, music, movies, and books, plus your phone's settings are backed up to the Google cloud. If you change devices, your new device reverts to the way you had your old device set up. A Samsung account does a similar thing, but it uses the Samsung ecosystem. Technically, you don't really need a Samsung account because a Google account provides everything you need. However, Samsung uses the Samsung account to enable certain Samsung-specific features on your Galaxy Note 3 (and other Samsung Android phones and tablets). These include Group Cast and Share Shot, which both involve sharing content in a group setting.

10. Enter the email address you used for your Samsung account.

11. Enter your Samsung account password.

12. Touch Sign In.

13. Touch to enable automatically backing up your data to your Samsung account.

14. Touch to first restore data previously backed up in the Samsung cloud to your Galaxy Note 3 before continuing.

15. Touch Next.

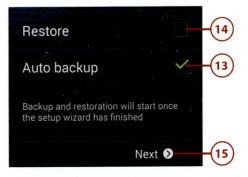

16. Touch Yes to log in to your Google account.

17. Enter your Google account email address (your Gmail address).

18. Enter your Google account password.

19. Touch to continue.

20. Check this box to restore settings previously saved in the Google cloud to your new Galaxy Note 3 before continuing.

21. Check this box to keep data on your Galaxy Note 3 backed up to the Google cloud.

22. Check this box if you are okay with Google collecting information about your geographic location at any time. Although this information is kept safe, if you are concerned about privacy rights, uncheck this box.

23. Check this box if you are okay with Google using your geographic location for Google searches and other Google services.

24. Touch to continue.

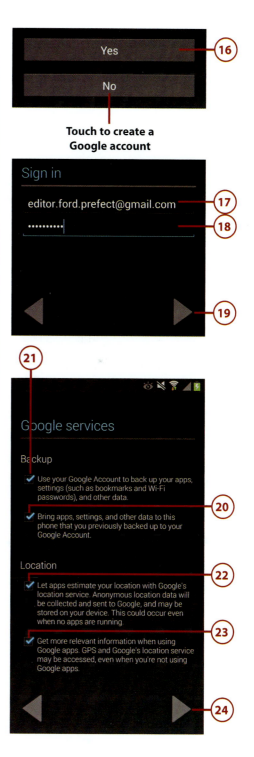

Touch to create a Google account

25. Touch to create a Dropbox account.

26. Touch to sign in to your existing Dropbox account.

27. Touch to skip using Dropbox and continue. If you choose to skip Dropbox, jump to step 31 to continue.

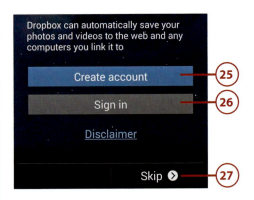

Do I Need Dropbox?

Dropbox is a company that provides cloud storage data. This means that you can use its storage to store your pictures, videos, and other files privately, and choose to share some of that content with your friends. You do not need to use Dropbox on your Galaxy Note 3. You can choose other cloud storage companies like Box.net, and even Google's cloud storage.

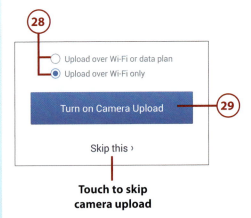

Touch to skip camera upload

28. Touch to choose whether to upload your camera photos when connected to only Wi-Fi, or anytime over Wi-Fi or cellular data.

What Is Camera Upload?

The Camera Upload feature lets your Note 3 upload all photos taken on your Note 3 camera into your Dropbox account automatically. In step 28 you choose when the photos are uploaded—when you're connected to either a Wi-Fi or cellular network, or only when you're connected to a Wi-Fi network.

29. Touch to enable Camera Upload.

30. Touch to allow Samsung access to your Dropbox files and folders.

Touch to cancel this action

31. Enter a name for your Note 3. This name is used whenever you are connecting to other devices.

32. Touch Finish.

Fundamentals of Android 4.3 and TouchWiz

Your Galaxy Note 3 is run by an operating system called Android. Android was created by Google to run on any smartphone, and your Galaxy Note 3 uses a version called Android 4.3 (or Jelly Bean). Samsung has made many changes to this version of Android by adding extra components and modifying many standard Android features. They call this customization TouchWiz.

The Lock Screen

If you haven't used your Galaxy Note 3 for a while, the screen goes blank to conserve battery power. This task explains how to interact with the Lock screen.

1. Press the Power button or Home button to wake up your Galaxy Note 3.

2. Slide your finger across the screen in any direction to unlock your Galaxy Note 3.

3. Touch the Missed Call notification and then swipe the screen to unlock and go directly to the call log.

4. Touch the Missed Text Message notification and then swipe the screen to unlock and go directly to the missed text message.

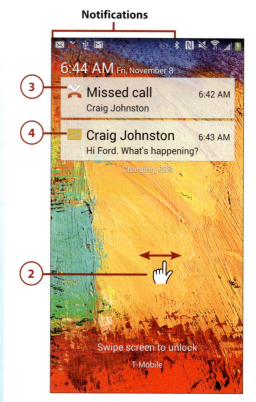

Working with Notifications and Settings on the Lock Screen

You can work with notifications and settings right on the Lock screen. If you see notifications in the Notification bar, pull down the Notification bar to view and clear them. Touching a notification takes you straight to the app that created them. Read more about the Notification bar later in this section.

Answering a Call from the Lock Screen

If your Galaxy Note 3 is locked when a call comes in, you have three choices: Drag the green icon to answer the incoming call; drag the red icon to reject the incoming call and send it straight to voice mail; or drag up from the bottom of the screen to reject the call and send a preset text message (SMS) to the caller.

Swipe down to see notifications and settings

Drag to answer   **Slide up to reject and send a text message**   **Drag to reject**

The Home Screen(s)

After you unlock your Galaxy Note 3, you are presented with the middle Home screen page. Your Galaxy Note 3 has five Home screen pages (although you can create more). The Home screen pages contain application shortcuts, a Launcher icon, Notification bar, Shortcuts, Favorites Tray, and widgets.

- **Notification bar**—The Notification bar shows information about Bluetooth, Wi-Fi, and cellular coverage, as well as the battery level and time. The Notification bar also serves as a place where apps can alert or notify you using notification icons.

- **Notification icons**—Notification icons appear in the Notification bar when an app needs to alert or notify you of something. For example, the Phone app can show the Missed Calls icon indicating that you missed a call.

- **Widgets**—Widgets are applications that run directly on the Home screens. They are specially designed to provide functionality and real-time information. An example of a widget is one that shows the current weather or provides a search capability. Widgets can be moved and sometimes resized.

- **App shortcut**—When you touch an app shortcut, the associated app launches.

- **App folders**—You can group apps together in a folder as a way to organize your apps and declutter your screen.

- **Favorites Tray**—The Favorites Tray is visible on all Home screen pages. You can drag apps to the Favorites Tray so that they are available no matter which Home screen you are looking at. Apps in the Favorites Tray can be rearranged and removed.

- **Launcher icon**—Touch to show application icons for all applications that you have installed on your Galaxy Note 3.

Work with Notifications

To interact with notifications that appear in the Notification bar, place your finger above the top of the screen and drag to pull down the Notification bar and reveal the notifications. Swipe individual notifications off the screen to the left or right to clear them one by one, or touch Clear to clear all of them at once. The Notification bar also includes Quick Settings such as the ability to turn on or off Wi-Fi or Bluetooth.

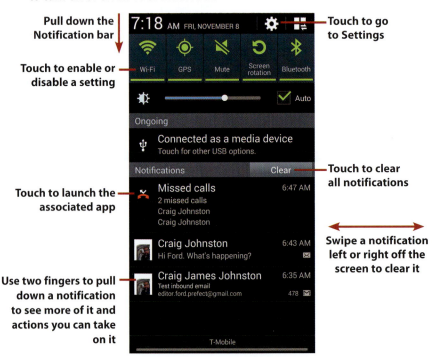

Pull down the Notification bar

Touch to go to Settings

Touch to enable or disable a setting

Touch to clear all notifications

Touch to launch the associated app

Swipe a notification left or right off the screen to clear it

Use two fingers to pull down a notification to see more of it and actions you can take on it

Create App Shortcuts

Touch the Launcher icon to see all of your apps. Touch and hold on the app you want to make a shortcut for. After the Home screens appear, drag the app shortcut to the location you want the shortcut to be on the Home screen, drag it to an App folder, or drag it left or right off the screen to move between Home screen pages. Release the icon to place it.

Touch and hold an app icon

Drag between Home screen pages

Drag to where you want it and release it

Create App Folders

To create a new App folder, touch and hold the first app shortcut you want in your folder. When the Create Folder icon appears, drag the app shortcut to that icon and release it. After you give your App folder a name, the folder displays on your Home screen. Now you can drag other app shortcuts into that folder. To open the folder, touch it to reveal the shortcuts in that folder.

Drag an app shortcut to the Create Folder icon

Give your folder a name

Drag app shortcuts to an existing folder

Creating a New Home Screen Page and Removing an App Shortcut

If you want to create a new Home screen page, touch and hold an app short-cut icon. Drag your app shortcut icon to the Create Page icon, and the short-cut is placed on a brand-new Home screen page. To remove an app shortcut icon, drag it to the Remove icon.

Drag an app shortcut icon to the Remove icon to delete it from the Home screen page

Drag an app shortcut icon to the Create Page icon to put it on a new Home screen page

Use the Touchscreen

You interact with your Galaxy Note 3 mostly by touching the screen, which is known as making gestures on the screen. You can touch, swipe, pinch, double-tap, and type.

- **Touch**—To start an application, touch its icon. Touch a menu item to select it. Touch the letters of the onscreen keyboard to type.

- **Touch and hold**—Touch and hold to interact with an object. For example, if you touch and hold a blank area of the Home screen, a menu pops up. If you touch and hold an icon, you can reposition it with your finger.

- **Drag**—Dragging always starts with a touch and hold. For example, if you touch the Notification bar, you can drag it down to read all of the notification messages.

- **Swipe or slide**—Swipe or slide the screen to scroll quickly. To swipe or slide, move your finger across the screen quickly. Be careful not to touch and hold before you swipe or you will reposition something. You can also swipe to clear notifications or close apps when viewing the recent apps.

- **Double-tap**—Double-tapping is like double-clicking a mouse on a desktop computer. Tap the screen twice in quick succession. For example, you can double-tap a web page to zoom in to part of that page.

- **Pinch**—To zoom in and out of images and pages, place your thumb and forefinger on the screen. Pinch them together to zoom out or spread them apart to zoom in (unpinching). Applications like Browser, Gallery, and Maps support pinching.

- **Rotate the screen**—If you rotate your Galaxy Note 3 from an upright position to being on its left or right side, the screen switches from Portrait view to Landscape view. Most applications honor the screen orientation. The Home screens and Launcher do not.

Use the Keyboard

Your Galaxy Note 3 has a virtual or onscreen keyboard for those times when you need to enter text. You might be a little wary of a keyboard that has no physical keys, but you will be pleasantly surprised at how well it works.

Some applications automatically show the keyboard when you need to enter text. If the keyboard does not appear, touch the area where you want to type and the keyboard slides up ready for use.

Touch to capitalize the next character

Double-tap to engage CAPS Lock

Touch for numbers and symbols

Touch to speak the text

Using the virtual keyboard as you type, your Galaxy Note 3 makes word suggestions. Think of this as similar to the spell checker you would see in a word processor. Your Galaxy Note 3 uses a dictionary of words to guess what you are typing. If the word you were going to type is highlighted, touch space or period to select it. If you can see the word in the list but it is not highlighted, touch the word to select it.

Touch to select an alternative suggested word

List of suggested words

Touch to see all suggested words

Touch space to accept the suggested word in the middle

To make the next letter you type a capital letter, touch the Shift key. To make all letters capitals (or CAPS), double-tap the Shift key to engage CAPS Lock. Touch Shift again to disengage CAPS Lock.

To type numbers or symbols, touch the Symbols key.

When on the Numbers and Symbols screen, touch the Symbols key to see extra symbols. There are three screens of symbols. Touch the ABC key to return to the regular keyboard.

Touch to see more symbols

Touch to return to letters

Quick Access to Symbols

If you want to type commonly used symbols, touch and hold the period key. A small window opens with those common symbols. Slide your finger over the symbol you want to type, and lift it to type that symbol.

Select a symbol to type

Touch and hold to see symbols

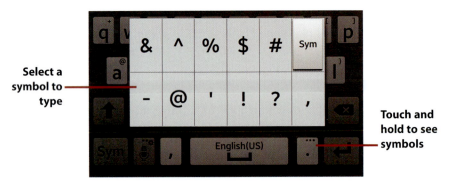

To enter an accented character, touch and hold any vowel or C, N, or S keys. A small window opens enabling you to select an accented or alternative character. Slide your finger over the accented character and lift your finger to type it.

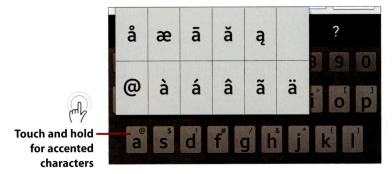

Touch and hold for accented characters

To reveal other alternative characters, touch and hold any other letter, number, or symbol.

Want a Larger Keyboard?

Turn your Galaxy Note 3 sideways to switch to a landscape keyboard. The landscape keyboard has larger keys and is easier to type on.

Swipe to Type

Instead of typing on the keyboard in the traditional way by touching each letter individually, you can swipe over the letters in one continuous movement. This is called Continuous Input. It is enabled by default; to use it, just start swiping your finger over the letters of the word you want to type. Lift your finger after each word. No need to worry about spaces because your Galaxy Note 3 adds them for you. To type a double letter (as in the word *toll*), loop around that letter on the keyboard.

Dictation—Speak Instead of Type

Your Galaxy Note 3 can turn your voice into text. It uses Google's speech recognition service, which means that you must have a connection to the cellular network or a Wi-Fi network to use it.

1. Touch the microphone key.

2. Wait until you see Speak Now and start speaking what you want to be typed. You can speak the punctuation by saying "comma," "question mark," "exclamation mark," or "exclamation point."

Touch to select a different dictation language

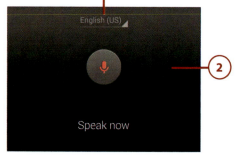

Edit Text

After you enter text, you can edit it by cutting, copying, or pasting the text. This task describes how to select and copy text so you can paste over a word with the copied text.

1. While you are typing, touch and hold a word you want to copy.

2. Slide the blue end markers until you have selected all of the text you want to copy.

3. Touch to copy the text.

4. Touch and hold the word you want to paste over.

5. Touch to paste what you copied earlier.

**Touch to
cut the text**

Placing a Cursor

You can also simply place a cursor on the screen and move it around to do manual text editing, such as backspace to delete letters or manually insert a new word. To do this, tap the screen in the text area. A single blue marker displays; drag that marker to the point in the text you want to make changes to. Now start typing or tap backspace, and the action occurs at the cursor position.

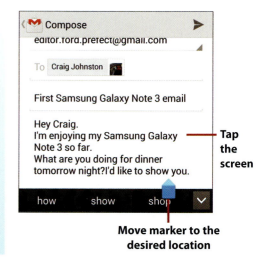

Tap the screen

Move marker to the desired location

Writing Instead of Typing

As discussed earlier in this chapter, your Galaxy Note 3 comes with the S Pen stylus. Instead of typing on the keyboard, you can use handwriting recognition to write. To enable Handwriting mode, pull out the S Pen from its holder and touch the Back key to dismiss the Air Command window. Then hover the S Pen over the screen in the text area until you see the handwriting icon. Touch the icon with your S Pen. Any text you have typed appears to be in handwriting. Now write in your own handwriting on the screen and it is turned into text. Touch Done to return to typing.

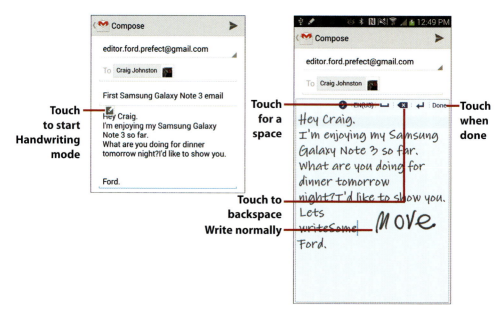

Touch to start Handwriting mode

Touch for a space

Touch to backspace

Write normally

Touch when done

Keyboard Tricks

You can write instead of typing, use emoticons (smiley faces), and enable a one-handed keyboard.

1. Touch and hold the microphone key (to the right of the Sym key).

2. Touch to see everything you have previously copied to the clipboard. If there is text, you can touch it to paste it at the cursor position.

3. Touch to change keyboard settings, including choosing a new keyboard.

4. Touch to type emoticons (smiley faces).

5. Touch to choose a one-handed keyboard.

ONE-HANDED TYPING

Your Galaxy Note 3 is a pretty large phone and unlike smaller phones that have 4-inch screens, you cannot type with one hand on your Galaxy Note 3. Samsung addresses this by enabling you to put the keyboard into one-handed typing mode. This mode squashes the keyboard to the left or right of the screen so that you can type with one thumb, or it lets you float the keyboard anywhere on the screen. To enable one-handed mode, follow steps 1 and 5 in the "Keyboard Tricks" task. Touch the arrow to switch between left-handed and right-handed modes.

>>>Go Further

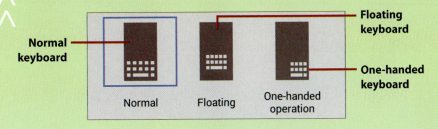

Drag the keyboard **Touch to switch between left-handed and right-handed modes**

Menus

Your Galaxy Note 3 has two types of menus: app menus and context menus. All applications use an app menu. To see the an app menu, touch the physical Menu button, which is to the left of the Home button.

A context menu applies to an item on the screen. If you touch and hold something on the screen (in this example, a link on a web page), a context menu appears. The items on the context menu differ based on the type of object you touched.

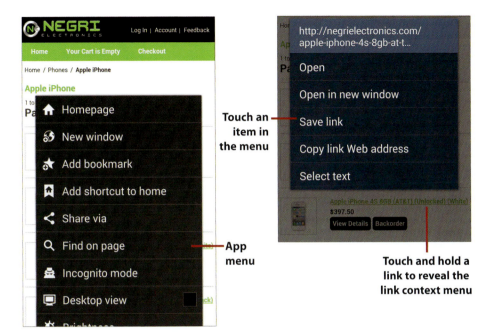

Touch an item in the menu

App menu

Touch and hold a link to reveal the link context menu

Switch Between Apps

You can switch between running apps and close apps using the multi-tasking feature.

1. Press and hold the Home button.

2. Scroll up and down the list of running apps.

3. Touch an app to switch to it.

4. Swipe an app left or right off the screen to close it.

Touch to open Google Now

Touch to close all apps

Run Two Apps at the Same Time

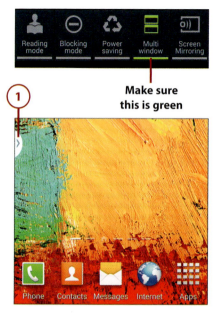

Make sure
this is green

Your Galaxy Note 3 has a feature called Multi Window that allows certain apps to run on the same screen at the same time.

Make Sure Multi Window Is Enabled

Before you start this section, make sure that Multi Window is enabled in the Quick Settings.

1. Touch the Multi Window handle to see apps.

2. Drag an app onto the screen but keep holding it.

Not All Apps Support Multi Window

Apps must be specially written to take advantage of Multi Window mode. This means that you might not see the apps you are looking for until the developer updates the app to support Samsung's Multi Window mode.

Scroll up and down
to see all apps

Touch to choose which window
of a multi-window app to use

3. Drag the app to either the top or bottom half of the screen and release it. If this is the first app you are choosing then just release it anywhere on the screen.

4. Drag the bar up or down to give more or less room to each app.

5. Touch the bar to reveal extra Multi Window features.

6. Touch to see all apps in the current window (if you have more than one).

7. Touch to swap the position of the apps on the screen.

8. Touch to enable dragging content between windows (like text or images).

9. Touch to close the selected window.

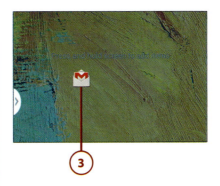

Touch to see the list of apps again

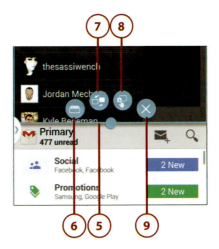

More Than One App in Each Window

You can have more than one app in each window. If you do have more than one and want to switch between them, touch the blue dot that is between the two windows, and touch the app selector icon (as shown in step 6). Then touch the app you want to switch to.

Choose the app you want to switch to

PRESETTING PAIRS OF APPS

>>>Go Further

You can create preset pairs of apps. This enables you to quickly open two apps on the screen without first dragging them onto the screen manually each time you open Multi Window. To do this, open the two apps that you want to work with (you can drag more apps into each window if you like so you have more than one in each window). Touch the Multi Window handle and touch Create. Either leave the pre-populated name and touch OK, or type in your own pair name. In the future when you open the Multi Window list, your preset app pairs will be right at the top.

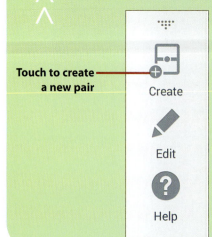

Touch to create a new pair

Name the new pair

Installing Synchronization Software

Because your Galaxy Note 3 is tightly integrated with Google and its services, all media that you purchase on your phone is stored in the Google cloud and accessible anywhere, anytime. However, you might have a lot of music on your computer and need to copy that to your Google cloud. To do that, you need to install the Google Music Manager software or the Android File Transfer app for your Mac to copy any file back and forth.

Install Android File Transfer (Apple Mac OS X)

You only need the Android File Transfer app when using a Samsung Android phone (like your Galaxy Note 3) on an Apple Mac running OS X.

1. From your Mac, browse to http://www.android.com/filetransfer/ and download the Android File Transfer app.

2. Click the Downloads icon.

3. Double-click the app in your Safari Downloads.

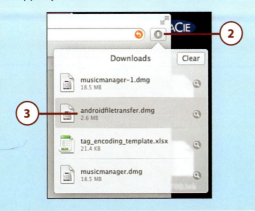

4. Drag the green Android to the Applications shortcut to install the app.

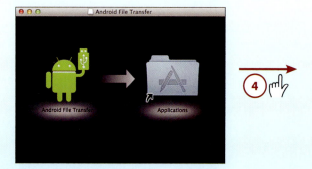

Install Google Music Manager (Apple Mac)

Don't install Google Music Manager unless you plan to upload files from your computer to the Google Music cloud.

1. Visit https://music.google.com/music/listen#manager_pl from your desktop web browser and log in to your Google account if you're prompted.

2. Click to download Music Manager.

3. Click the Downloads icon.

4. Double-click the app in your Safari Downloads.

5. Drag the Music Manager icon to the Applications shortcut to install the app.

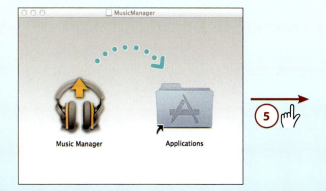

6. Double-click the Music Manager icon in the Applications folder.

7. Skip to the "Configure Music Manager" section to complete the installation.

Install Google Music Manager (Windows)

Don't install Google Music Manager unless you plan to upload files from your computer to the Google Music cloud.

1. Visit https://music.google.com/music/listen#manager_pl from your desktop web browser and log in to your Google account if you're prompted.

2. Click to download Music Manager.

3. Double-click the app in your Downloads folder.

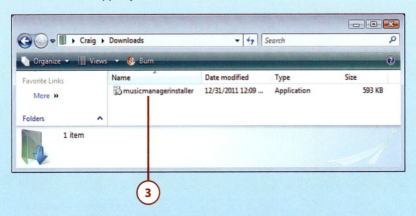

4. Skip to the "Configure Music Manager" section to complete the installation.

Configure Music Manager (Windows and Apple Mac)

1. Click Continue.

2. Enter your Google (Gmail) email address.

3. Enter your Google (Gmail) password.

4. Click Continue.

5. Choose where you keep your music.

6. Click Continue.

7. Choose whether to upload all of your music or just some of your playlists. Remember that you can only upload 20,000 songs for free. Skip to step 12 if you chose to upload all music.

8. Check if you want to also upload podcasts.

9. Click Continue.

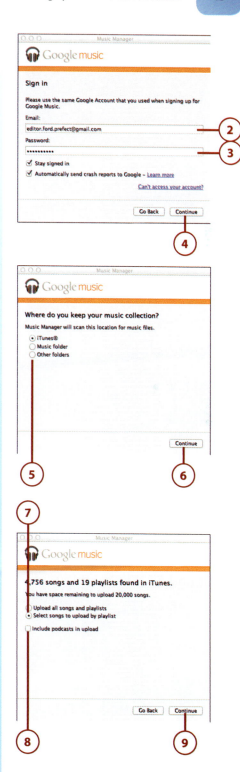

10. Select one or more music playlists.

11. Click Continue.

12. Choose whether you want to automatically upload any new music that is added to your computer.

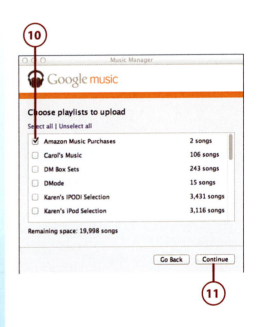

13. Click Continue.

14. Click Close.

Touch to turn
Wi-Fi on and off

Touch to turn NFC
on and off

In this chapter, you discover the connectivity capabilities of your Galaxy Note 3, including Bluetooth, Wi-Fi, VPN, and NFC. Topics include the following:

→ Pairing with Bluetooth devices
→ Connecting to Wi-Fi networks
→ Working with virtual private networks (VPN)
→ Using your Galaxy Note 3 as a Wi-Fi hotspot
→ Using Near Field Communications (NFC) and beaming

Connecting to Bluetooth, Wi-Fi, and VPNs

Your Galaxy Note 3 can connect to Bluetooth devices, such as headsets, computers, and car in-dash systems, as well as to Wi-Fi networks, and 2G, 3G, and 4G cellular networks. It has all the connectivity you should expect on a great smartphone. Your Galaxy Note 3 can also connect to virtual private networks (VPNs) for access to secure networks, and can even share its cellular data connection with other devices over Wi-Fi.

Connecting to Bluetooth Devices

Bluetooth is a great personal area network (PAN) technology that allows for short-distance wireless access to all sorts of devices, such as headsets, other phones, computers, and even car in-dash systems for hands-free calling. The following tasks walk you through pairing your Galaxy Note 3 to your device and configuring options.

Pair with a New Bluetooth Device

Before you can take advantage of Bluetooth, you need to connect your Galaxy Note 3 with that device, which is called pairing. After you pair your Galaxy Note 3 with a Bluetooth device, the two devices can connect to each other automatically in the future.

Putting the Bluetooth Device into Pairing Mode First

Before you pair a Bluetooth device to your Galaxy Note 3, you must first put it into Pairing mode. If you are pairing with a Bluetooth headset, you normally have to hold the button on the headset for a certain period of time. Please consult your Bluetooth device's manual to find out how to put that device into Pairing mode.

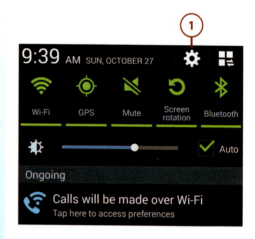

1. Pull down the Notification bar and touch the Settings icon.

2. Touch the Connections tab.

3. Touch Bluetooth.

4. Touch Scan if you don't see the device you want to connect to in the list of discovered devices.

5. Touch the Bluetooth device you want to connect to. In this example, we are going to connect to the Pebble Smartwatch (Pebble 1984).

Your Galaxy Note 3's Bluetooth name

Devices you are already paired with

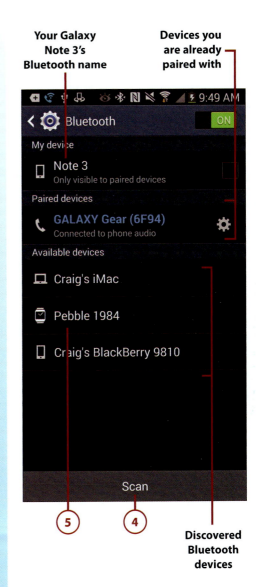

Discovered Bluetooth devices

6. If all went well, your Galaxy Note 3 should now be paired with the new Bluetooth device.

Bluetooth Passkey

If you are pairing with a device that requires a passkey, such as a car in-dash system, smartwatch, smartphone, or a computer, the screen shows a passkey. Make sure the passkey is the same on your Galaxy Note 3 and on the device you are pairing with. Touch OK on your Galaxy Note 3 and confirm the passkey on the device you are pairing with.

All Zeros

If you are pairing with an older Bluetooth headset, you might be prompted to enter the passkey. Try using four zeros; it normally works. If the zeros don't work, refer to the headset's manual.

Successfully paired

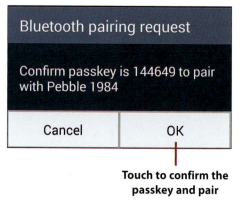

Touch to confirm the passkey and pair

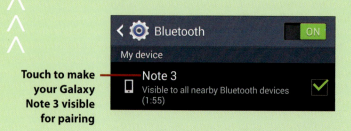

>>>Go Further

REVERSE PAIRING

The steps in this section describe how to pair your Galaxy Note 3 with a Bluetooth device that is in Pairing mode, listening for an incoming pairing command. You can pair Bluetooth another way in which you put your Galaxy Note 3 in Discovery mode. To do this, touch the Bluetooth name of your Galaxy Note 3 on the screen (this is normally "Note 3" unless you have changed it). Your Galaxy Note 3 goes into Pairing mode for two minutes.

Touch to make your Galaxy Note 3 visible for pairing

Extra Bluetooth Options

1. Press the Menu button.

2. Touch to change how long your Galaxy Note 3 stays visible when pairing.

3. Touch to see any files people have sent you over the Bluetooth network.

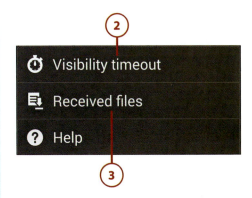

Change Bluetooth Device Options

After a Bluetooth device is paired, you can change a few options for some of them. The number of options depends on the Bluetooth device you are connecting to. Some have more features than others.

1. Touch the Settings icon to the right of the Bluetooth device.

2. Touch to rename the Bluetooth device to something more descriptive.

3. Touch to disconnect and unpair the Galaxy Note 3 from the Bluetooth device. If you do this, you won't be able to use the Bluetooth device again until you redo the pairing as described in the "Pair with a New Bluetooth Device" task.

4. Touch to enable and disable using this device for phone calls. Sometimes Bluetooth devices have more than one profile. You can use this screen to select which ones you want to use.

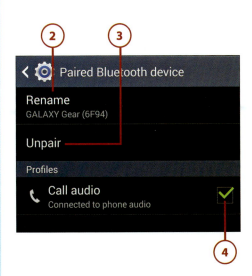

Bluetooth Profiles

Each Bluetooth device can have one or more Bluetooth profiles. Each Bluetooth profile describes certain features of the device. This tells your Galaxy Note 3 what it can do when connected to the device. A Bluetooth headset normally only has one profile, such as Phone Audio. This tells your Galaxy Note 3 that it can only use the device for phone call audio. Some devices might have this profile but also provide other features such as a Phone Book Access profile, which would allow it to synchronize your Galaxy Note 3's address book. The latter is typical for a car in-dash Bluetooth device.

Quick Disconnect

To quickly disconnect from a Bluetooth device, touch the device on the Bluetooth Settings screen and then touch OK.

Wi-Fi

Wi-Fi (Wireless Fidelity) networks are wireless networks that run within free radio bands around the world. Your local coffee shop probably has free Wi-Fi, and so do many other places, such as airports, train stations, malls, and other public areas. Your Galaxy Note 3 can connect to any Wi-Fi network and provide you faster Internet access speeds than the cellular network.

Connect to Wi-Fi

The following steps explain how to find and connect to Wi-Fi networks. After you have connected your Galaxy Note 3 to a Wi-Fi network, you automatically are connected to it the next time you are in range of that network.

1. Pull down the Notification bar and touch the Settings icon.

2. Touch the Connections tab.

3. Touch Wi-Fi.

4. Touch to turn Wi-Fi on if the slider is in the off position.

5. Touch the name of the Wi-Fi network you want to connect to. If the network does not use any security, you can skip to step 8.

6. Enter the Wi-Fi network password.

7. Touch to connect to the Wi-Fi network.

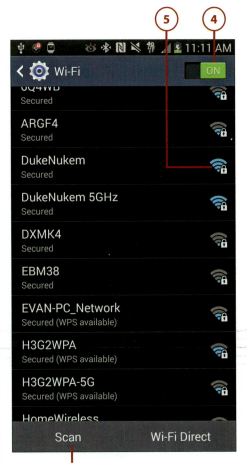

Touch to scan manually

Touch to use special proxy settings

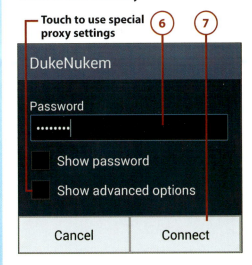

Adding a Hidden Network

If the network you want to connect to is not listed on the screen, it might be purposely hidden. Hidden networks do not broadcast their names (which are known as their service set identifier [SSID]). You need to scroll down to the bottom of the listed Wi-Fi networks and touch Add Wi-Fi Network, type in the SSID, and choose the type of security that the network uses. You need to get this information from the network administrator before you try to connect.

8. If all goes well, you see the Wi-Fi network in the list with the word Connected under it.

Can't Connect to Wi-Fi?

If all does not go well, you might be typing the password or encryption key incorrectly. Verify this with the person who owns the Wi-Fi network. Sometimes there is a lot of radio interference that causes problems. Ask the person who owns the Wi-Fi network to change the channel it operates on and try again.

Type network name (SSID)

Choose type of security used (if any)

Type network password (if needed)

Indicates Wi-Fi signal strength

Wi-Fi Network Options

1. Touch a Wi-Fi network to reveal a pop-up that shows information about your connection to that network.

2. Touch Forget to tell your Galaxy Note 3 to not connect to this network in the future.

3. Touch and hold on a Wi-Fi network to reveal two actions.

4. Touch to forget the Wi-Fi network and no longer connect to it.

5. Touch to change the Wi-Fi network password or encryption key that your Galaxy Note 3 uses to connect to the network.

Advanced Wi-Fi Options

Your Galaxy Note 3 enables you to configure a few advanced Wi-Fi settings that can actually help preserve your battery life.

1. Touch the Menu button.

2. Touch Advanced.

3. Touch to enable or disable the ability for your Galaxy Note 3 to automatically notify you when it detects a new Wi-Fi network.

4. Touch to let your Note 3 automatically connect to Wi-Fi networks that support Passpoint.

5. Touch to change the the sort order of Wi-Fi networks. By default they are sorted alphabetically.

6. Touch to change the Wi-Fi sleep policy. This enables you to choose if your Galaxy Note 3 should keep its connection to Wi-Fi when it goes to sleep.

7. Touch to choose whether to allow Google and apps running on your Note 3 to scan for Wi-Fi networks, even if you have turned Wi-Fi off.

8. Touch to choose whether to allow your Note 3 to automatically switch between Wi-Fi and cellular data networks.

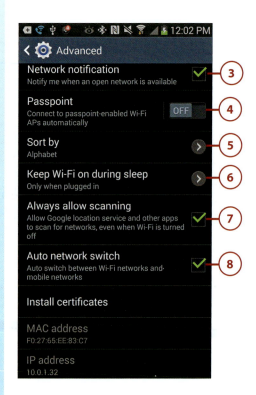

Should You Keep Wi-Fi on During Sleep?

In step 6 of the "Advanced Wi-Fi Options" task, you can choose how your Galaxy Note 3 handles its connection to Wi-Fi when it goes to sleep. Because Wi-Fi is much faster and more efficient than 3G or 4G and is free, you should keep this set to Always. However, battery usage can be affected by always being connected to Wi-Fi, so you might want to set this to Only When Plugged In, which means that if your Galaxy Note 3 is not charging, and it goes to sleep, it switches to the cellular network for data; when the Galaxy Note 3 is charging and it goes to sleep it stays connected to Wi-Fi. If you choose Never for this setting, when your Galaxy Note 3 goes to sleep, it switches to using the cellular network for all data. This can lead to more data being used out of your cellular data bundle, which might cost extra, so be careful.

9. Touch to install certificates provided by your administrator that are stored on the SD Card (external memory) in your Note 3.

10. Use this Wi-Fi MAC address if you need to provide a network administrator with your MAC address in order to be able to use a Wi-Fi network.

11. This shows the IP address that has been assigned to your Galaxy Note 3 when it connected to the Wi-Fi network.

12. Touch to save your changes and return to the previous screen.

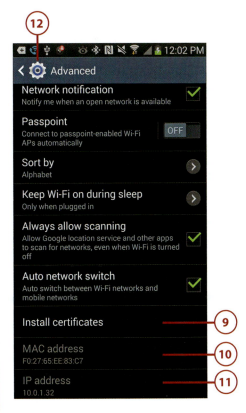

>>>Go Further

WHAT ARE IP AND MAC ADDRESSES?

A MAC address is a number burned into your Galaxy Note 3 that identifies its Wi-Fi adapter. This is called the physical layer because it is a physical adapter. An IP address is a secondary way to identify your Galaxy Note 3. Unlike a Physical Layer address or MAC address, the IP address can be changed anytime. Modern networks use the IP address when they need to deliver some data to you. Typically when you connect to a network, a device on the network assigns a new IP address. On home networks, this is typically your Wi-Fi router.

Some network administrators use a security feature to limit who can connect to their Wi-Fi network. They set up their network to only allow connections from Wi-Fi devices with specific MAC addresses. If you are trying to connect to such a network, you will have to give the network administrator your MAC address, and he will add it to the allowed list.

What Is Passpoint?

Passpoint is a technology that is being used increasingly by operators of Wi-Fi hotspots, and its purpose is to let your Note 3 (and other Passpoint-enabled smartphones and tablets) to automatically roam onto the hotspots with no need for you to search for them or log in to them using the typical hotspot login web page. Simply based on the SIM card in your Note 3, you are automatically authenticated onto these hotspots and provided a secure encrypted connection.

Wi-Fi Direct

Wi-Fi Direct is a feature that allows two Android devices running version 4.1 (Jelly Bean) or later to connect to each other using Wi-Fi so they can exchange files. Because Wi-Fi is much faster than Bluetooth, if you are sending large files, using Wi-Fi Direct makes sense.

Send a File Using Wi-Fi Direct

Follow these steps to connect two Android devices running version 4.1 (Jelly Bean) or later via Wi-Fi Direct and send them files from your Note 3.

1. Ask the other person to enable Wi-Fi Direct on his Android device. The Wi-Fi Direct screen is normally under the Wi-Fi Settings.

2. Touch the Share icon for the item you want to send. This can be a picture in the Gallery app, for example.

3. Touch the Wi-Fi Direct icon.

4. Touch the device name to invite it to connect with your Galaxy Note 3 via Wi-Fi Direct and send the file to that device.

Does Wi-Fi Direct Work for All Android Devices?

Theoretically, all Android devices running version 4.1 should be able to send or receive files via Wi-Fi Direct; however, some devices have reported issues. For example, as of the writing of this book, the HTC One wouldn't operate properly on Wi-Fi Direct.

5. Ask the other person to touch Accept or Connect on the device you are inviting.

6. If the Wi-Fi Direct connection is made successfully, the file is sent to the other device.

Receive a File Using Wi-Fi Direct

Follow these steps to connect two Android devices running version 4.1 (Jelly Bean) or later via Wi-Fi Direct and receive one or more files.

1. Pull down the Notification Bar and touch Settings.

2. Touch Wi-Fi under the Connections tab.

3. Touch Wi-Fi Direct and wait for the other person to invite you.

4. Touch Connect when the other person invites you to connect using Wi-Fi Direct. One or more files should now start copying to your Note 3.

5. Pull down the Notification Bar and touch the Files Received notification.

6. Touch a received file to open it.

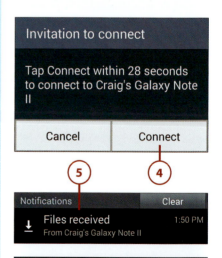

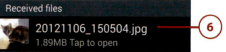

Near Field Communications (NFC)

Your Galaxy Note 3 has the ability to swap data via its NFC radio with other phones that use NFC or read data that is stored on NFC tags. You can also use NFC to pay for items you have purchased. Android Beam and Samsung S Beam also use NFC to send files between Android devices by setting up the sending process automatically via NFC, and continuing it via Bluetooth or Wi-Fi Direct.

Enable NFC, Android Beam, and S Beam

To get the full benefit from NFC, you need to enable the NFC radio. You should also enable Android Beam and S Beam.

1. Pull down the Notification bar and touch the Settings icon.

2. Touch to enable NFC.

3. Touch to enable S Beam.

4. Touch NFC to see more settings.

5. Touch to enable Android Beam. (See the next section for more about Android Beam.)

6. Touch to save your changes and go back to the Connections tab.

>>>Go Further

WHAT IS ANDROID BEAM?

All Android devices running version 4.0 (Ice Cream Sandwich) or later have a feature called Android Beam. This feature sends small bits of data via NFC (such as links to YouTube videos or links to apps in Google Play) to enable you to effectively share content, but it also automates sending actual files (such as pictures and videos) between devices like via Bluetooth.

Use Android Beam to Send Links to Content

You can use Android Beam to send links to content—such as apps, music, and video in the Google Play Store or website links—to another device. Android Beam only works between devices that are both running Android 4.0 (Ice Cream Sandwich) or later.

1. Open a website that you'd like to share the link to. Put the back of your Galaxy Note 3 about 1" from the back of another NFC-enabled phone. You know that the two devices have successfully connected when the web page zooms out.

2. Touch the web page after it zooms out.

3. The browser on the other device opens and immediately loads the link you shared.

Beam Google Play Content and YouTube Videos

If you like a song, movie, book, or app that is in the Google Play Store, you can beam it to someone. Simply open the song, movie, book, or app in Google Play, touch your devices together, and touch to beam. To beam a YouTube video, open the video in the YouTube app, touch the devices together, and touch to beam. The other device opens YouTube and jumps directly to the video.

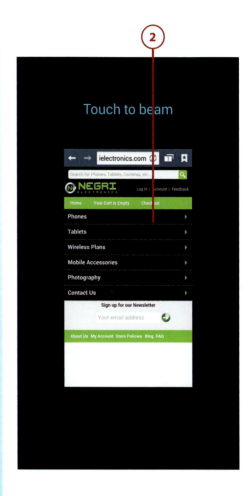

Use Android Beam to Send Real Files

You can also use Android Beam to send real content such as pictures, music, and video that's stored on your Galaxy Note 3. This only works between devices that are running Android 4.1 (Jelly Bean) or later. This task describes how to beam a picture.

1. Open the picture you want to beam. (The picture must reside on your Galaxy Note 3 and not in the Google Cloud.) Then put the back of your Galaxy Note 3 about 1" from the back of another NFC-enabled phone. You know that the two devices have successfully connected when the picture zooms out.

2. Touch the picture after it zooms out.

3. Your Galaxy Note 3 sends the picture to the other device. The file is sent using Bluetooth in the background.

It's Not All Good

Beaming to Non-Samsung Devices

Android Beam is designed to work between any Android devices running version 4.1 (Jelly Bean) or later; however, Samsung included a feature called S Beam that works in a slightly different way to Android Beam. If you want to beam files from your Galaxy Note 3 to a non-Samsung Android device, you must disable S Beam first. If you don't disable S Beam, your Galaxy Note 3 simply tries to use S Beam instead of Android Beam, and the beaming fails. You need to reenable S Beam when trying to use S Beam between your Galaxy Note 3 and another Samsung device.

Use Samsung S Beam to Send Files

Samsung S Beam is Samsung's version of Android Beam, and you can use it to send real content—such as pictures, music, and video—that's stored on your Galaxy Note 3. Samsung S Beam only works between Samsung Android devices that also support S Beam. This task describes how to beam a picture.

1. Open the picture you want to send via S Beam. (Note that the picture must reside on your Galaxy Note 3 and not in the Google Cloud.) Put the back of your Galaxy Note 3 about 1" from the back of another S Beam–enabled Samsung device. You know that the two devices have successfully connected when the picture zooms out.

2. Touch the picture after it zooms out.

3. Separate the two devices as instructed on the screen.

4. Your Galaxy Note 3 sends the picture to the other device. The file is sent using Wi-Fi Direct in the background.

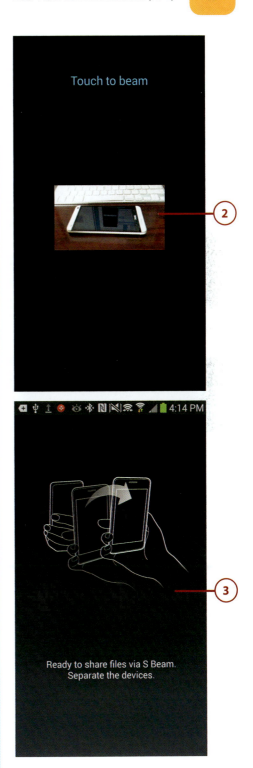

Cellular Networks

Your Galaxy Note 3 can connect to many different cellular networks around the world. The exact networks that it can connect to are determined by the variant of Galaxy Note 3 you have because not all carriers use the same technology. To complicate things even more, many devices use different frequencies from one another.

Change Mobile Settings

Your Galaxy Note 3 has a few options when it comes to connecting to cellular (or mobile) networks.

1. Pull down the Notification bar and touch the Settings icon.

2. Touch More Networks on the Connections tab.

3. Touch Mobile Networks.

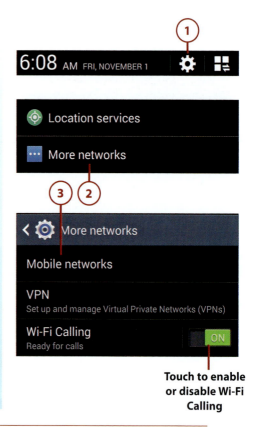

Touch to enable or disable Wi-Fi Calling

What Is Wi-Fi Calling?

Wi-Fi Calling, also known as Unlicensed Mobile Access (UMA), is provided by some cellular carriers to both augment their coverage and to provide free calls over Wi-Fi. This is not Voice over IP (VoIP) calling but a regular GSM voice call, routed via a Wi-Fi hotspot, over the Internet, to your carrier. Because the call is not using the cellular network infrastructure, the calls are free, and because of the speeds at which Wi-Fi networks operate, the call quality is much higher because much less compression is needed. To read more about UMA, try this online article: http://crackberry.com/saving-call-charges-recession-your-blackberry.

4. Touch to enable or disable cellular data. If this option is unchecked, your Galaxy Note 3 is able to use only Wi-Fi networks for data.

5. Touch to enable or disable cellular data roaming. If this is unchecked, your Galaxy Note 3 does not attempt to use data while you roam away from your home cellular network.

6. Touch to view, edit, and add APNs. It is unlikely that you need to make any APN changes.

7. Touch to change the network mode. This setting enables you to choose to force your Note 3 to connect to a slower 2G network to save battery or always to a faster 3G or 4G network for the best speed, or to leave it set to Auto mode and let your phone choose for you.

8. Touch to view and choose mobile operators to use manually.

9. Touch to save your changes and return to the previous screen.

What Is an APN?

APN stands for Access Point Name. You normally don't have to make changes to APNs, but sometimes you need to enter them manually to access certain features. For example, if you need to use tethering, which is where you connect your laptop to your Galaxy Note 3 and your Galaxy Note 3 provides Internet connectivity for your laptop, you might be asked by your carrier to use a specific APN. Think of an APN as a gateway to a service.

Can I Disable Mobile Data?

If you disable mobile data, you can save on battery life; however, you effectively kill the functionality of any app that needs to be connected all the time, such as instant messaging apps (Yahoo! or Google Talk) or apps like Skype. You also stop receiving email in real time. When this feature is disabled, about 5 minutes after your Galaxy Note 3 goes to sleep, it disconnects from the mobile data network; however, it remains connected to the mobile voice network.

>>>Go Further

WHY SELECT OPERATORS MANUALLY?

When you are roaming in your home country, your Galaxy Note 3 automatically selects your home cellular provider. When you are roaming outside your home country, your Galaxy Note 3 registers on a cellular provider based on its name and how it scores alphabetically. The lowest score always wins. For example, a carrier whose name starts with a number is always chosen over carriers whose names start with letters. A carrier whose name starts with the letter *A* is chosen over a carrier whose name starts with the letter *B*, and so on. As you roam, your home carrier might not have a good roaming relationship with a carrier that your Galaxy Note 3 has chosen based on its name, so it's better for you to choose the carrier manually to ensure the best roaming rates and, many times, basic connectivity. You will notice that sometimes carriers are represented not by their names but by their operator codes (or Public Land Mobile Network [PLNM] number). For example, 53024 is actually 2Degrees in New Zealand, and 53005 is Telecom New Zealand.

Virtual Private Networks (VPNs)

Your Galaxy Note 3 can connect to virtual private networks (VPNs), which are normally used by companies to provide a secure connection to their inside networks or intranets.

Add a VPN

Before you add a VPN, you must first have all the information needed to set it up on your Galaxy Note 3. Speak to your network administrator to get this information ahead of time (and save yourself some frustration). The information you need includes the type of VPN protocol used, the type of encryption used, and the name of the host to which you are connecting.

1. Pull down the Notification bar and touch the Settings icon.

2. Touch More Networks on the Connections tab.

3. Touch VPN.

4. Touch OK to set up a screen lock PIN, pattern, or password. If you already have a screen lock PIN or password, you won't be prompted at this point, and you can proceed to step 6.

Why Do You Need to Set a PIN or Password?

If you don't already have a screen lock PIN, password, or pattern set up before you create your first VPN network connection, you are prompted to create one. This is a security measure that ensures your Galaxy Note 3 must first be unlocked before anyone can access a stored VPN connection. Because VPN connections are usually used to access company data, this is a good idea.

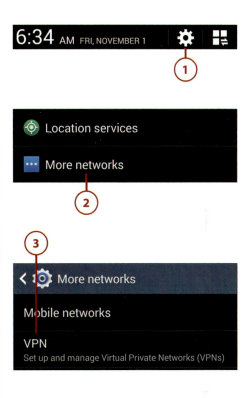

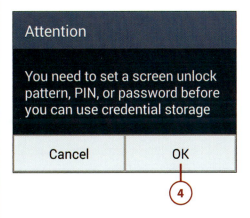

5. Choose either a pattern, PIN, or password to unlock your Galaxy Note 3 and follow the steps to create it.

6. Touch Add VPN Network.

7. Enter a name for your VPN network. You can call it anything like Work VPN or the name of the provider like PublicVPN.

8. Touch to choose the type of encryption the VPN network uses.

9. Enter the remaining parameters that your network administrator has provided.

10. Touch Save.

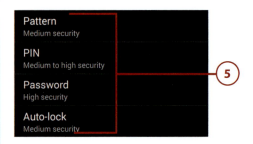

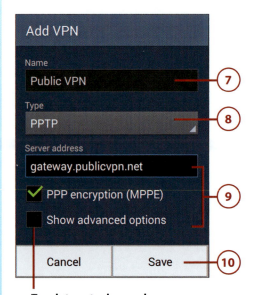

Touch to set advanced options like DNS and forwarding

Connect to a VPN

After you have created one or more VPN connections, you can connect to them when the need arises.

1. Pull down the Notification bar and touch the Settings icon.

2. Touch More Networks on the Connections tab.

3. Touch VPN.

4. Touch a preconfigured VPN connection.

5. Enter the VPN username.

6. Enter the VPN password.

7. Touch Connect. After you're connected to the VPN, you can use your web browser and other applications normally, but you now have access to resources at the other end of the VPN tunnel, such as company web servers or even your company email.

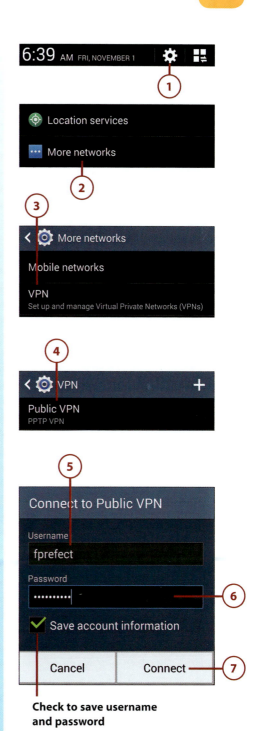

Check to save username and password

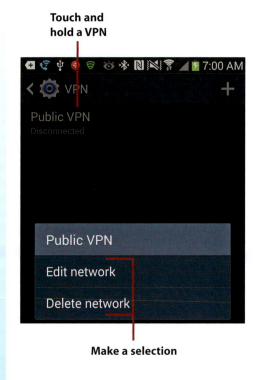

>>>Go Further

HOW CAN YOU TELL IF YOU ARE CONNECTED?

After your Galaxy Note 3 successfully connects to a VPN network, you see a key icon in the Notification bar. This indicates that you are connected. If you pull down the Notification bar, you can touch the icon to see information about the connection and to disconnect from the VPN.

Connected to VPN

Editing or Deleting a VPN

You can edit an existing VPN or delete it by touching and holding the name of the VPN. A window pops up with a list of options.

Touch and hold a VPN

Make a selection

It's Not All Good

No Quick Way to Start a VPN Connection

Unlike the Galaxy Note II, the Galaxy Note 3 does not have a way to add a shortcut to your Home screen to jump straight to the VPN screen. There may be third-party solutions in the form of apps you can install that will add this functionality. Check the Google Play Store.

Mobile Wi-Fi Hotspot

Your Galaxy Note 3 has the ability to share its cellular data connection with up to eight devices over Wi-Fi. Before you use this feature, you need to normally sign up for a tethering or hotspot plan with your cellular provider, which is normally an extra monthly cost.

Start Your Mobile Wi-Fi Hotspot

1. Pull down the Notification bar and touch the Settings icon.

2. Touch Tethering and Mobile HotSpot on the Connections tab.

3. Touch Mobile HotSpot to configure the settings.

What Is USB Tethering?

USB tethering is a feature that enables you to share your Note 3's Internet connection with a computer via the USB port. To use this, connect your Note 3 to the computer using the supplied USB cable and enable USB tethering. On the computer there will be some extra setup to do, which includes choosing your Note 3 as an Internet access point. (And on older Windows computers you might need to install a device driver. Please consult the computer's manual for instructions.)

Touch to enable USB tethering

4. Touch to choose whether to allow any device to connect or only devices you allow.

5. Touch Configure.

6. Choose a network name (also known as the SSID) for your mobile hotspot. You can leave it set to the auto-generated name or change it to something more friendly.

7. Touch to enable or disable broadcasting your Wi-Fi HotSpot's network name (also called its SSID). If you choose not to broadcast it, your network will be hidden, but it requires more steps to connect to it.

8. Touch to choose the type of security to use for your mobile hotspot or choose Open to use no security.

9. Enter a password for your portable hotspot if you chose to use a security method in step 8.

10. Touch to change the maximum number of devices that can connect to your HotSpot.

11. Touch to save your settings.

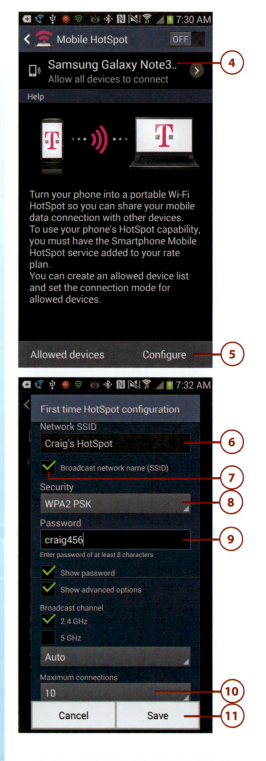

12. Touch to enable your portable hotspot.

13. Provide the network connection information to anyone you want to have connecting to your hotspot.

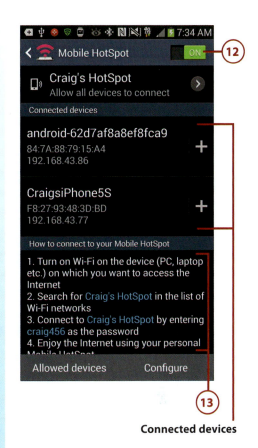

Connected devices

Limit Who Can Connect

People can only connect to your hotspot after you give them the connection information; however, you can further limit who can connect to your hotspot by allowing only certain devices.

1. Touch to add an already connected device to the allowed devices list.

2. Touch to add devices to the allowed list manually.

3. Touch to add a new allowed device using its MAC address. You need to ask the person who owns the device to give you his Wi-Fi MAC address ahead of time.

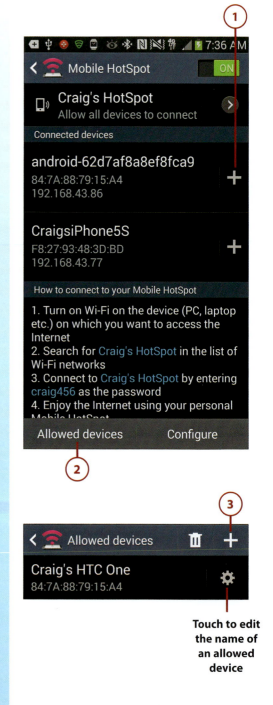

Touch to edit the name of an allowed device

Choose a new wallpaper

In this chapter, you find out how to customize your Galaxy Note 3 to suit your needs and lifestyle. Topics include the following:

→ Using wallpapers and live wallpapers

→ Replacing the keyboard

→ Adjusting sound and display settings

→ Setting region and language

2

Customizing Your Galaxy Note 3

Your Galaxy Note 3 arrives preconfigured to appeal to most buyers; however, you might want to change the way some of the features work, or even personalize it to fit your mood or lifestyle. Luckily your Galaxy Note 3 is customizable.

Changing Your Wallpaper

Your Galaxy Note 3 comes preloaded with a cool wallpaper. You can install other wallpapers, use live wallpapers that animate, and even use pictures in the Gallery application as your wallpaper.

1. Touch and hold in an open area on the Home screen.

2. Touch Set Wallpaper.

3. Select where you want to change the wallpaper.

4. Touch the type of wallpaper you want to use. Use the steps in one of the following three sections to select your wallpaper.

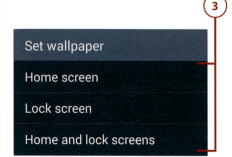

Wallpaper from Gallery Pictures

You can use any picture in your Gallery as a wallpaper.

1. Select the photo you want to use as your wallpaper.

2. Touch Crop Picture.

3. Touch Just Once.

4. Move the crop box to the part of the photo you want to use.

5. Adjust the size of the crop box to include the part of the photo you want.

6. Zoom in and out of the picture using the pinch gesture.

7. Touch Done to use the cropped portion of the photo as your wall-paper.

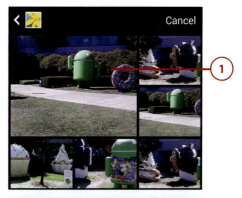

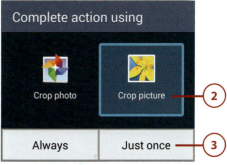

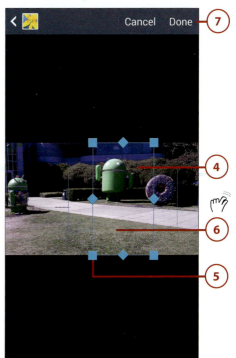

Live Wallpaper

Live wallpaper is wallpaper with some intelligence behind it. It can be a cool animation or even an animation that keys off things such as the music you are playing on your Galaxy Note 3, or it can be something simple such as the time. There are some very cool live wallpapers in Google Play that you can install and use.

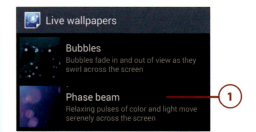

1. Touch the live wallpaper you want to use.

2. Touch Set Wallpaper to use the live wallpaper.

Finding More Wallpaper

You can find wallpaper or live wallpaper in the Google Play Store. Open the Google Play Store app and search for "wallpaper" or "live wallpaper." Read more on how to use the Google Play Store in Chapter 11, "Working with Android Apps."

Wallpaper

Choose a static wallpaper that is pre-loaded and sized correctly for your screen.

1. Scroll left and right to see all of the wallpapers.

2. Touch Set Wallpaper to use the wallpaper.

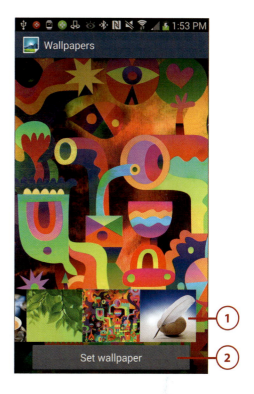

Wallpaper from Photos

You can make wallpaper from any picture that is stored in your Google+ Photos service.

1. Select the photo you want to use as your wallpaper.

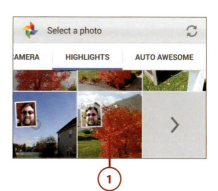

2. Move the crop box to the part of the photo you want to use.

3. Adjust the size of the crop box to include the part of the photo you want.

4. Touch Save to use the cropped portion of the photo as your wallpaper.

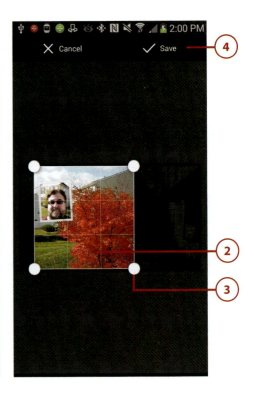

Changing Your Keyboard

If you find it hard to type on the standard Galaxy Note 3 keyboard, or you just want to make it look better, you can install replacement keyboards. You can download free or purchase replacement keyboards from the Google Play Store. Make sure you install a keyboard before following these steps.

1. Pull down the notification bar and touch the Settings icon.

2. Touch Language and Input on the Controls tab.

3. Check the box next to a keyboard you have previously installed from the Google Play Store (in this example, we used SwiftKey Trial) to make that keyboard available for use.

4. Touch OK to change the input method.

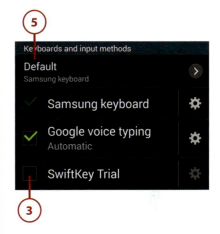

Doing Your Research

When you choose a different keyboard in step 3, the Galaxy Note 3 gives you a warning telling you that nonstandard keyboards have the potential for capturing everything you type. Do your research on any keyboards before you download and install them.

5. Touch Default to change the default keyboard to the one you have just enabled.

6. Touch the name of your new keyboard to select it to be the default.

What Can You Do with Your New Keyboard?

Keyboards you buy in the Google Play Store can do many things. They can change the key layout, change the color and style of the keys, offer different methods of text input, and even enable you to use an old T9 predictive input keyboard that you might have become used to when using an old "dumb phone" that only had a numeric keypad.

7. Touch the Settings icon for a keyboard to make changes, including customizing it.

8. Touch to save your changes.

Adding Widgets to Your Home Screens

Some applications that you install come with widgets that you can place on your Home screens. These widgets normally display real-time information, such as stocks, weather, time, and Facebook feeds. Your Galaxy Note 3 also comes preinstalled with some widgets. Here is how to add and manage widgets.

Add a Widget

Your Galaxy Note 3 should come preinstalled with some widgets, but you might also have some extra ones that have been added when you installed other applications. Here is how to add those widgets to your Home screens.

1. Touch and hold an open area on the Home screen.

2. Touch Apps and Widgets.

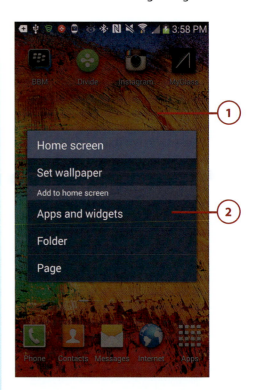

3. Touch the Widgets tab.

4. Touch and hold a widget to move it to the Home screen. Keep holding the widget as you move to step 5. This example uses the Calendar (Month).

Scroll left and right to see all widgets

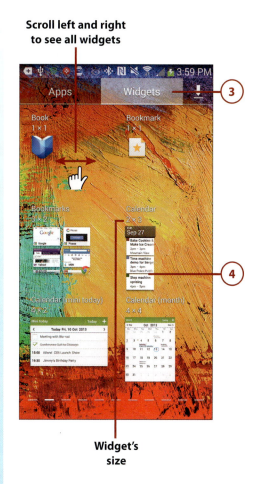

Widget's size

5. Position the widget where you want it on the Home screen.

6. Drag the widget between sections of the Home screen.

7. Release your finger to place the widget. Some widgets ask you a few questions after they are positioned.

How Many Widgets Can I Fit?

Each part of the Home screen is divided into four blocks across and four blocks down. In the figure for steps 3 and 4, notice that each one shows its size in blocks across and down (such as 2×3). From that, you can judge if a widget is going to fit on the screen you want it to be on, but it also helps you position it in step 4.

Resizing Widgets

Some (not all) widgets can be resized. To resize a widget, touch and hold the widget until you see an outline and then release it. If the widget can be resized, you see the resizing borders. Drag them to resize the widget. Touch anywhere on the screen to stop resizing.

Drag to resize the widget

Faint preview of how much space it will require

Remove and Move a Widget

Sometimes you want to remove a widget, resize it, or move it around.

1. Touch and hold the widget until you see a blue shadow, but continue to hold the widget.

2. Drag the widget to the word Remove to remove it.

3. Drag the widget around the screen or drag it between sections of the Home screen to reposition it.

4. Release the widget.

Setting the Language

If you move to another country or want to change the language used by your Galaxy Note 3, you can do so with a few touches.

1. Pull down the Notification bar and touch the Settings icon.

2. Touch Language and Input on the Controls tab.

3. Touch Language.

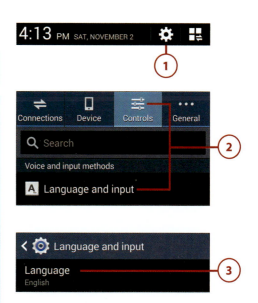

4. Touch the language you want to switch to.

What Obeys the Language Setting?

When you switch your Galaxy Note 3 to use a different language, you immediately notice that all standard applications and the Galaxy Note 3 menus switch to the new language. Even some third-party applications honor the language switch. However, many third-party applications ignore the language setting on the Galaxy Note 3. So you might open a third-party application and find that all of its menus are still in English.

Changing Accessibility Settings

Your Galaxy Note 3 includes built-in settings to assist people who might otherwise have difficulty using some features of the device. The Galaxy Note 3 has the ability to provide alternative feedback, such as vibration and sound. It can even read menu items aloud to you.

1. Pull down the Notification bar and touch the Settings icon.

2. Touch Accessibility on the Device tab.

3. Touch to enable automatic screen rotation. When disabled, the screen does not rotate between Portrait and Landscape modes.

4. Touch to set how many minutes of inactivity your Galaxy Note 3 waits before timing out the screen.

5. Touch to enable or disable the feature where your Note 3 speaks your passwords as you type them.

6. Touch to choose whether to use the Home key to answer calls or answer calls with a voice command. You can also designate to use the power key to end calls.

7. Touch to enable or disable the feature where you can simply touch the icons on the Lock or Home screen instead of having to drag them.

8. Touch to enable or disable the feature where you can press and hold the power key to jump straight to this Accessibility settings screen.

9. Touch to export your accessibility settings as a file or update them from a file. You can also share your exported accessibility file with others.

10. Scroll down for more settings.

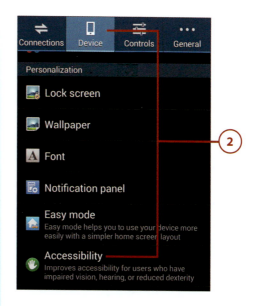

11. Touch to enable or disable TalkBack. When enabled, TalkBack speaks everything, including menus.

12. Touch to set the font size used on your Galaxy Note 3. You can choose sizes ranging from tiny to huge.

13. Touch to enable or disable magnification gestures, which include the ability to magnify any screen by double-tapping it. When a screen is magnified, you can pan around it.

14. Touch to enable or disable negative colors where all colors displayed on your Galaxy Note 3 are reversed.

15. Touch to enable the Color Adjustment Wizard that helps you adjust the screen colors if you have difficulty seeing it.

16. Touch to enable or disable the notification reminder that beeps to remind you that you have unread notifications (such as a new email notification).

17. Touch to enable or disable the accessibility shortcut. When it's enabled, you can access accessibility features by doing certain gestures.

18. Touch to change the settings for the text-to-speech service provided by Samsung.

19. Scroll down for more settings.

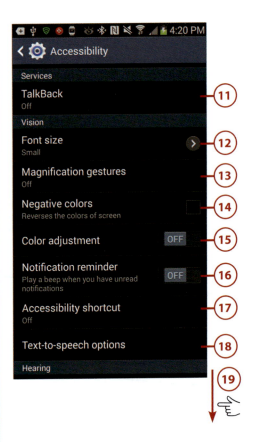

20. Touch to adjust the balance of audio played when wearing earphones.

21. Touch to use mono audio when wearing one earphone.

22. Touch to turn off all sounds.

23. Touch to enable or disable improving the sound quality if you use a hearing aid.

24. Touch to enable or disable making your Note 3 light up the camera flash when you have a new notification.

25. Touch to enable or disable a special assistant menu that stays on the screen at all times.

26. Touch to change how long you have to hold when you perform a touch-and-hold on the screen.

27. Scroll down for more settings.

28. Touch to enable or disable interaction control, which includes blocking areas of the screen so they do not respond to touch.

29. Touch to save your changes.

More About Text-to-Speech

By default, your Galaxy Note 3 uses the Samsung Text-to-Speech service with an option to use the Samsung service to speak any text that you need to read. You can install other text-to-speech software by searching for them in the Google Play Store. After you've installed the software, you'll have multiple choices in step 18.

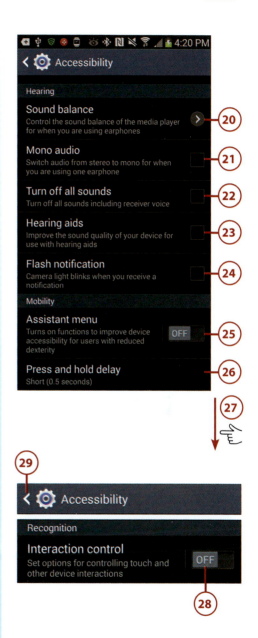

Adjusting Sound Settings

You can change the volume for games, ringtones, and alarms, change the default ringtone and notification sound, plus control what system sounds are used.

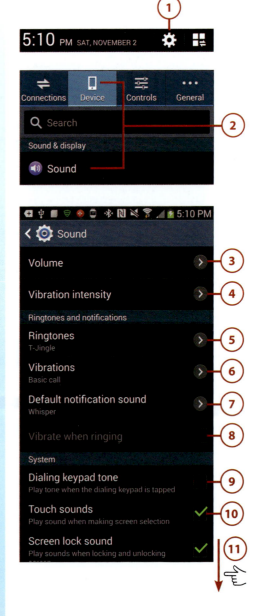

1. Pull down the Notification bar and touch the Settings icon.

2. Touch Sound on the Device tab.

3. Touch to change the volume for games and media, such as videos and music, ringtones and notifications, and alarms.

4. Touch to choose the intensity of vibrations for incoming calls, notifications, and haptic feedback.

5. Touch to choose the default notification ringtone or add new ones.

6. Touch to choose the vibration pattern used for notifications or create your own.

7. Touch to choose the sound that plays for notifications.

8. Touch to enable or disable playing a sound and vibration when being notified. This option is only available when you have your Galaxy Note 3 in Sound mode.

9. Touch to enable or disable playing touch-tone sounds when typing numbers on the phone keypad.

10. Touch to enable or disable the touch sounds that play when you touch something on the screen or a menu.

11. Scroll down for more settings.

12. Touch to enable or disable the screen lock sound that plays when your Galaxy Note 3 locks the screen after the inactivity timeout.

13. Touch to enable or disable Haptic feedback, which is a vibration that indicates that you have success- fully touched the Menu and Back keys.

14. Touch to choose the sound that plays when you remove or put back the S Pen. Learn more about the S Pen in the Prologue.

15. Touch to enable or disable a sound that plays when you tap keys.

16. Touch to enable or disable a vibra- tion that is triggered when you tap keys.

17. Touch to select Stereo or Surround sound when media is played via the HDMI cable.

18. Touch to adapt the sound output for calls and music, by taking a quick audio ear exam.

19. Touch to save your changes and return to the previous screen.

Creating Your Own Vibration Patterns

In step 6, you can choose the vibration pattern to be used when you are noti- fied, but you can also create your own. Touch Create. On the next screen, touch in the area where it reads Tap to Create, and then tap out your vibration pattern on the screen using short taps for short vibrations and long taps for longer vibra- tions. The example in the figure uses Morse Code for SOS. You can literally cre- ate any vibration pattern you want.

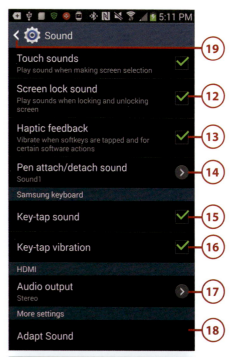

Touch to play back your vibration pattern

Touch to save it

Modifying Display Settings

You can change many display settings including the screen brightness or set it to automatic, change the screen mode, change how long to wait before your Galaxy Note 3 goes to sleep, change the size of the font used, and change whether to use the Pulse notification light.

1. Pull down the Notification bar and touch the Settings icon.

2. Touch Display under the Device tab.

3. Touch to change the screen brightness manually or set it to automatic. When on automatic, your Galaxy Note 3 uses the built-in light sensor to adjust the brightness based on the light levels in the room.

4. Touch to choose how many minutes of inactivity must pass before your Galaxy Note 3 puts the screen to sleep.

5. Touch to set how long the backlight behind the Menu and Back touch keys remain illuminated after you either touch the screen or touch one of the Touch keys.

6. Touch to choose the Screen mode, which is how the screen represents colors. You can choose Dynamic, Standard, Professional Photo, Movie, or leave it set to Adapt Display, which means your Note 3 chooses the best settings based on usage.

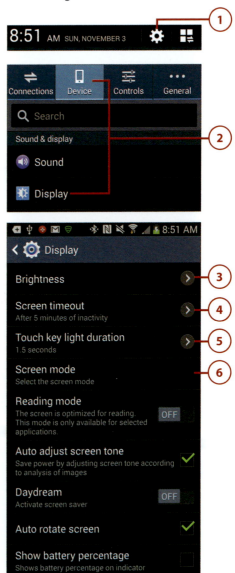

Is Adapt Display Mode Good?

If you leave your screen mode set to Adapt Display, you should know that your Note 3 adjusts the color range, saturation, and sharpness of the screen for the Gallery, Camera, Internet Web Browser, Samsung Video, Samsung WatchON, and Google Play Books apps only. All other system apps and apps that you install are not optimized. With this in mind, you might prefer to manually select an appropriate screen mode in step 6.

7. Touch to set Reading mode on or off. Reading mode adjusts the screen so its easier on your eyes, typically for reading books or working with apps that require you to look at the screen for a long time.

8. Touch to add or remove apps that, when run, automatically start Reading mode.

9. Touch to enable or disable automatically adjusting the tone of the screen based on the kinds of images being shown.

10. Touch to enable or disable Daydream mode. Daydream mode is essentially a screensaver.

11. Touch to select which screen saver to use, and manage its settings. You can also choose when the Daydream mode activates.

12. Touch to enable or disable a feature that uses the front-facing camera to determine the orientation of the screen based on the orientation of your face.

13. Touch to enable or disable displaying the battery level as a percentage as well as showing the level graphically.

14. Scroll down for more settings.

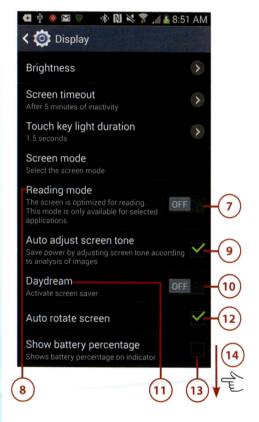

Aren't Screensavers Obsolete?

In steps 10 and 11 you can enable and manage the Daydream mode, which is essentially a screensaver as we remember it from desktop computers. For many years now, screensavers have not been needed because we no longer use Cathode Ray Tube (CRT) monitors and screens. In the days when we used CRTs, if an image remained in one spot for a long time, it would be burned into the front of the screen. Having a screensaver on a CRT monitor made sense because the images were moving and changing constantly. Screensavers continued to be used because people liked seeing the patterns and images in the screensavers. This is why Daydream mode is on your Note 3. Once activated, it can display your photos or cool color patterns after a period of inactivity, when you plug your Note 3 into a dock, or when it is charging.

15. Touch to enable editing a screen-captured image right after you take the screen capture. Learn more about screen captures in the Prologue.

16. Touch to save your changes and return to the previous screen.

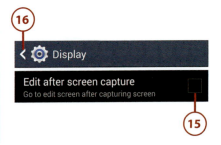

Adjusting Samsung-Specific Settings

On top of the regular Android features, Samsung has added some that only work on Samsung phones. Here is how to set those settings. For this section, assume that all screens start on the Settings screen.

Multi Window Mode

When Multi Window mode is enabled, you can use two apps at the same time on the same screen. You can read more about Multi Window mode in the Prologue.

1. Touch the Device tab.

2. Touch to enable or disable Multi Window mode.

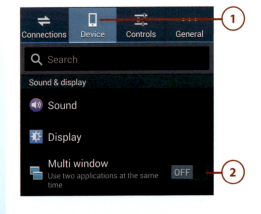

LED Indicator

In the LED Indicator screen you can decide when the LED is used.

1. Touch the Device tab.

2. Touch LED Indicator.

3. Select when the LED Indicator is triggered.

4. Touch to save your changes.

Easy Home Screen Mode

Home Screen mode changes which widgets are placed on your Home screen and how many you have on the Home screen. When Easy mode is enabled, it places a lot of widgets that have shortcuts to many apps and makes the icons larger.

1. Touch the Device tab.

2. Touch Easy Mode.

3. Touch to enable Easy mode, or disable it and return to Basic mode.

Blocking Mode

Blocking mode enables you to choose a time period when notifications are blocked. This would normally be while you are asleep, but it could be anytime you choose.

1. Touch the Device tab.

2. Touch to enable or disable Blocking mode.

3. Touch to configure Blocking mode.

4. Touch to enable or disable blocking all incoming calls while in Blocking mode.

5. Touch to enable or disable blocking all notifications while in Blocking mode.

6. Touch to enable or disable blocking all alarms and timers while in Blocking mode.

7. Touch to enable or disable blocking the LED indicator while in Blocking mode.

8. Touch to set the Blocking mode to Always. Uncheck to set it for a specific period.

9. Set the period of time when Blocking mode is automatically enabled and disabled.

10. Touch to configure which contact's calls will get through when Blocking mode is enabled.

11. Touch to save your changes and return to the previous screen.

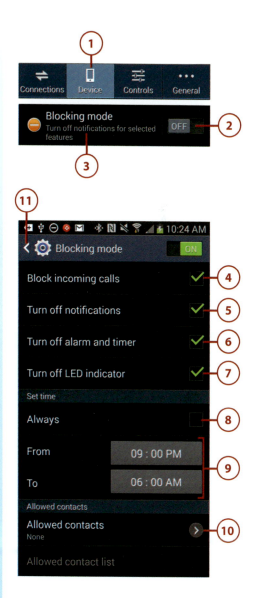

S Pen

The S Pen Settings screen enables you to configure how your S Pen behaves and even makes it possible for your Galaxy Note 3 to alert you if you leave your S Pen on the desk and walk away.

1. Touch Controls.

2. Touch S Pen.

3. Touch to disable S Pen detection, which saves the battery. S Pen detection enables your Galaxy Note 3 to detect when you remove the S Pen from its holder.

4. Touch to enable or disable S Pen Keeper that alerts you if you set down your S Pen and walk away without it.

5. Touch to enable or disable showing a pointer on the screen marking where the S Pen is hovering.

6. Touch to enable or disable a feature that opens Popup Note, which is a mini version of S Note, when you detach your S Pen. This can be useful for writing quick notes.

7. Touch to change what app is launched when you detach the S Pen. You can choose None, Action Memo, or Air Command. Learn more about Air Command in the Prologue.

8. Touch to change the sound that is played when you detach your S Pen.

9. Touch to save your changes and return to the previous screen.

Motion Control

Your Note 3 has a number of Motion Control features that enable you to use hand movements and phone movements to show information and perform certain functions.

1. Touch Controls.

2. Scroll down to Motion Control and touch to configure Motion.

3. Touch to enable or disable Air Gesture, and manage which air gestures are enabled.

4. Touch to enable or disable Air View and manage which Air View options are enabled.

>>>Go Further

AIR GESTURES

Air Gestures keep monitoring the front-facing sensor on your Note 3 to enable the following features:

• Quick Glance displays key information such as number of missed calls, number of unread emails, and battery percentage if you reach toward your phone while the screen is off.

• Air Jump enables you to scroll up and down through web pages and emails by moving your hand up or down over the sensor.

• Air Browse enables you to move left and right through items on the screen by moving your hand left and right over the sensor.

• Air Call-Accept enables you to answer a call by making a specific gesture over the sensor.

>>>Go Further

AIR VIEW

Air View enables you to hover your finger or the S Pen close the screen to perform certain functions, such as previewing information, list scrolling, and more.

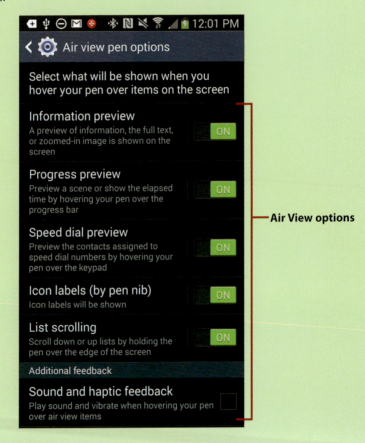

Air View options

5. Touch to enable or disable Air Command, which enables you to perform additional functions by pressing the button on the S Pen while you hover it over the screen.

6. Touch to enable or disable Motions that allow your Note 3 to do certain things when you pick it up, tilt it, pan it, or turn it over.

7. Touch to enable or disable Smart Screen and decide which Smart Screen functions are enabled. Smart Screen uses the front sensor to track your eyes and perform certain functions based on where you are looking.

8. Touch to increase touch sensitivity so you can use your Note 3 with gloves on.

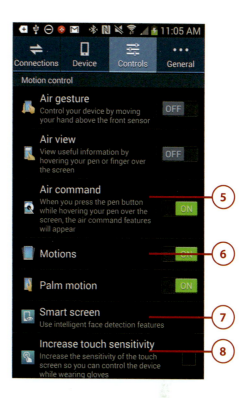

MOTIONS

Motions is a feature that allows your Note 3 to do certain things when you pick it up, tilt it, pan it, or turn it over including

- Direct Call enables you to lift the phone to your ear to automatically place a call to a contact whose phone number is on the screen.

- Smart Alert vibrates the phone as you pick it up if you have missed any calls or messages.

- Tilt to Zoom enables you to tilt your phone to zoom in and out of images.

- Pan enables you to move around a zoomed-in image by moving your phone rather than swiping around the image.

>>>Go Further

- Turn Over enables you to mute or pause sounds by turning your Note 3 face down on a surface.

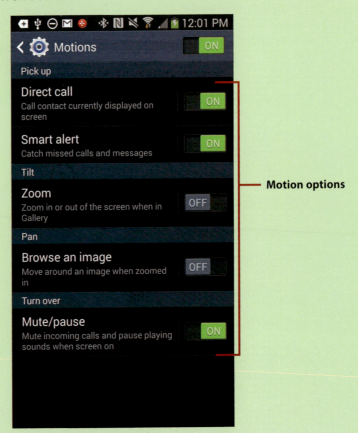

Motion options

>>>Go Further

SMART SCREEN

Smart screen uses the front sensor to watch your eyes and face to do the following things:

- Smart Stay keeps the screen on as long as you are looking at it.

- Smart Rotation watches your face and rotates the screen between portrait and landscape based on your face's orientation.

- Smart Pause pauses a video when it detects that you have looked away from the screen.

- Smart Scroll scrolls what you are looking at based on the angle you tilt your head.

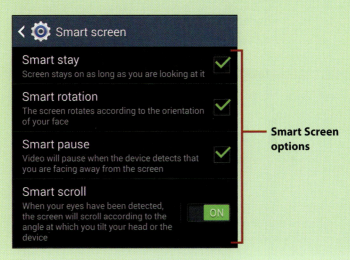

Smart Screen options

Browse without leaving traces using the Incognito feature

In this chapter, you discover how to browse the World Wide Web using the Chrome browser app that comes with your Galaxy Note 3. Topics include the following:

→ Bookmarking websites

→ Using tricks to browse quickly

→ Keeping track of websites you have visited

→ Configuring Chrome to work your way

Browsing the Web

Your Galaxy Note 3 comes with not one, but two web browsers to enable you to explore the Web on its large screen. This chapter shows you how to use Chrome, a browser developed by Google. You can bookmark sites you want to revisit, hold your Galaxy Note 3 in landscape orientation so you can see more on the screen, and even share your GPS location with sites.

Navigating with Chrome

The Chrome browser app enables you to access sites quickly, book-mark them for future use, and return instantly to the sites you visit most frequently. You can even sync your open Chrome tabs among your Galaxy Note 3, your other portable devices, and your computer.

1. Touch the Chrome icon. This icon might be on the Apps screen or in the Google folder on the Apps screen.

2. Touch the omnibox—a combined address box and search box—to type in a new web address. If the website has moved the previous page up so that the omnibox is hidden, drag the web page down so that the omnibox appears again.

3. Touch to navigate among your tabs. Read more about tabs later in this chapter.

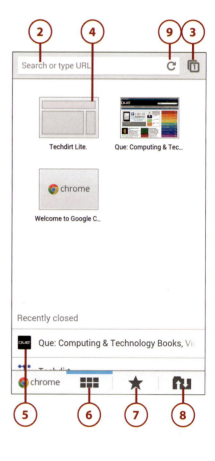

4. Touch a thumbnail to go to one of your Most Visited sites.

5. Touch to display one of the pages you have closed most recently. You might need to scroll down to reach the button for the page you want.

6. Touch to display the list of Most Visited sites.

7. Touch to display your bookmarks.

8. Touch to display your Other Devices list, which shows the tabs open on your other phones, tablets, and computers that use Chrome and sign in to your Google account.

9. Touch to refresh the display of the current page. You'd normally do this either if a page failed to load completely or to load updated information, such as fresh news.

10. Touch the Menu button to display more options for working with Chrome and web pages.

Web Page Options

While a web page is open, you have a number of options, such as creating a bookmark for the page or finding text on the page.

1. Touch the Menu button to display the menu.

2. Touch to go back to the previous web page you visited on this tab.

3. Touch to go forward again in the chain of pages you've browsed on this tab. Touching this button takes you to the last web page from which you went back (as described in step 2). This button is unavailable until you go back from a page.

4. Touch to add a bookmark for this page.

5. Touch New Tab to open a new tab.

6. Touch New Incognito Tab to open a new Incognito tab for private browsing. Incognito tabs are covered later in this chapter.

7. Touch Bookmarks to display your bookmarks.

8. Touch Other Devices to display your Other Devices list.

9. Touch History to display the History screen, which contains a list of the pages you have visited. This list comes from each device that signs into the same Chrome account.

10. Touch Share to share this web page with other people using apps such as Email, Gmail, Facebook, Messaging, or Twitter. The Share Via dialog shows all the apps you can use to share the web page.

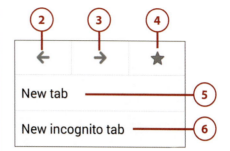

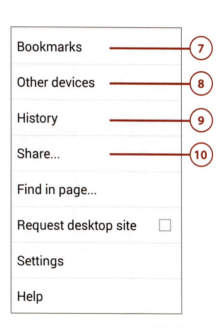

11. Touch Find in Page to search this page for specific text you type.

12. Touch Request Desktop Site to enable or disable forcing websites to show the regular view of a web page designed for full-size screens instead of a mobile view designed for small screens.

13. Touch to change the settings for the Chrome browser.

14. Touch to get help.

Bookmarks

Other devices

History

Share...

Find in page... ⸺ 11

Request desktop site ☐ 12

Settings ⸺ 13

Help ⸺ 14

Browser Tricks

The Chrome browser app has some neat tricks to help you browse regular websites comfortably on your Galaxy Note 3's screen.

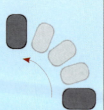

DIY hardware hacking...easy as Pi ®!
Raspberry Pi is taking off like a rocket! You can use this amazing, dirt-cheap, credit card-sized computer to learn powerful hardware hacking techniques as you build incredibly creative and useful projects! This complete, full-color guide requires absolutely no experience with either hardware hacking or computer programming. Colorful photos guide you through each project, and the step-by-step instructions are stunningly clear and easy!
1. Start with the absolute basics:
. Discover why millions of people are so passionate about the Pi!
. Tour the hardware, including storage, connections, and networking
. Install and run Raspbian, Raspberry Pi's Linux-based operating system
. Manage devices and configuration files
. Network Raspberry Pi and add Wi-Fi
. Program Raspberry Pi using Python, Scratch, XHTML, PHP, and MySQL
2. Next, build all these great projects:
. Media Center

Portrait

1. Rotate your Galaxy Note 3 so that its long edge is sideways. This puts the screen into what's called *landscape orientation*. Your Galaxy Note 3 automatically switches the screen to Landscape mode.

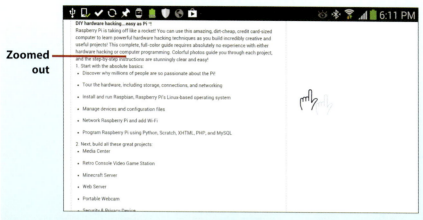

Zoomed out

Landscape

2. Double-tap the screen to zoom in and out.

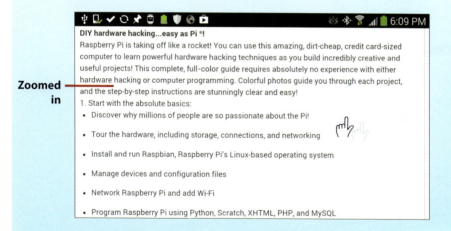

Zoomed in

If Chrome does not switch to landscape mode when you rotate the Galaxy Note 3, you need to turn on screen rotation. Pull down the notification panel and tap the Quick Settings icon to display the Quick Settings screen and then tap Screen Rotation, turning the arrow green.

Pinch to Zoom

When you need to zoom in further, or zoom in to exactly the degree you want, use the alternative way to zoom. Place your thumb and forefinger on the screen and spread them apart to zoom in. Move them back together to zoom out.

Managing Bookmarks, Most Visited Sites, and Other Devices

The Chrome app enables you to bookmark your favorite websites for quick access, but it also keeps a list of the sites you visit most often so you can return to them at the tap of an icon. The app also syncs your open tabs among your devices that run Chrome and sign in to the same Google account, so you can quickly pick up browsing on your Galaxy Note 3 exactly where you left it on your desktop computer, laptop, or tablet—or vice versa.

Manage Bookmarks

1. Touch the Menu button.

2. Touch Bookmarks. Normally, the Mobile Bookmarks folder opens. If not, you can navigate to it manually.

3. Touch to display the main Bookmarks folder. From there, you can touch a bookmark it contains or another bookmarks folder.

4. Touch a bookmarks folder to display the bookmarks it contains.

5. Touch a bookmark to display the web page it marks.

6. Touch and hold a bookmark to display a menu of extra actions you can take with it.

7. Touch Open in New Tab to open the bookmarked web page in a new tab.

8. Touch Open in Incognito Tab to open the bookmark in an Incognito tab.

9. Touch Edit Bookmark to edit the bookmark. For example, you can change the bookmark's name or move it to a different folder.

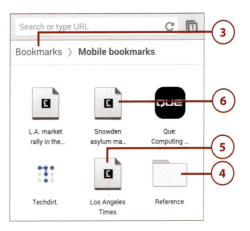

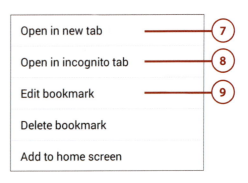

10. Touch Delete Bookmark to delete the bookmark.

11. Touch Add to Home Screen to add the bookmark to your Galaxy Note 3's Home screen, where you can quickly access it without having to switch to Chrome first. This is a great move for bookmarks that point to your most valued sites.

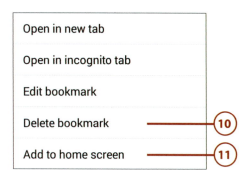

Create a Bookmark

1. Navigate to the page you want to bookmark.

2. Touch the Menu button to open the menu.

3. Touch to start creating a new bookmark.

4. Change the bookmark name if you want to. The default is the web page's title; you might prefer a shorter name.

5. Edit the address if necessary. If you went to the right page in step 1, you do not need to change the address.

6. Select the folder in which to save the bookmark. You can create new folders as needed.

7. Touch Save.

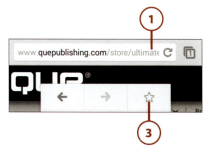

Manage the Most Visited Sites List

The Chrome app's Most Visited sites list enables you to quickly return to sites you visit frequently but that you have not necessarily bookmarked.

1. Touch the Menu button.

2. Touch Bookmarks to display the Bookmarks screen.

3. Touch to display the Most Visited screen.

4. Touch to open one of the pages in the current tab.

5. Touch and hold a page thumbnail to display further options.

6. Touch to open in a new tab.

7. Touch to open in an Incognito tab.

8. Touch to remove the web page from the Most Visited list.

Manage the Other Devices List

The Other Devices list gives you instant access to the tabs open in Chrome on your other devices, such as your tablet and your PC or Mac.

1. Touch the Menu button.

2. Touch Other Devices.

3. Touch a heading to expand or collapse the list of pages on a device.

4. Touch a page to open it.

Managing Multiple Tabs

The Chrome app can have multiple web pages open at the same time, each in a different tab. This enables you to open multiple web pages at once and switch between them.

1. Touch the tab icon in the Chrome app.

2. Touch to open a new tab.

3. Touch to close an existing tab.

4. Touch a tab to switch to it.

Browsing in Secret

If you want to visit a website in secret, you can. Visiting a website in secret means that the site you visit does not appear in your browser history or search history and does not otherwise leave a trace of itself on your Galaxy Note 3. To browse secretly, create a new Incognito browser tab by touching the Menu button and then touching New Incognito Tab. Inside that browser tab, all sites you visit are in secret.

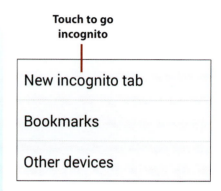

Touch to go incognito

Customizing Browser Settings

You can customize Chrome to make it behave the way you want. Here are the various settings you can change.

1. Touch the Menu button.

2. Touch Settings.

3. Touch your Google account name.

4. Touch Sync to turn sync on or off. If you turn sync on, you can choose which items to sync: Autofill data, bookmarks, history, passwords, open tabs, or everything. You can also choose whether to use encryption.

5. Touch Chrome to Mobile to enable or disable sending web pages from your computer to the Chrome app on your Galaxy Note 3.

6. Touch Auto Sign-In to enable or disable automatically signing in to Google sites. Signing in automatically saves you time and typing but decreases your privacy.

7. Touch to return to the Settings screen.

8. Touch Search Engine to choose your search engine. Your choices might include Google, Yahoo!, Bing, Ask, and AOL.

9. Touch Autofill Forms to enable or disable the Autofill Forms feature. This feature lets you add profile information—your name, address, and so on—and credit card information for the Chrome app to fill in automatically on web forms. This means you can complete web forms and spend your money with even less effort.

10. Touch Save Passwords to enable or disable the Chrome app's ability to save your passwords so it can enter them for you.

11. Touch Privacy to display the Privacy screen.

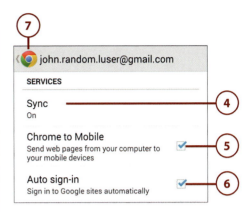

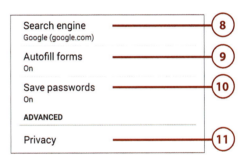

12. Touch Navigation Error Suggestions to enable or disable showing suggestions for web addresses that you enter incorrectly or that Chrome cannot locate.

13. Touch Search and URL Suggestions to enable or disable showing related queries and popular websites similar to those you type in the omnibox.

14. Touch Network Action Predictions to enable or disable the Network Action Predictions feature. See the nearby sidebar for details.

Privacy

Navigation error suggestions
Show suggestions for alternatives when a web address does not resolve or a connection cannot be made — (12)

Search and URL suggestions
Use a prediction service to show related queries and popular websites as you type in the address bar — (13)

Network action predictions
Improve page load performance — (14)

Usage and crash reports
Never send

'Do Not Track'
Off

CLEAR BROWSING DATA

>>>Go Further

WHAT ARE NETWORK ACTION PREDICTIONS?

Network Action Predictions is a feature that allows the Chrome app to preload web pages you are likely to want to load. The app does this in two ways. First, when you start typing an address in the omnibox, the Chrome app preloads a matching web page if it has high confidence that you will want it—for example, because you have visited that page before. Second, when you are on a particular web page, the app might preload the pages whose links you are most likely to click—for example, the top few search results.

If Chrome has predicted correctly and loaded the correct pages into memory, when you touch a link, that page renders straight from your Galaxy Note 3's memory instead of first loading over the network. Although this can be a time-saver, it means that your Galaxy Note 3 might preload pages that you will not look at, which can lead to wasted data usage. When you enable Network Action Predictions, you can choose Only on Wi-Fi on the Bandwidth Management screen to allow the Chrome app to preload pages only when your Galaxy Note 3 is connected to Wi-Fi, not when it's connected via a cellular data connection.

15. Touch Usage and Crash Reports to choose whether to send usage and crash reports to Google. Your choices are Always Send, Only Send on Wi-Fi, and Never Send. If you are happy to provide this data, choosing Only Send on Wi-Fi is usually the best choice because it prevents the reports from consuming your cellular data allowance.

16. Touch 'Do Not Track' to choose whether to turn on the Do Not Track feature. This feature requests that the websites you visit not track you, but websites are not bound to honor the request.

17. Touch Clear Browsing Data to display the Clear Browsing Data dialog.

18. Touch Clear Browsing History to enable or disable clearing your browsing history. This clears the history of websites you have visited using the Chrome app on your Galaxy Note 3.

19. Touch Clear the Cache to enable or disable clearing the cache, data that Chrome stores so that it can redisplay web pages more quickly when you visit them again.

20. Touch Clear Cookies, Site Data to enable or disable clearing your cookies and website data. Browser cookies are used by websites to personalize your visit by storing information specific to you in the cookies.

21. Touch Clear Saved Passwords to enable or disable clearing your saved passwords.

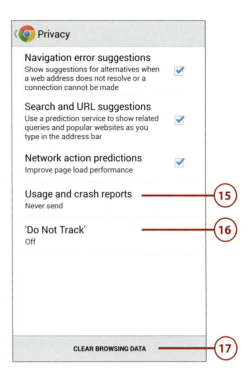

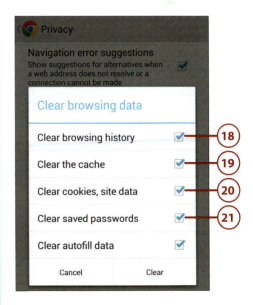

22. Touch Clear Autofill Data to enable or disable clearing your Autofill data.

23. Touch Clear to clear the items whose boxes you checked in the Clear Browsing Data dialog.

24. Touch to return to the Settings screen.

25. Touch Accessibility.

26. Drag the Text Scaling slider to make the text in the Preview box appear at a comfortable size for reading. This is the minimum size to which the Chrome app zooms the text when you double-tap a paragraph.

What Is Text Scaling?

When you use text scaling, you instruct your Galaxy Note 3 to always increase or decrease the font sizes used on a web page by a specific percentage. For example, you can automatically make all text 150% larger than was originally intended.

27. Touch Force Enable Zoom to turn on or off Chrome's ability to zoom in on a website that prevents zooming. Some websites turn off zooming because their creators consider design to be more important than readability.

28. Touch to return to the Settings screen.

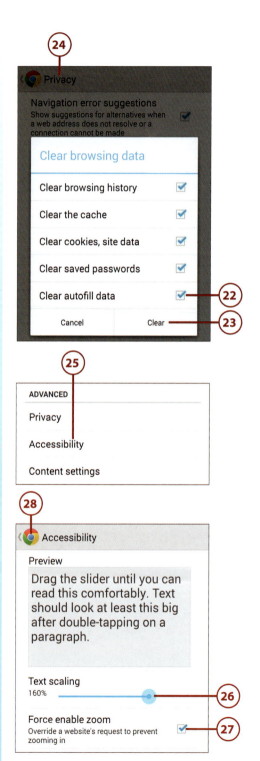

29. Touch Content Settings to display the Content Settings screen.

30. Touch Accept Cookies to enable or disable accepting cookies. Browser cookies are used by websites to personalize your visit by storing information specific to you in the cookies.

31. Touch Enable JavaScript to enable or disable JavaScript. JavaScript is used on many web pages for formatting and other functions, so you might want to leave this enabled.

32. Touch Block Pop-Ups to enable or disable blocking pop-up windows. Pop-up windows are almost always advertisements, so keeping this enabled is a good idea; however, some websites might not work correctly if pop-up blocking is on.

33. Touch Voice and Video Calling to enable or disable giving websites access to your Galaxy Note 3's microphone and camera through Chrome. If you don't need this capability, it's best to disable it.

34. Touch Google Translate to enable or disable the Google Translate service, which you can use to translate web pages.

35. Touch Google Location Settings to allow or disallow websites access to your GPS information. Providing your location to websites is helpful when you need information related to where you are, but at other times, you might prefer to keep your location private.

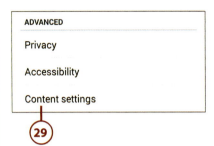

ADVANCED

Privacy

Accessibility

Content settings

(29)

Content settings

Accept cookies — (30)
Allow sites to save and read cookie data

Enable JavaScript — (31)
Allow sites to run JavaScript

Block pop-ups — (32)
Block pop-ups from all sites

Voice and Video calling — (33)
Allow sites to access microphone and camera

Google Translate — (34)
On

Google location settings — (35)
Allow sites to request access to your location

Website settings
Advanced settings for individual websites

36. Touch to view the list of websites that are storing data on your Galaxy Note 3. You can then clear the data for a specific website if necessary.

37. Touch to return to the Settings screen.

38. Touch Bandwidth Management to display the Bandwidth Management screen.

39. Touch Preload Webpages to open the Preload Webpages dialog. (Refer to the "What Are Network Action Predictions" sidebar for more information about preload-ing webpages.)

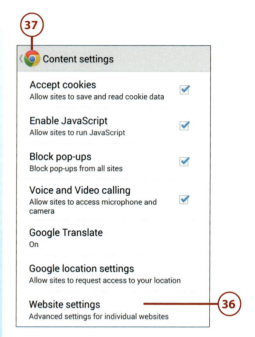

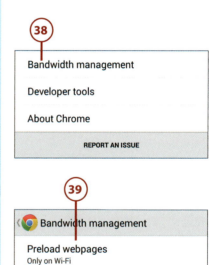

40. Touch to preload pages over both Wi-Fi and cellular connections.

41. Touch to preload pages over Wi-Fi only.

42. Touch to turn off preloading. You would normally do this only if you need to minimize data use on your Wi-Fi connection.

43. Touch to return to the Settings screen.

What Are the Developer Tools in Chrome Settings?

The Chrome app's Developer Tools screen offers two features intended for people developing apps for Android, but one of the features is useful for nondevelopers as well. The Enable Tilt Scrolling feature enables you to scroll through your open tabs in Chrome by tilting your Galaxy Note 3 backward and forward. The Enable USB Web debugging option lets developers use Chrome on a PC or Mac to hunt down bugs in Chrome on Android.

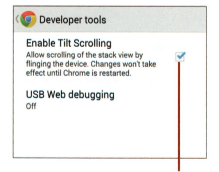

Touch to turn on tilt scrolling for tab

Touch to open
Gmail email only

Touch to open email

In this chapter, you discover your Galaxy Note 3's email applications for Gmail and other accounts, such as POP3, IMAP, and even Microsoft Exchange. Topics include the following:

→ Sending and receiving email
→ Working with attachments
→ Working with Gmail labels
→ Changing settings

4

Email

Your Galaxy Note 3 has two email programs: the Gmail app, which only works with Gmail, and the Email app that works with POP3, IMAP, and Microsoft Exchange accounts.

Gmail

When you first set up your Galaxy Note 3, you set up a Gmail account. The Gmail application enables you to have multiple Gmail accounts, which is useful if you have a business account and a personal account.

Add a Google Account

When you first set up your Galaxy Note 3, you added your first Google (Gmail) account. The following steps describe how to add a second account.

1. Pull down the Notification bar and touch the Settings icon.

2. Touch Accounts under the General tab.

3. Touch Add Account.

4. Touch Google.

5. Touch Existing if you already have a Google account.

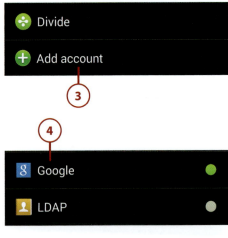

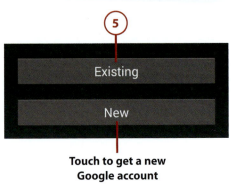

Touch to get a new Google account

6. Enter your existing Google account name. This is your Gmail address.

What If I Don't Have a Second Google Account?

If you don't already have a second Google account but want to set one up, in step 5, touch Get a Google Account. Your Galaxy Note 3 walks you through the steps of choosing a new Google account.

7. Enter your existing Google password.

8. Touch the right-pointing arrow to move to the next screen.

9. Touch to allow or disallow Google from emailing you news and offers from Google Play and then touch the right-pointing arrow at the bottom of the screen (not shown).

10. Touch Not Now to skip the step to save credit-card information to Google Wallet. Right now you just want to set up the email account.

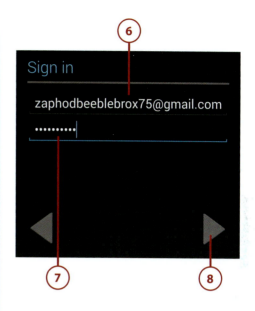

11. Select what components of your Google account you want to synchronize with your Galaxy Note 3.

12. Touch the right-pointing arrow to finish the Google account setup.

Why Multiple Google Accounts?

You are probably wondering why you would want multiple Google accounts. Isn't one good enough? Actually, it is not that uncommon to have multiple Google accounts. It can be a way to compartmentalize your life between work and play. You might run a small business using one account, but email only friends with another. Your Galaxy Note 3 supports multiple accounts, but still enables you to interact with them in one place.

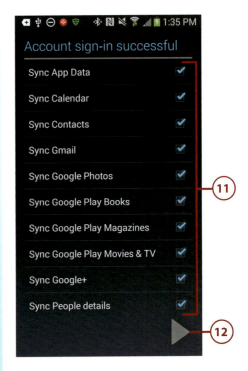

Navigate the Gmail App

This task shows you how to navigate the main screen of the Gmail app.

1. Touch the Gmail icon.

2. Touch to switch between Gmail accounts (if you use more than one) or switch from the Inbox label to one of your other labels.

3. Touch to compose a new email.

4. Touch to search the current label for an email.

5. Pull down and release the list to manually refresh the current view.

6. Touch the Menu button and touch Label settings to manage your labels.

7. Touch the star to add the email to the Starred label.

Indicates that the email is important

Stars and Labels

Gmail allows you to use stars and labels to help organize your email. In most email clients, you can create folders in your mailbox to help you organize your emails. For example, you might create a folder called "emails from the boss" and move any emails you receive from your manager to that folder. Gmail doesn't use the term folders; instead, it uses the term labels. You can create labels in Gmail and choose an email to label. When you do this, the email moves to a folder with that label, but the email is also still in the Inbox with a label that distinguishes it from other emails. And email that you mark with a star is actually just getting a label called "starred." But when viewing your Gmail, you see the yellow star next to an email. People normally add a star to an email as a reminder of something important.

Compose Gmail Email

1. Touch the Compose icon.

2. Touch to change the Gmail account from which the message is being sent (if you have multiple Gmail accounts).

3. Type names in the To field. If the name matches someone in your Contacts, the name is displayed and you can touch it to select it.

Can You Carbon Copy (Cc) and Blind Carbon Copy (Bcc)?

While you are composing your email, you can add recipients to the To field, as shown in the figure for step 3; however, there are no Carbon Copy (Cc) and Blind Carbon Copy (Bcc) fields shown. You can add these fields by touching the Menu button and touching Add Cc/Bcc. After you do that, the Cc and Bcc fields display.

4. Type a subject for your email.

5. Type the body of the email.

6. Touch to send the email.

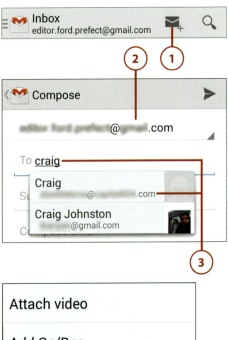

Touch to show the
Cc and Bcc fields

Add Attachments to Messages

Before sending an email, you can add one or more attachments. You can attach pictures or videos, but if you use Dropbox you can attach any file that is in your Dropbox folders. If you use OfficeSuite for your Microsoft Office documents, you can attach files from there, too.

1. With an email message open, touch the Menu button.

2. Touch Attach Picture or Attach Video (they do the same thing).

3. Touch Gallery. For this example we will attach a picture from the Gallery.

4. Navigate the Gallery app to find the picture you want to attach.

Attach picture

Attach video

Touch to attach any file type stored in your Dropbox

Choose type of attachment

Dropbox

Gallery

Photos

Samsung Link

Touch to attach a picture stored in your Google+ Photos account

Touch to attach any file stored in your Samsung Link account

ShareViaWiFi(2)

Camera(7)   5 February 2...(4)

5. Attachments are listed below the body of the email.

Touch to remove the attachment

Indicates attachments

Rich text formatting is preserved

Read Gmail Email

1. Touch an email to open it.

2. Touch to reply to the sender of the email. This does not reply to anyone in the Cc field.

3. Touch the Menu button to do a Reply All (reply to all recipients) or Forward the email.

4. Touch to expand the email header to see all recipients and all other email header information.

5. Touch to "star" the email, which adds it to the star label. Read more about labels earlier in this chapter.

6. Touch to move the email to the Gmail Archive folder.

7. Touch to permanently delete the email.

8. Touch to change the label of the email. Read more about labels earlier in this chapter.

9. Touch to mark the message as unread and return to the message list.

More Email Actions

1. With an email message open, touch the Menu button.

2. Touch to report the email as spam.

3. Touch to mute the email conversation. Once the email is muted, you no longer see emails in the conversation.

4. Touch to report the email as a phishing scam.

5. Touch to mark the message as not important or important.

| Change labels |
| Mark not important — ⑤ |
| Mute — ③ |
| Revert auto-sizing |
| Report spam — ② |
| Report phishing — ④ |

>>>Go Further

CAN I UNMUTE?

In step 3 you can mute a conversation, which means you hide it and any new emails in that conversation. You will never see those emails again. You can unmute conversations by switching to the All Mail label, opening the muted conversation, touching the Menu button, and then choosing Move to Inbox. This effectively unmutes the conversation, and it will appear back in your Inbox. You'll also see all future emails in that conversation.

What Is Important?

Gmail tries to automatically figure out which of the emails you receive are important. As it learns, it might guess wrong. If an email is marked as important but it is not important, you can manually change the status to not important as described in step 5. Important emails have a yellow arrow, whereas emails that are not important have a clear arrow.

What Are Conversations?

Conversations are Gmail's version of email threads. When you look at the main view of the Gmail app, you see a list of email conversations. The conversation might have only one email in it, but to Gmail that's a conversation. As you and others reply to that original email, Gmail groups those emails in a thread, or conversation.

What Happens to Your Spam and Phishing Emails?

When you mark an email in Gmail as spam or a phishing scam, two things happen. The message gets a label called Spam. In addition, a copy of that email is sent to Gmail's spam servers so they are now aware of a possible new spam or phishing scam email that is circulating around the Internet. Based on what the servers see for all Gmail users, they block that spam or phishing email from reaching other Gmail users. So the bottom line is that you should always mark spam and phishing emails because it helps all of us.

Modify Gmail Settings

You can customize the way Gmail accounts work on your Galaxy Note 3, including changing the email signature and choosing which labels synchronize.

1. Touch the Menu button.

2. Touch Settings.

Email Signature

An email signature is a bit of text that is automatically added to the bottom of any emails you send from your Galaxy Note 3. It is added when you compose a new email, reply to an email, or forward an email. A typical use for a signature is to automatically add your name and maybe some contact information at the end of your emails. Email signatures are sometimes referred to as email footers.

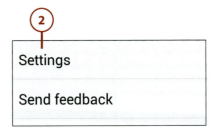

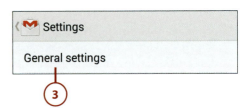

3. Touch General Settings.

4. Touch to change what happens if you swipe your finger over a conversation list. You can set it so that the conversation is only archived, only deleted, or archived and deleted at the same time.

5. Touch to enable or disable swiping a message to archive it.

6. Touch to enable or disable showing the email sender's contact list image beside his or her's name.

7. Touch to enable or disable making Reply All the default action when replying to emails. Normally only Reply is used. Reply All replies to the sender and all recipients.

8. Touch to enable or disable Auto-fit. When enabled, Auto-fit shrinks all emails so that they fit on the screen, but you can use the unpinch gesture to zoom in.

9. Touch Auto-advance to select which screen your Galaxy Note 3 must show after you delete or archive an email. Your choices are Newer Conversation, Older Conversation, and Conversation List.

10. Touch to change the behavior of the message actions bar as you scroll through a message. Your choices are to keep it at the top of the screen as you scroll, only keep it at the top of the screen when in Portrait mode, or don't show it at all.

11. Touch to enable or disable confirmation before deleting a message or entire conversation.

12. Scroll down for more options.

13. Touch to enable or disable confirmation before archiving a message or entire conversation.

14. Touch to enable or disable confirmation before sending an email.

15. Touch to return to the main Settings screen.

16. Touch one of your Gmail accounts to change settings specific to that account.

17. Touch to enable or disable showing your Priority Inbox instead of your regular Inbox when opening the Gmail app.

18. Touch to enable or disable getting notified when new email arrives for this Gmail account.

19. Touch to select how to get notified when new email arrives for this account.

20. Touch to enter a signature that will appear at the end of all emails composed using this account.

21. Touch to change how this account is synchronized, what is synchronized, or remove it entirely.

22. Touch to select how many days of mail to synchronize with your Galaxy Note 3.

23. Touch to manage labels. Read more about managing labels in the next task.

24. Touch to enable or disable downloading attachments while connected to a Wi-Fi network.

25. Touch to return to the main Settings screen.

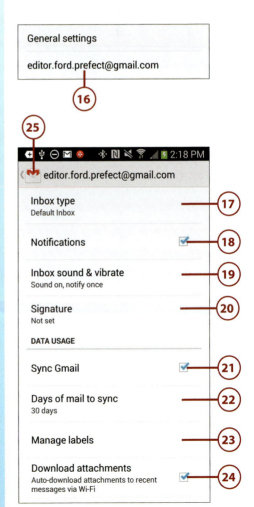

Manage Gmail Labels

Gmail labels are Google's name for email folders. You can manage how each of them synchronize and alert you.

1. Touch the Menu button.
2. Touch Settings.
3. Select an account to manage labels for.
4. Touch Manage Labels.
5. Touch a label to manage it.

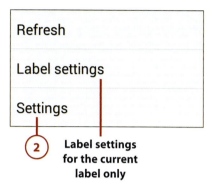

2 **Label settings for the current label only**

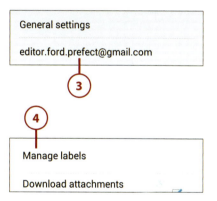

3

4

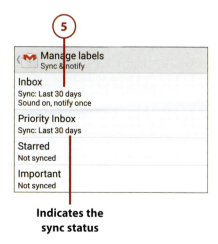

5

Indicates the sync status

6. Touch to enable synchronization of this label to your Galaxy Note 3 and whether to synchronize 30 days of email or all email. After synchronization is enabled, the rest of the settings on this screen become available.

7. Touch to enable or disable being notified when new email arrives in this label.

8. Touch to select the ringtone that plays when you are notified of new email in this label.

9. Touch to choose whether to also vibrate when new email arrives in this label.

10. Touch to enable or disable notifying you once when multiple emails arrive in this label, as opposed to notifying for each one.

11. Touch to save your changes.

Email Application

The Email application supports all email accounts with the exception of Gmail. This includes any corporate email accounts that use Microsoft Exchange or corporate email systems, such as Lotus Domino/Notes, that have an ActiveSync gateway. In addition to corporate email accounts, the Email application also supports POP3 and IMAP accounts. These are typically hosted by your Internet service provider, but also by places like Yahoo! or Hotmail.

Add a Work Email Account

Your Galaxy Note 3 can synchronize your contacts from your work email account as long as your company uses Microsoft Exchange or an email gateway that supports Microsoft ActiveSync (such as Lotus Traveler for Lotus Domino/Notes email systems). It might be useful to be able to keep your work and personal contacts on one mobile device instead of carrying two phones around all day.

1. From the Home screen, pull down the Notification bar and touch the Settings icon.

2. Touch Accounts under the General tab.

3. Touch Add Account.

4. Touch Microsoft Exchange ActiveSync.

5. Enter your full corporate email address.

6. Enter your corporate network password.

7. Touch Next.

Error Adding Account? Guess the Server.

Your Galaxy Note 3 tries to work out some information about your company's ActiveSync setup. If it can't, you are prompted to enter the ActiveSync server name manually. If you don't know what it is, you can try guessing it. If, for example, your email address is dsimons@allhitradio.com, the ActiveSync server is most probably webmail.allhitradio.com or autodiscover.allhitradio.com. If options like these don't work, ask your email administrator.

8. Touch to agree that your mail administrator may impose security restrictions on your Galaxy Note 3 if you proceed.

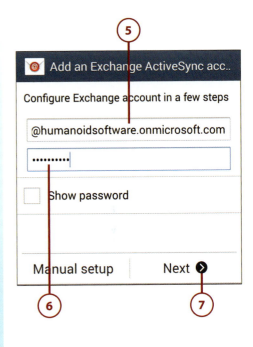

9. Touch to choose how often your corporate email is delivered to your Galaxy Note 3. Push means that as it arrives in your Inbox at work, it is delivered to your phone. You can set it to Manual, which means that your work email is only delivered when you open the Email app on your phone. You can also set the delivery frequency from every 5 minutes to every hour.

10. Touch to choose how email is synchronized to your Galaxy Note 3.

11. Touch to choose how much of an email is retrieved.

12. Touch to choose how many days calendar items are synced to your Note 3.

13. Touch to enable or disable being notified when new email arrives from your corporate Inbox.

14. Touch to enable or disable syncing your corporate email to your Note 3.

15. Scroll down to see more settings.

16. Touch to enable or disable syncing corporate contacts to your Note 3.

17. Touch to enable or disable synchronizing your corporate calendar to your Galaxy Note 3.

18. Touch to enable or disable syncing your corporate tasks to your Note 3.

19. Touch to enable or disable synchronizing SMS (text) messages you receive on your Galaxy Note 3 to your corporate Inbox.

20. Touch to enable or disable automatically downloading email attachments when your Galaxy Note 3 is connected to a Wi-Fi network.

21. Touch Next.

22. Touch Activate to allow your company's mail server to act as a device administrator for your Note 3.

23. Enter a name for this email account. Use something meaningful that describes the purpose of the account, such as Work Email.

24. Touch Done to complete the setup.

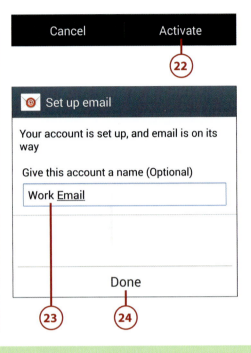

CAN YOU TRULY KEEP WORK AND PRIVATE DATA SEPARATE?

More and more companies are adopting a Bring Your Own Device (BYOD) policy, which means that they expect you to use your personal phone to get access to company emails, contacts, calendar, and internal apps. As we have seen, your Galaxy Note 3 fully supports accessing your company's email system, but when you activate, you have to agree to allow your administrator control over your phone. This is not ideal as the administrator can see what apps you have installed, and he can send a self-destruct command to your Galaxy Note 3, which means you lose all your private data and apps. Dual Persona is fast becoming the way for you to truly keep your private data private and not allow your company to wipe your phone or see what you have installed. A few companies today provide this service, including Enterproid (the product is called DIVIDE), Good Technology (the product is called GOOD), and Samsung (the system is called KNOX). The idea is that your Galaxy Note 3 has two personalities—a work persona and a private persona. All work data is kept in its own separate area on your phone, and administrators from your company have no control over the rest of your phone.

Switch to KNOX —

Switch to Divide —

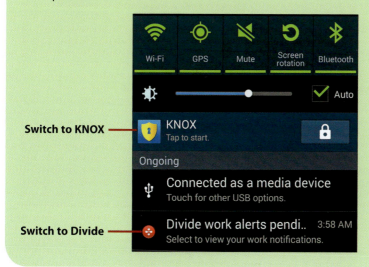

Add a New POP3 or IMAP Account

1. Pull down the Notification bar and touch the Settings icon.

2. Touch Accounts under the General tab.

3. Touch Add Account.

4. Touch Email.

5. Enter your email address.

6. Enter your password.

7. Touch Next.

Why Manual Setup?

Your Galaxy Note 3 tries to figure out the settings to set up your email account. This works most of the time when you are using common email providers such as Yahoo! or Hotmail. It also works with large ISPs such as Comcast, Road Runner, Optimum Online, and so on. It might not work for smaller ISPs, in smaller countries, or if you have created your own website and set up your own email. In these cases, you need to set up your email manually.

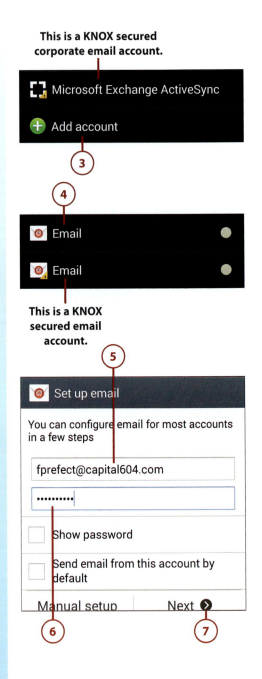

This is a KNOX secured corporate email account.

Microsoft Exchange ActiveSync

Add account

This is a KNOX secured email account.

Email

Email

Set up email

You can configure email for most accounts in a few steps

fprefect@capital604.com

·········

Show password

Send email from this account by default

Manual setup   Next

8. Touch POP3 or IMAP. IMAP has more intelligence to it, so select that when possible.

9. Ensure that the information on the outgoing server screen is accurate.

10. Touch Next.

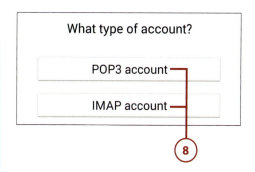

Where Can I Find This Information?

If you need to manually set up your email account, you must have a few pieces of information. Always check your ISP's, or email service provider's, website, and look for instructions on how to set up your email on a computer or smartphone. This is normally under the Support section of the website.

Username and Password

On the Incoming Server and Outgoing Server screens, your username and password should already be filled out because you typed them in earlier. If not, enter them.

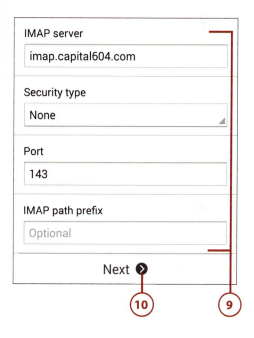

11. Ensure that the information on the incoming server screen is accurate.

12. Touch Next.

13. Touch to change the frequency in which email from this account synchronizes to your Note 3.

14. Touch to check the box if you want email to synchronize between this account and your Note 3.

15. Touch to check the box if you want email to be sent from this account by default.

16. Touch to check the box if you want to be notified when new email arrives into this account.

17. Touch to check the box if you want attachments to be automatically downloaded when you are connected to a Wi-Fi network.

18. Touch Next.

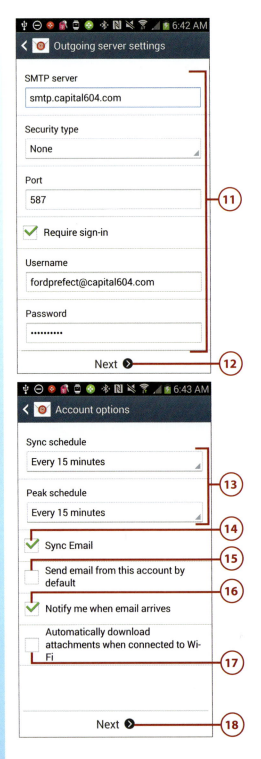

19. Enter a friendly name for this account, like Home Email.

20. Enter your full name or the name you want to be displayed when people receive emails sent from this account.

21. Touch Done to save the settings for this account and return to the Add Accounts screen.

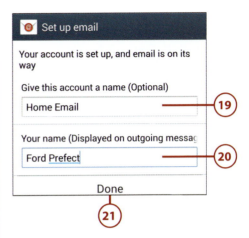

Be Secure If You Can

If your mail provider supports email security, such as Secure Sockets Layer (SSL) or Transport Layer Security (TLS), you should strongly consider using it. If you don't, emails you send and receive go over the Internet in plain readable text. Using SSL or TLS encrypts the emails as they travel across the Internet so nobody can read them. Set this under the Advanced settings for the incoming and outgoing servers.

Working with the Email App

Now that you have added two new accounts, you can start using the Email application. Everything you do in the Email application is the same for every email account. The Email app enables you to either work with email accounts separately or in a combined view.

Navigate the Email Application

Before you learn how to compose or read emails, you should become familiar with the Email application.

1. Touch to launch the Email app.

2. Touch to switch between email accounts or select the Combined View, which shows all emails from all accounts.

3. Touch the star to mark an email as flagged.

4. Each color represents a specific email account.

5. Check boxes next to emails to select more than one. Then you can take actions against multiple emails at once, such as Mark as Unread, Delete, or Move to a New Folder.

6. Touch to compose a new email.

Working in Batches

When you select multiple emails by checking the boxes next to them, you can take action on all the selected messages at once. You can mark the messages as unread, move them to a different folder, or delete them.

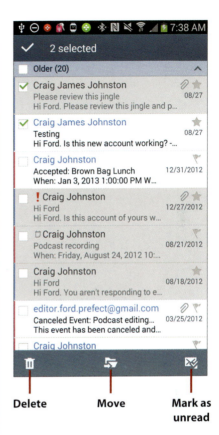

Delete   Move   Mark as unread

Landscape Mode

Because your Galaxy Note 3 has such a large screen, Samsung rewrote the Email app to support a Landscape mode. If you rotate your Galaxy Note 3 sideways, the Email app reconfigures to show the email list on the left and the actual email you are reading on the right.

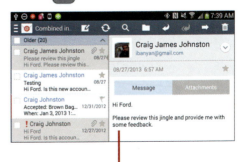

Email app in landscape view

Compose an Email

1. Touch to compose a new email.

2. Enter one or more recipients. As you type, your Galaxy Note 3 tries to guess who you want to address the message to. If you see the correct name, touch it to select it. This includes names stored on your Galaxy Note 3 and in your company's corporate address book.

3. Enter a subject.

4. Enter the body of the message. Use the formatting icons to change the font, font size, color, and other properties.

5. Touch to send the message.

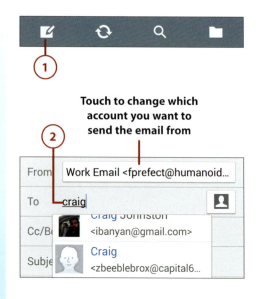

Touch to change which account you want to send the email from

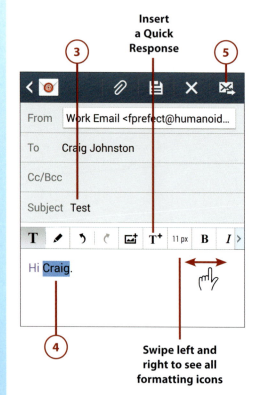

Insert a Quick Response

Swipe left and right to see all formatting icons

Drawing in Your Email

Instead of just typing your email, you can draw in it. Pull out your S Pen and touch the Drawing Mode icon. Then draw in the area indicated. Touch the Pen Settings icon to change the style of instrument (brush, pen, and so on) and the color of the ink. Touch the Eraser icon and use the S Pen to erase parts of your drawing. Touch the Insert icon to insert images from the Gallery.

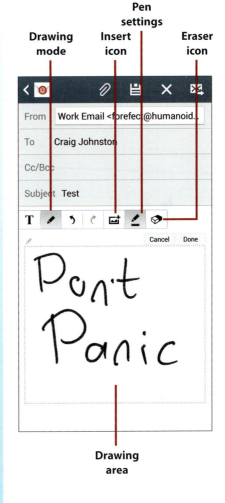

Pen settings

Drawing mode   Insert icon   Eraser icon

Drawing area

Add Attachments to a Message

Before you send your message, you might want to add one or more attachments. You can attach any type of file, including pictures, video, audio, contacts, and location.

1. Touch the Attach icon.

2. Choose the type of attachment.

3. Touch to remove an attachment.

4. Touch to send your email.

Scroll down to see all attachment types

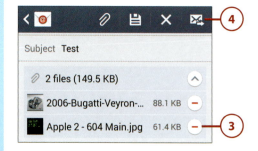

Read Email

Reading messages in the Email application is the same regardless of which account the email has come to.

1. Touch an email to open it.

2. Touch to reply to the sender of the email. This does not reply to anyone in the Cc field.

3. Touch to forward the email.

4. Touch to expand the email header to see all recipients and all other email header information.

5. Touch to mark the message as flagged.

6. Touch to delete the message.

7. Touch to see the attachments.

8. Touch to play or view the attachment. In this example it is an audio file.

9. Touch to save the attachment to your phone.

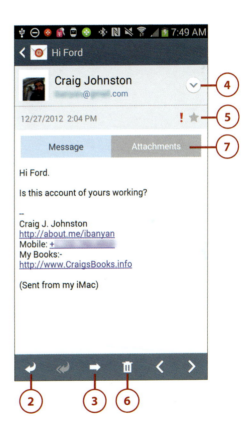

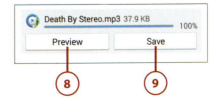

10. Touch the Menu button to see more options.

11. Touch to mark the message as unread.

12. Touch to mark the message as spam or junk mail.

13. Touch to move the message to a different folder.

14. Touch to save the email as a file on your phone (outside the Email app).

15. Touch to add the sender to the Priority Sender list. Email from people in the Priority Sender list are displayed in the Priority Sender view.

16. Touch to create a new filter rule based on the header and contents of the email.

17. Touch to print the email on a Samsung printer available on the Wi-Fi network.

18. Touch to compose a new email.

19. Touch to change the font size used when reading the message.

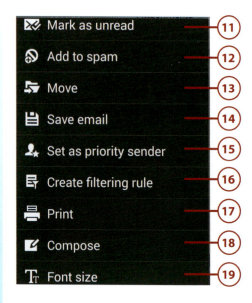

Change Email App Settings

1. Touch the Menu button.

2. Touch Settings.

3. Touch to change how many lines of the email are shown in the preview, what shows in the title line, and enable auto-fit (which shrinks emails so they fit on the screen properly when you read them).

4. Touch to edit your Quick Responses, default image size when you attach images, and enable and control delayed email sending.

5. Touch to change how auto-advance works. You can choose to either advance to a newer message, older message, or back to the message list.

6. Touch to enable or disable email deletion confirmation.

7. Touch to manage the Priority Sender list.

8. Touch to manage your spam address list.

9. Touch to manage your mailbox rules that enable actions to be taken on arriving emails based on certin criteria.

Quick Responses

Quick responses are words, phrases, sentences, or paragraphs of text that you create ahead of time and save as Quick Responses. While you are composing an email, you can choose to insert one or more of your Quick Responses. The idea is that it saves on typing the same things over and over.

10. Touch to enable or disable Split View mode when you rotate your Galaxy Note 3 on its side.

11. Scroll up to see your email accounts.

What Is the Priority Sender List?

Emails received from people who you have listed in the Priority Sender list are shown in the Priority Sender Inbox as well as in the regular Inbox. Opening the Priority Sender Inbox folder shows only emails from these people, which can be a way of filtering email so that you respond to the important people first and then switch to the regular Inbox and respond to everyone else.

Corporate Account Settings

You are able to change your email signature as well as control what components are synchronized and how often they are synchronized. Repeat steps 1 and 2 from the "Change Email App Settings" task to get started.

1. Touch Account Settings.

2. Touch your corporate email account.

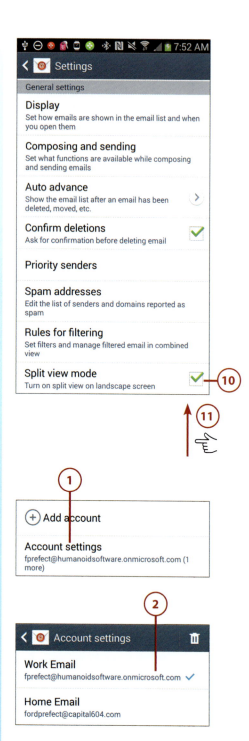

3. Touch to manage synchronization settings, which include the schedule to sync your email, how far back in the past to sync, and the size of the portion of each email to retrieve.

4. Touch to enable or disable using an email signature, add an email signature, or edit a signature.

5. Touch to set whether you are out of the office and your out-of-office message. This synchronizes to the Out-of-office on your corporate mailbox so your out-of-office messages will be sent by your mail server.

6. Touch to enable or disable using this account as the default account when composing email.

7. Touch to update your password, such as when your company requires you to change your password.

8. Touch to enable or disable being notified when new emails arrive for this account.

9. Touch to select the ringtone that plays when you are notified of new email for this account.

10. Touch to enable or disable also vibrating when the notification ringtone plays.

11. Touch for more settings.

12. Touch to change the friendly name for this account.

13. Touch to choose whether to always Bcc or Cc yourself on emails you send.

14. Touch to enable or disable automatically loading embedded images in emails sent to you on this account.

15. Touch to enable or disable automatically downloading email attachments when your Note 3 is connected to Wi-Fi.

16. Touch to manage how many times your Note 3 retries sending emails if something causes them to fail to be sent.

17. Touch to choose which folders (excluding Inbox and Outbox) you want to synchronize from your office email account and when they synchronize based on the peak and off-peak schedule.

18. Touch to choose how far back in the past your calendar synchronizes.

19. Touch to empty your Trash folder on the email server back in the office.

20. Scroll down for more settings.

Why Empty the Office Trash Folder?

Step 20 describes how you can choose to empty your Trash folder back in the office. The reason that this is useful is sometimes your email administrator sets a limit on the size of your mailbox, and when you reach that limit, you are unable to send emails. By emptying your Trash folder back at the office, you might be able to clear a little bit of space in your mailbox so you can send that important email.

21. Touch to change which device wins if there is a conflict between your phone and your email account back at the office.

How Are There Conflicts?

A conflict can occur if you (or someone who has delegate access on your email account) makes a change in your mail-box using the desktop email client (like Outlook)—for example, your delegate moves an email to a folder—and you make a change on your Galaxy Note 3—say you delete that same email. Now there is a conflict because an email has been both moved and deleted at the same time. If you set the server to have priority then the conflict is resolved using your rule that the server wins. In this example, the email is not deleted, but it is moved to a folder.

22. Touch to set advanced security options, including whether you want to encrypt your emails, sign emails with an electronic signa-ture, and email certificates to use with S/MIME (if your company supports it).

23. Select what to synchronize between your Note 3 and your office email account.

24. Touch to enable or disable view-ing emails in a conversation view (also known as threaded).

25. Touch to change the Exchange mail server settings for this account. This includes your account username and password if this has changed.

26. Touch to return to the Settings main screen.

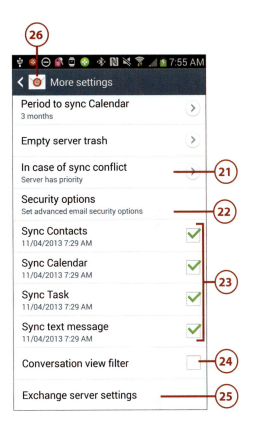

POP/IMAP Account Settings

1. Touch a POP or IMAP account.

2. Touch to manage synchronization settings that include the schedule to sync your email, how far back in the past to sync, and the size of the portion of each email to retrieve.

3. Touch to enable or disable using an email signature, add an email signature, or edit a signature.

4. Touch to enable or disable using this account as the default account when composing email.

5. Touch to update your password.

6. Touch to enable or disable being notified when new emails arrive for this account.

7. Touch to select the ringtone that plays when you are notified of new email for this account.

8. Touch to enable or disable also vibrating when the notification ringtone plays.

9. Touch for more settings.

10. Touch to change the friendly name for this account.

11. Touch to edit the name that is displayed when you send email to others.

12. Touch to choose whether to always Bcc or Cc yourself on emails you send.

13. Touch to enable or disable automatically loading embedded images in emails sent to you on this account.

14. Touch to set advanced security settings for this account, including choosing to encrypt emails, sign them with a digital signature, and manage encryption keys on your phone for use with encrypting emails.

15. Touch to set how many emails to load.

16. Touch to enable or disable automatically downloading email attachments when your Note 3 is connected to Wi-Fi.

17. Touch to manage how many times your Note 3 retries sending emails if something causes them to fail to be sent.

18. Scroll down for more settings.

19. Touch to change the incoming server settings for this account.

20. Touch to change the outgoing server settings for this account.

21. Touch to return to the Settings main screen.

Search Google

See your sports scores

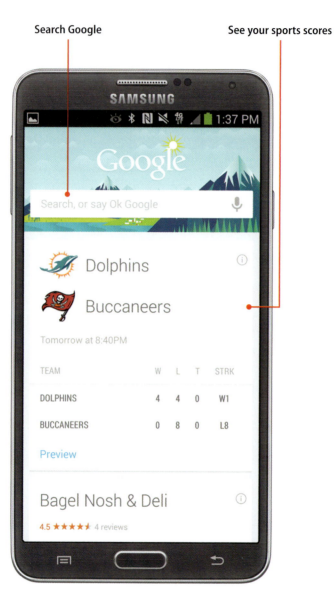

In this chapter, you find out how to use Google Maps, Navigation, and Google Now. Topics include the following:

→ Getting to know Google Now
→ Working with Google Maps
→ Using Google Maps with no data coverage
→ Getting around with Navigation

5

Google Now and Navigation

Your Galaxy Note 3 can be used as a GPS Navigation device while you are walking or driving around. The Galaxy Note 3 also includes a new app called Google Now that offers to provide you all the information you need when you need it.

Google Now

You can access Google Now from the Lock screen or from any screen and it enables you to search the Internet. The app also provides you information, such as how long it will take to drive to work and game scores from your favorite teams.

Accessing Google Now

Access Google Now anytime by pressing and holding the Home button and then touching the Google logo.

Touch and hold

**Touch to launch
Google Now**

Understand the Google Now Screen

1. Cards automatically appear based on your settings. Possibilities include teams you follow, upcoming meetings, weather where you work, and traffic on the way to work.

2. Touch and speak a request or search. You can also just say "Google" and then speak your request. Cards relevant to your search or request appear.

**Touch to change
card settings**

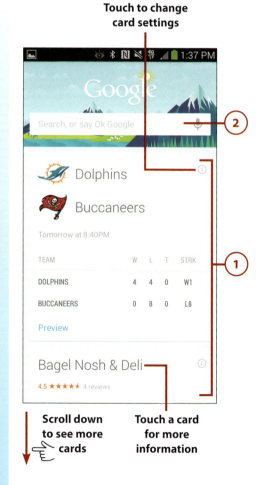

**Scroll down
to see more
cards**

**Touch a card
for more
information**

Set Up Google Now

1. Touch the Menu button.

2. Touch Settings.

3. Touch Google Now to choose what cards Google Now displays and configure how some of the cards work.

4. Touch to choose what notifications you want to receive (like public alerts, heavy traffic, and more).

5. Touch to set your home and work address, reminders, your sports teams, and stocks you want to follow.

6. Touch Voice.

7. Touch to choose the language that Google Now uses.

8. Touch to set when Google Now speaks the search results. The choices are Always, Only When the Information Is Informative, or Only When You Are Using a Hands-free Device.

9. Touch to block or allow offensive words. Turning this on causes the Voice Search feature to hide any search results that contain offensive words.

10. Touch to enable or disable Hotword detection. When this option is enabled and while Google Now is running, it is always listening for you to say "OK, Google." When you do, a voice search launches.

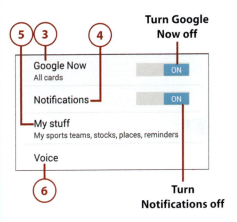

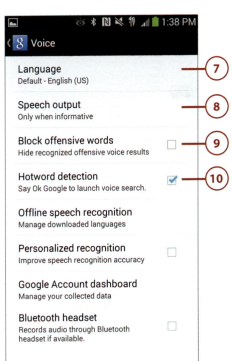

11. Touch to download speech recognition software so you can do voice searches even when you're not connected to the Internet. You can download multiple languages.

12. Touch to enable or disable personalized voice recognition. When enabled, Google tries to better understand your accent to make for more accurate searches.

13. Touch to see your Google dashboard, which shows you all of your Google account information and enables you to manage settings for all of the Google services you use.

14. Touch to allow Google Now to listen for your voice when you are using a Bluetooth headset.

15. Touch to save your changes and return to the main Settings screen.

16. Touch to choose which apps installed on your Galaxy Note 3 are searched when you search using Google Now.

17. Touch to change which Google account you want to use for Google Now, and set whether you want to report your location information. (Disabling this severely limits the usefulness of Google Now.)

18. Touch to save your changes and return to Google Now.

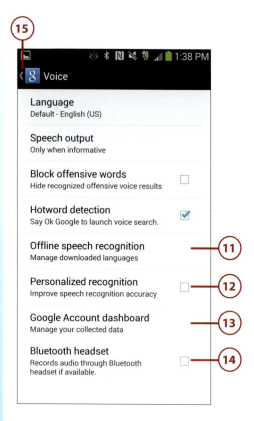

Google Maps

Google Maps enables you to see where you are on a map, find points of interest close to you, give you driving or walking directions, and provide extra layers of information, such as a Satellite view and traffic.

1. Touch to launch Google Maps.

2. Touch to type a search term. This screen also helps you find local restaurants, coffee shops, bars, and attractions.

3. Touch to get walking or driving directions from one location to another. You can also choose to use public transit or biking paths to get to your destination.

4. Touch to zoom the map into your current location.

5. Touch to add layers to the Map view. Layer options include a satellite view, transit lines, and biking paths.

6. Touch to see information about your profile and any special offers in the area where you are (coupons, discounts, and so on).

Your current location

Get Directions

Most people use Google Maps to get directions to where they want to go. Here is how.

1.   Touch the Directions icon.

2.   Touch to set the starting point or leave it as My Location (which is your current location).

3.   Touch to choose a previous destination that you searched for.

4.   Type in the destination address or business name.

5.   Touch to use driving directions.

6.   Touch to use public transportation.

7.   Touch to use bike paths (if available).

8.   Touch to walk to your destination.

9.   Touch to reverse the directions.

Public Transportation

If you choose to use public transportation to get to your destination, you have two extra options to use. You can choose the type of public transportation, including bus, subway, train, or tram/light rail. You can also choose the best route, including fewer transfers and less walking.

Alternatively, you can search for something

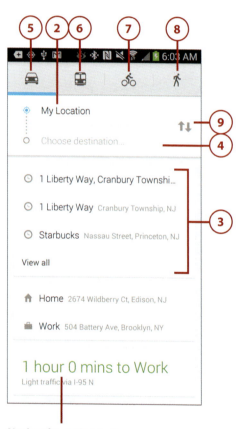

Notice the estimated time to get to work

10. Scroll down to see all route options.

11. Touch to return to the map and prepare to start your navigation.

12. Touch to cancel the navigation.

13. Touch to return to the previous screen and make changes to your trip.

14. Touch to start the turn by turn navigation.

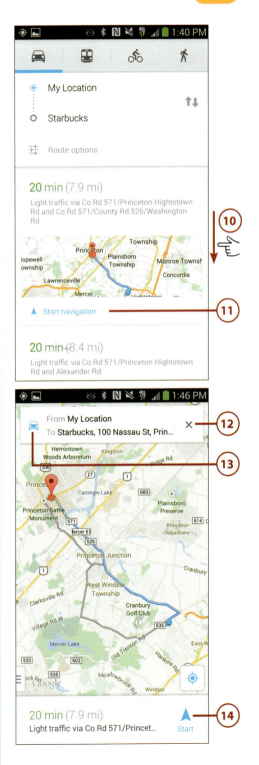

15. Follow the audio and visual prompts that will guide you to your destination.

16. Touch to get a route preview, the full list of step-by-step directions, mute the audio prompts, or enable the satellite view.

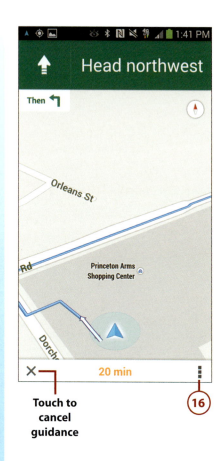

Touch to cancel guidance

(16)

Adjust Google Maps Settings

1. Touch the drawer icon.

2. Touch Settings.

(1)

(2)

3. Touch to switch to another Google account to use Google Maps.

4. Touch to edit your home and work addresses.

5. Touch to improve your location on the map if you are having issues with it.

6. Touch to see your map history and delete selected searches and directions.

7. Touch to change the unit of distance manually (to miles or kilometers), or let it get set automatically based on where you are.

8. Touch to write some feedback about Google Maps to Google.

9. Touch to enable or disable the ability to simply shake your Galaxy Note 3 to bring up the feedback screen.

10. Touch to change your Google Map location setting.

11. Touch to enable or disable letting Google access your location at any time. With this disabled, Maps and Google Now become useless.

12. Touch to enable or disable reporting your location from your Galaxy Note 3.

13. Touch to enable location history where Google Maps keeps track of where you have been. Having this enabled makes Google Now much better.

14. Touch to save your changes and return to the previous screen.

Use Offline Google Maps

Google Maps enables you to download small parts of the global map to your Galaxy Note 3. This is useful if you are traveling and need an electronic map but cannot connect to a network to download it in real time.

1. Find an area that you would like to save locally on your Note 3.

2. Touch search and scroll to the bottom of the screen.

3. Touch Make This Map Area Available Offline.

How Much Map Can I Take Offline?

When selecting the area of the map to take offline, you are limited to about 100Mb of map data. However, you don't need to worry about the size of the data because if you have selected an area that is too large, Google Maps gives you a warning.

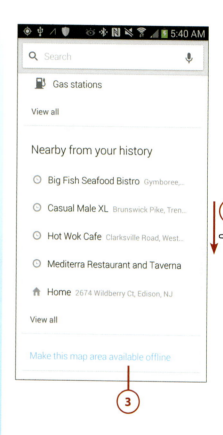

Warning that the selection area is too large

It's Not All Good

Offline Maps Have Limited Use

If you download some map data to your Galaxy Note 3, you can use it to zoom in and out of the area you downloaded and also see where you are on the map in real time while you have no network coverage. You cannot, however, get directions within the downloaded map area or use the Navigation app to get turn-by-turn directions. You also cannot search for things in the downloaded map area or see points of interest. So how useful is having map data already downloaded to your Galaxy Note 3? It is useful to a point because it provides an electronic map while you're offline, but to be much more useful, you need a network connection for directions and navigation. Because the map data is already downloaded, if you were to get a network connection and use that for driving directions, at least Google Maps would not need to download the map data in real time, which could save you a lot of money in data roaming charges.

The Clock app in
Bedside/Dock mode

In this chapter, you find out how to set the time, use the Clock application, and use the S Planner calendaring application. Topics include the following:

→ Synchronizing to the correct time

→ Working with the Clock application

→ Setting alarms

→ Waking up with the latest weather, news, and your schedule

→ Working with S Planner

6

Working with Date, Time, and S Planner

Your Galaxy Note 3 has a Clock application you can use as a bedside alarm. The S Planner application synchronizes with your Google or Microsoft Exchange calendars and enables you to create events and meetings while on the road and to always know where your next meeting is.

Setting the Date and Time

Before you start working with the Clock and S Planner applications, make sure that your Galaxy Note 3 has the correct date and time.

1. Pull down the Notification panel.

2. Touch the Settings icon to display the Settings screen.

3. Touch General to display the General screen.

4. Touch Date and Time.

5. Touch to enable or disable synchronizing time and date with the wireless carrier. It is best to leave this enabled as it automatically sets date and time based on where you are traveling.

Does Network Time Sync Always Work?

In some countries, on some carriers, time synchronization does not work. This means that when you get off the plane and turn Airplane mode off (see the Prologue for information on Airplane mode), after a reasonable amount of time your time, date, and time zone will still be incorrect. In these instances, it is best to disable automatic date and time and manually set the time, date, and time zone yourself, and try it on automatic in the next country you visit or when you are back in your home country.

6. Touch to set the date if you choose to disable network synchronization.

7. Touch to set the time if you choose to disable network synchronization.

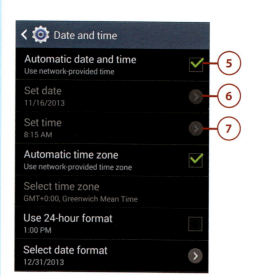

8. Touch to enable or disable synchronizing the time zone with the wireless carrier. It is best to leave this enabled as it automatically sets the time zone based on where you are traveling.

9. Touch to set the time zone manually if you choose to disable network synchronization.

10. Touch to enable or disable the use of 24-hour time format. This format makes your Galaxy Note 3 represent time without a.m. or p.m. For example, 1:00 p.m. becomes 13:00 in 24-hour format.

11. Touch to change the way in which the date is represented. For example, people in the United States normally write the date with the month first (12/31/2010). You can make your Galaxy Note 3 display the date with the day first (31/12/2010) or with the year first (2010/12/31).

Clock Application

The Clock application is preinstalled on your Galaxy Note 3 and provides the functionality of a bedside clock and alarm clock.

Navigate the Clock Application

1. Touch the Clock icon on the Apps screen.

2. Touch the + to create an alarm.

3. Touch Alarm to view and edit your alarms.

4. Touch World Clock to see the World Clock and manage the clocks on that screen.

5. Touch Stopwatch to use the Stopwatch.

6. Touch Timer to use the Timer.

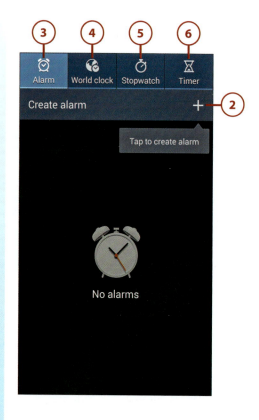

Manage Alarms

The Clock application enables you to set multiple alarms. These can be one-time alarms or recurring alarms. Even if you exit the Clock application, the alarms you set still trigger.

1. Touch to create a new alarm.

2. Touch the up/down arrows to set the hours and minutes.

3. Touch the AM/PM button to toggle between a.m. and p.m.

4. Touch the days of the week when you want the alarm to trigger. In this example, the alarm will sound on all days of the workweek but not on Saturday and Sunday.

5. Check the Repeat Weekly box if you want the alarm to repeat every week.

6. Touch Alarm Type to change the type of alarm. Your choices are Melody, Vibration, and Vibration and Melody.

7. Touch Alarm Tone to change the alarm tone or melody that plays.

8. Move the Volume slider to adjust the volume of the alarm.

9. Scroll down to see the extra settings.

10. Touch to enable or disable Location Alarm. If you enable this, you are setting the alarm to trigger only when you are at the chosen location.

11. Touch to enable or disable the Snooze feature and set how long the snooze lasts.

12. Touch to enable or disable Smart Alarm. Smart Alarm plays a tune ahead of the alarm time to slowly start waking you up.

13. Touch to give the alarm a name.

14. Touch to save your new alarm.

Cancel location alarm

Turning Off an Alarm

When the alarm goes off, touch the red circled X and drag it to either side to turn off the alarm.

Editing or Deleting an Alarm

To edit or delete an alarm, touch and hold the alarm you want to edit or delete. When the pop-up window appears, make your choice. If you just want to quickly enable or disable an alarm, touch the Alarm Clock icon on the far right of an alarm.

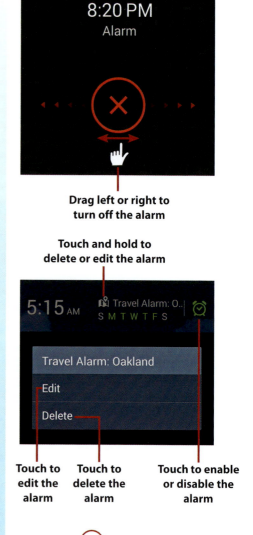

Drag left or right to turn off the alarm

Touch and hold to delete or edit the alarm

Touch to edit the alarm **Touch to delete the alarm** **Touch to enable or disable the alarm**

Use the World Clock

The World Clock enables you to keep track of time in multiple cities around the world.

1. Touch World Clock to display the World Clock screen.

2. Touch the + to add a new city.

3. Type in a partial city name to find the city you want to add.

4. Touch a city to add it to the World Clock screen.

Managing Cities

To delete a city from your World Clock screen, or to rearrange the cities you've saved, touch the Menu button and choose Delete to select which cities to delete or Change Order to rearrange them.

Use Dock Mode and the Desk Clock

When you insert your Galaxy Note 3 into a Samsung dock, the phone automatically switches to Dock mode. This mode turns the Clock app into a desk clock or a bedside clock. At this writing, you cannot switch to Dock mode manually.

1. Insert your Galaxy Note 3 into a Samsung dock.

2. If the Complete Action Using dialog opens, touch Desk Clock, and then touch Always if you want to use the Desk Clock every time you dock the Galaxy Note 3 or Just Once if you want to choose among the dock options each time.

Touch to see a shortlist of cities based on your current location

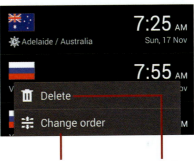

Touch to rearrange the list of cities   **Touch to choose cities to delete**

Touch Always to use the Desk Clock each time you dock the phone   **Touch Just Once to choose a docking option each time**

3. Touch to switch the sound between playing through the Galaxy Note 3's speaker and through the dock.

4. Touch to exit Dock mode without removing the Galaxy Note 3 from the dock. You can also simply remove the Galaxy Note 3 from the dock.

Using Low-Power Dock Mode

After one minute of inactivity in Dock mode, the Galaxy Note 3 dims its screen to suit the light level in the room and displays just the date, time, and weather. Touch anywhere on the screen to switch back to the full Dock mode display.

Touch an app to launch that app

Touch a day to display it in S Planner

Touch anywhere to restore the full Dock mode display

Customize Dock Mode

You can customize Dock mode to suit your needs better. You can change the shortcuts displayed, hide the shortcuts if you don't want to see them, and choose which other items appear.

1. In Dock mode, touch the Menu button to display the menu.

2. Touch Edit Shortcuts to unlock the shortcuts so that you can change them.

3. Touch to remove a shortcut.

4. Scroll to the right.

5. Touch to add a new shortcut. The Select Activity dialog opens.

6. Scroll down as needed to see all available apps.

7. Touch to select an app to create a new shortcut.

8. Touch the Back button to apply the new shortcut (not shown).

9. Touch the Menu button to display the menu.

10. Touch Settings to display the Settings screen.

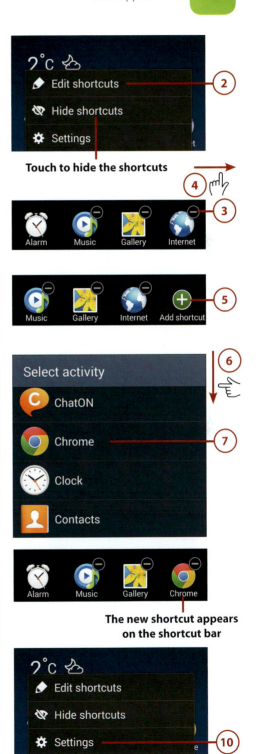

Touch to hide the shortcuts

The new shortcut appears on the shortcut bar

11. Touch to hide the status bar when in Dock mode.

12. Touch Wallpaper to choose the background displayed in Dock mode. You can choose the default Dock wallpaper, choose an image from the Gallery app, or set it to use whatever you have chosen as the wallpaper for your Home screen.

13. Touch the Calendar check box to enable or disable showing the calendar in Dock mode.

14. Touch the Weather switch to enable or disable showing the weather on the Dock screen.

15. Touch Weather (anywhere apart from the switch) to choose Fahrenheit or Celsius and whether the weather is periodically updated.

16. Touch to display the Accessory screen, which includes a section of settings for Dock mode.

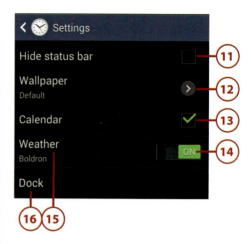

Displaying the Accessory Screen Without a Dock Attached

When you don't have a Dock attached to your Galaxy Note 3, you can still open the Accessory screen and choose Dock settings. To do so, pull down the Notification bar and touch Settings to open the Settings app. Touch General to display the General screen, and then touch Accessory to display the Accessory screen.

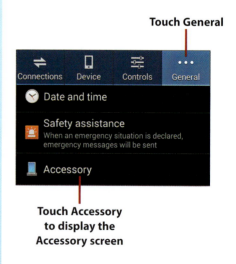

Touch General

Touch Accessory to display the Accessory screen

17. Check the Dock Sound box to enable or disable playing a sound when you insert your Galaxy Note 3 into the dock. Playing the sound can be helpful if you find it difficult to insert the Galaxy Note 3 in the dock.

18. Touch to enable or disable using external speakers connected to the dock when docked and playing audio.

19. Touch to enable or disable automatically showing the Dock screen when you insert your Galaxy Note 3 into the dock. If unchecked, you just see the regular Home screen.

20. Touch to choose what kind of audio is output via the High-Definition Multimedia Interface (HDMI) cable when the Galaxy Note 3 is docked. Choose Stereo if you have a standard two-speaker rig or Surround if you have a surround-sound setup, such as a 5.1 speaker set (five directional speakers and a nondirectional subwoofer) or a 7.1 setup (seven speakers and a subwoofer).

21. Touch the Back button to save your settings and return to the Settings screen for Dock mode.

22. Touch the Back button to leave the Settings screen and return to the Dock mode desktop.

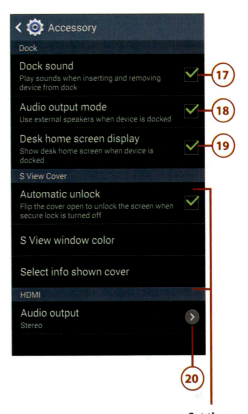

Set these options if you use an S View cover

Using the S Planner Calendaring Application

The S Planner calendaring application enables you to synchronize all your Google Calendars under your primary Google account to your Galaxy Note 3. You can accept appointments and create and modify appointments right on your phone. Any changes are automatically synchronized wirelessly back to your Google Calendar.

Navigate the S Planner Main Screen

The main screen of the S Planner app shows a one-day, one-week, or one-month view of your appointments. S Planner also shows events from multiple calendars at the same time.

1. Touch the S Planner icon on the Apps screen.

2. Swipe left to go backward in time.

3. Swipe right to go forward in time.

4. Touch to show today's date.

5. Touch Year, Month, Week, Day, List, or Task to choose a calendar view.

6. Touch to switch to Writing mode, where you can draw over the calendar with the S Pen.

7. Touch to create a new event.

The circle marks today's date

DRAWING ALL OVER YOUR CALENDAR

>>>Go Further

Instead of adding events to your calendar, you can just draw on the calendar as if it were a wall calendar or a page in a notebook. This feature only works when you are viewing the Month view and you are holding your Galaxy Note 3 in portrait orientation. When you switch into Writing mode as described in step 6, you can draw anything anywhere on the month. This is simply free-form drawing and is not translated into real events in your calendar; however, it's an easy and creative way to mark the calendar for yourself.

Event Colors

S Planner can display one calendar or many calendars at the same time. If you choose to display multiple calendars, events from each calendar are color coded so you can tell which events are from which calendar.

Choose Which Calendars and Task Lists to View

If you have set up multiple accounts, which might each have multiple calendars or task lists, you can choose which calendars S Planner shows at the same time.

1. Touch the Menu button to open the menu.

2. Touch Calendars to display the Calendars screen.

3. Check the All Calendars box to display all calendars and task lists from all accounts.

4. Touch to expand an account to see all calendars and task lists it has.

5. Touch to collapse an expanded account.

6. Touch to enable or disable displaying the calendar or task list.

7. Touch to return to the main S Planner screen.

Add a new account

Change S Planner Settings

1. Touch the Menu button.

2. Touch Settings.

3. Touch View Styles to choose the way that the calendar shows events when you touch to view them in the Month view and Week view. For Month view, your choices are to have a pop-up showing the Event view or a list of the events at the bottom of the screen. For Week view, your choices are to have a Timeline view where the days are across the top and the hours of the day are below, or an Analog view where the days are all shown on the screen at once. Try each style and see which you prefer.

4. Touch First Day of Week to set the first day of your week. You can choose Saturday, Sunday, or Monday. You can also choose Locale Default, which means the locale determined by the time zone you are in controls what the first day of the week is.

5. Touch Hide Declined Events to enable or disable hiding events you have declined.

6. Touch Lock Time Zone to enable or disable using your home time zone when displaying the calendar and event times. When this is enabled, your home time zone is always used even when you are not traveling in it.

7. Touch Select Time Zone to set your home time zone if you enabled Lock Time Zone in step 7.

8. Touch Show Week Number to enable or disable showing the week number. For example, March 26 is in week 13.

9. Check the Hide Completed Tasks box if you want to hide tasks you have completed. Hiding what you've done may make it easier to see what you still have left to do.

10. Check the Weather box if you want to display the weather on the calendar.

11. Scroll down for more settings.

12. Touch Set Alerts and Notifications to enable or disable notifications for calendar events. You can also set whether you are alerted only in the Notification bar or with a pop-up alert.

13. Touch Select Ringtone to choose the ringtone to play when you are being alerted for calendar events.

14. Touch Vibration to choose whether your Galaxy Note 3 should also vibrate when the event ringtone plays.

15. Touch Quick Responses to edit the four built-in Quick Responses. Read more about Quick Reponses later in this chapter.

16. Touch the Back button to save your settings and return to the main S Planner screen.

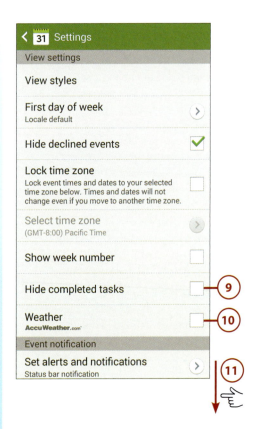

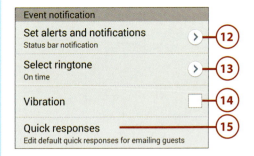

Add a New Event

While you're on the road, you can add a new appointment or event—and even invite people to it. Events you add synchronize to your Google and corporate calendars in real time.

1. Touch to add a new event.

A Quicker Way to Add an Event

You can quickly add a new event by touching and holding on the day on which you want to create the event and the time of day you want to create it.

2. Touch the color swatch to choose the color to assign to the event. You can use colors to make important events more conspicuous.

3. Touch Title to enter a title for your event.

4. Check the All Day box to mark the event as an all-day event.

5. Touch the From box to select the start date and time of the event.

6. Touch the To box to select the end date and time of the event.

7. Touch Calendar to select the calendar to add the event to.

8. Touch Sticker to choose a sticker for your event. The stickers have images that help you visually categorize events.

Touch and hold the time   Choose the calendar

Type the event title   Touch OK

9. Touch Repeat to set this as a recurring event. You can make it repeat daily, weekly, or monthly on the same date each month, but you can also set a meeting to repeat, for example, monthly but only every last Thursday regardless of the date.

10. Touch the + on the Reminder line to add a reminder for the event.

11. Touch to set the timing of the reminder.

12. Touch to change the type of reminder (Email or Notification).

13. Touch the – to remove the reminder.

14. Scroll down to reach more event settings.

15. Touch Location to specify where the event will take place. This can be a full physical address, which is useful because most smartphones can map the address.

16. Touch Description and type a description for the event.

17. Touch to add invitees from your Contacts list. You can also add invitees by typing their names or email address in the text box.

18. Touch to remove an invitee.

19. Scroll down to reach more event settings.

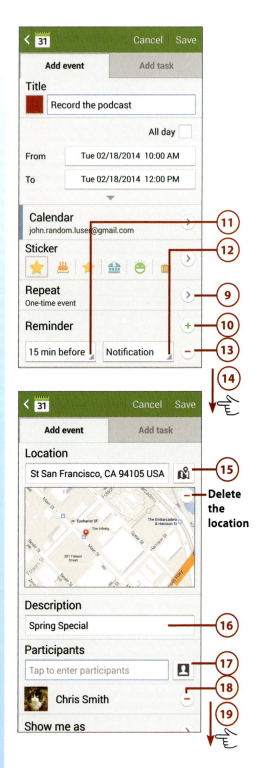

Delete the location

20. Touch to choose how to show your availability during this event. You can choose Busy or Available.

21. Touch to choose the privacy of the event. You can choose Public or you can choose Private so only you can see it. If the event is being created on your corporate calendar, setting the event to Private means that people can see you are busy, but they cannot see the event details.

22. Touch to save the event. Any attendees that you have added are automatically sent an event invitation.

Editing and Deleting an Event

To edit or delete a calendar event, touch the event to see the event preview and then touch the event preview. After the event opens, touch the Menu button and choose either Edit or Delete. When you successfully delete an event to which someone has invited you, S Planner sends an event decline notice to the event organizer. So you don't have to first decline the meeting before deleting it because this is all taken care of automatically.

Respond to a Google Event Invitation

When you are invited to an event, you can choose your response right on your Galaxy Note 3 in the invitation email itself, or you can use the S Planner app.

Respond from the Email

The Google event invitation email allows you to respond in the email itself.

1. Touch to open the event invitation email.

2. Touch Yes, Maybe, or No to indicate whether you will attend.

Touch More Options for other options, such as setting a reminder

Respond from S Planner

When you receive an invite, it is automatically inserted into your Google calendar but with no response selected.

1. Touch the new event.

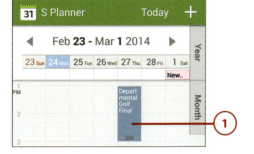

2. Touch the event location to have it mapped in Google Maps or another mapping app that you have installed (such as Google Earth).

3. Touch Attend? to choose your response.

4. Choose Accept, Tentative, or Decline.

5. Back on the Meeting Invitation screen, touch the Back button to return to the main S Planner screen.

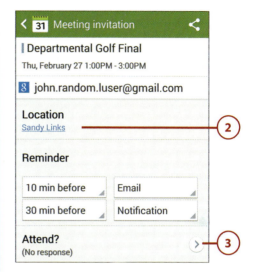

Respond to a Corporate Event Invitation

When you receive an invitation to an event, choose your response in the invitation email itself.

1. Touch to open the event invitation email.

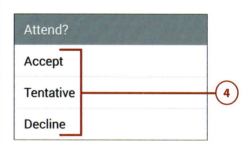

2. Touch to see the invitation responses.

3. Touch Accept, Decline, or Maybe to indicate whether you will attend.

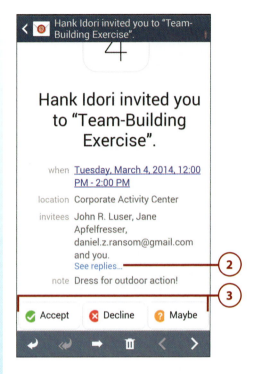

Use Quick Responses

When you are notified of an upcoming event on your Galaxy Note 3, you can choose to Snooze or Email Guests. When you choose to Email Guests, you can choose a Quick Response to send them.

1. Pull down the Notification bar.

2. Touch Email Guests to open the Select a Quick Response dialog.

Touch to snooze the reminder

3. Choose one of your Quick Responses or write a custom message.

4. Touch the email app you want to use to send the Quick Response.

Add a Task

In addition to calendar events, you can add tasks you need to complete.

1. Touch to add a new task.

2. Touch Add Task.

3. Touch Title and type the title for the task.

4. Touch Due Date and then specify when the task is due. If the task needs no due date, check the No Due Date box instead.

5. Touch Task and then choose the account to add the task to.

6. Touch Reminder to choose when you want to be reminded of the task.

7. Touch Priority to choose the task's priority.

8. Touch Description and then type a description for the task.

9. Touch Save to save the task.

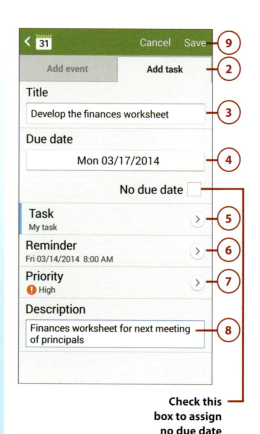

Check this box to assign no due date

Marking a Task as Completed

To mark a task as completed, switch to Task view. Check the box to the left of the task to mark it as completed.

Check the box to mark the task as completed

Add, search, and
manage your contacts

In this chapter, you become familiar with your Galaxy Note 3's contact-management application, which is called Contacts. You find out how to add contacts, synchronize contacts, join duplicate contacts together, and even how to add a contact to your Home screen. Topics include the following:

→ Importing contacts
→ Adding contacts
→ Synchronizing contacts
→ Creating favorite contacts

Contacts

On any smartphone, the application for managing contacts is essential because it is where you keep all of your contacts' information. On the Galaxy Note 3, this application is called simply Contacts. It is the central hub for many activities, such as calling and sending text messages (SMS), multimedia messages (MMS), or email. You can also synchronize your contacts from many online sites, such as Facebook and Gmail, so as your friends change their Facebook profile pictures, their pictures on your Galaxy Note 3 change as well.

Adding Accounts

Before you look around the Contacts app, add some accounts to synchronize contacts from. You already added your Google account when you set up your Galaxy Note 3 in the Prologue.

Adding Facebook, Twitter, LinkedIn, and Other Accounts

To add accounts for your online services such as Facebook, Twitter, LinkedIn, and so on to your Galaxy Note 3, you might need to install the apps for those services from the Google Play Store. Please see how to install apps in Chapter 11, "Working with Android Apps." After the apps are installed and you have signed in to them, if you visit the Accounts settings as shown in the following sections, you see new accounts for each online service.

Your accounts appear on the Accounts screen in the Settings app

1. From the Home screen, pull down the Notification bar.

2. Touch the Settings icon.

3. Touch General to display the General screen.

4. Touch Accounts to display the Accounts screen.

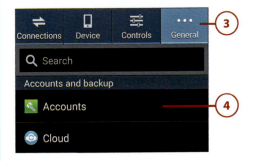

5. Touch Add Account to display the Add Account screen.

6. Touch Microsoft Exchange ActiveSync to display the Add an Exchange ActiveSync Account screen.

7. Type the email address for the account.

8. Touch Password and type the password.

9. Touch Show Password if you want to see the password rather than the dots the Galaxy Note 3 shows for security. Seeing the password can be helpful when entering complex passwords.

10. Touch Next. The Settings app tries to set up the account with the information you've provided.

Dealing with Exchange ActiveSync Setup Problems

Your Galaxy Note 3 tries to work out some information about your company's ActiveSync setup. If it can't, it displays the Setup Could Not Finish dialog to explain the problem. Often, you will see the Authentication Failed message.

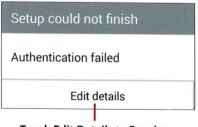

Touch Edit Details to Resolve the Authentication Problem

Need Domain Name?

On the Exchange Server Settings screen that appears, type the domain name before your username, separating the two with a backslash (for example, CORP\john). Type the Exchange Server's name in the Exchange Server box. Then touch Next to try the credentials again with this extra information.

11. In the Remote Security Administration dialog, touch OK to agree that your mail administrator may impose security restrictions on your Galaxy Note 3 after you connect to the Exchange Server.

What Is Remote Security Administration?

Remote Security Administration says that when you activate your Galaxy Note 3 against your work email servers, your email administrator can add restrictions to your phone. These can include forcing a device password, imposing the need for a very strong password, and requiring how many letters and numbers the password must contain. Your Exchange administrator can also remotely wipe your Galaxy Note 3, restoring it to factory defaults. This is normally done if you lose your phone or it is stolen.

Type the domain name if the administrator says you need it

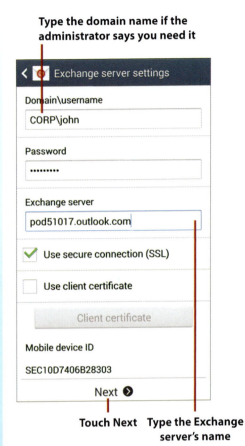

Touch Next   **Type the Exchange server's name**

12. Touch Period to Sync Email to choose how many days, weeks, or months in the past email is synchronized to your Galaxy Note 3 or set it to All to synchronize all email in your Inbox.

13. Touch Sync Schedule to choose how often overall your Galaxy Note 3 syncs your Exchange email.

Push and Other Options for Getting Email

Push means that as email arrives in your Inbox at work, it is delivered to your phone. You can set it to Manual, which means that your Galaxy Note 3 checks for email only when you open the Email app. You can also set the delivery frequency from every 5 minutes to every 12 hours.

14. Touch Peak Schedule to choose how often your Galaxy Note 3 receives Exchange email during peak hours. You may want to check email more frequently during peak hours than off-peak hours.

15. Touch Emails Retrieval Size to choose the largest email size to retrieve. You can choose from 0.5KB to 100KB, choose All to retrieve all messages no matter how big they are, or choose Automatic to use the server's settings. 50KB or 100KB is a reasonable size unless you get vast numbers of messages.

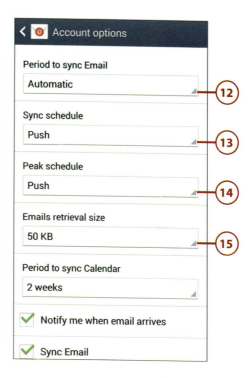

16. Touch Period to Sync Calendar to choose how long a period of calendar appointments to synchronize. Your choices are 2 weeks, 1 month, 3 months, 6 months, or All Calendar.

17. Check the Notify Me When Email Arrives box to receive a notification when email messages arrive. This notification can be helpful, but you might find it overkill if you receive many messages.

18. Check the Sync Email box to sync your email messages with the server. Normally, you will want to do this.

19. Scroll down the screen to see more settings.

20. Check the Sync Contacts box to enable synchronizing your corporate contacts to your Galaxy Note 3.

21. Check the Sync Calendar box to enable synchronizing your corporate calendar to your Galaxy Note 3.

22. Check the Sync Task box to enable synchronizing your corporate task list to your Galaxy Note 3.

23. Check the Sync Text Message box to enable synchronizing your SMS messages to your Galaxy Note 3.

24. Check the Automatically Download Attachments When Connected to Wi-Fi box to make your Galaxy Note 3 automatically download email attachments when it's connected to a Wi-Fi network.

25. Touch Next. The Activate Device Administrator? screen appears.

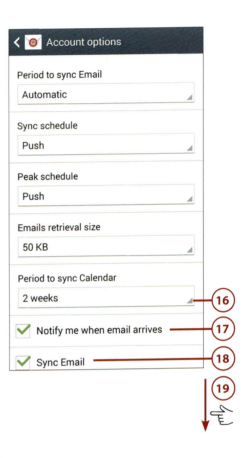

What to Synchronize

You might decide that you don't want to synchronize all your work information to your Galaxy Note 3. You might decide to just synchronize email, and not the calendar, or maybe just the calendar but not the contacts and email. Unchecking these boxes enables you to choose the information you don't want to synchronize.

26. Read the details of the powers you're about to assign to the Exchange server. Scroll down to see the full list of horrors.

27. Touch Activate.

28. Enter a name for this email account. Use something meaningful that describes the purpose of the account such as Exchange (Work).

29. Touch Done to complete the setup.

Removing an Account

To remove an account, open the Settings screen and touch General to display the General screen. Touch Accounts to display the Accounts screen and then touch the account to be removed. On the screen for the account, touch the account in the Accounts list and then touch Remove Account on the screen that appears.

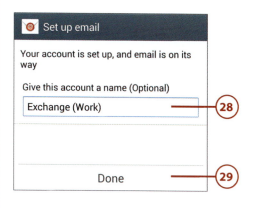

Navigating Contacts

The Contacts app consists of four screens: Phone, Groups, Favorites, and Contacts. Normally, the Contacts app displays the Contacts screen first, showing your list of contacts, but you can navigate to any of the other screens by touching its tab.

1. From the Home screen, touch the Contacts icon.

2. Touch to add a new contact.

3. Touch Phone to switch to the Phone app. From the resulting screen, you can dial a number on the keypad.

4. Touch Groups to see your contact groups. See more information about creating contact groups in the later section titled "Create Contact Groups."

5. Touch Favorites to see your list of favorite contacts.

6. Touch Contacts to see all contacts.

7. Touch to search for a contact.

8. Touch a contact to see all information about her.

9. Touch a contact picture (or picture placeholder) to see the Quick Connect bar.

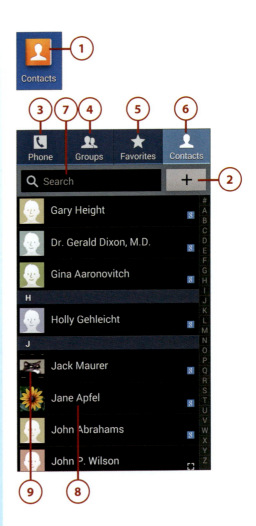

Quick Connect Bar

When you touch a contact picture, the Quick Connect bar displays. This bar enables you to quickly access different ways of communicating with the contact. If the icon list extends off the screen, swipe left to reveal further icons.

Phone Video Internet
call   call   call   Email Address

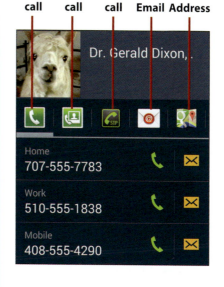

Check a Contact's Status

If you have added contacts that belong to social networks such as Facebook, you can check their statuses right from the Contacts app.

1. Touch a contact.

2. Touch to view the contact's Facebook profile.

Edit a Contact

When you need to, you can easily change a contact's existing information or add further information to it.

1. Touch the contact you want to edit.

2. Touch to open the contact record for editing.

3. Touch to enter a name prefix, middle name, or name suffix.

4. Touch a – sign next to an existing field to delete it.

5. Touch to change the field sub-category. For example, you can change a phone number's subcategory from Mobile to Home.

6. Touch + to add a new field in a specific category. In this example, touching + enables you to add a new phone number and choose its subcategory, such as Work.

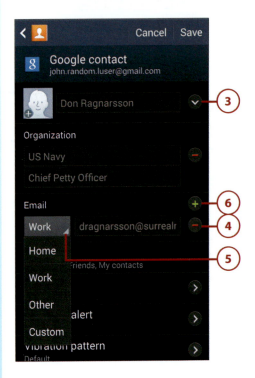

7. Touch Groups to put the con-
    tact in a contact group. The
    Galaxy Note 3 comes with
    built-in groups, including ICE –
    Emergency Contacts, Co-Workers,
    Family, and Friends. But you can
    also create as many other groups
    as you need.

8. Touch Ringtone to assign a differ-
    ent ringtone to calls from the con-
    tact. By giving important contacts
    distinctive ringtones, you can eas-
    ily identify important calls.

9. Touch Message Alert to assign a
    distinctive alert to instant mes-
    sages from the contact.

10. Touch Vibration Pattern to assign
    a different vibration pattern to
    calls from the contact. Vibration
    patterns help you identify impor-
    tant calls when you have silenced
    the ringer.

11. Touch Add Another Field to add
    a new field to the contact record.
    Extra fields include things such as
    the contact's phonetic name (to
    help you pronounce it correctly),
    IM (Instant Messaging) addresses,
    Notes, and Relationship, which
    you use to specify how someone
    is related to the contact—for
    example, an assistant or manager.

12. Touch Save to save the changes to
    the contact record.

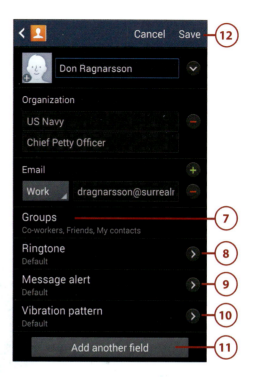

Add a Contact Photo

A contact record on your Galaxy Note 3 includes a contact photo when you link a social network account to the contact or when you import a contact record that includes a photo (for example, from a vCard file). You can manually add a picture as needed, either from an existing file or by taking a photo.

1. Touch the contact.

2. Touch the contact photo to open the Contact Photo dialog.

3. Touch to add a photo already saved on your Galaxy Note 3.

4. Touch the album that contains the photo.

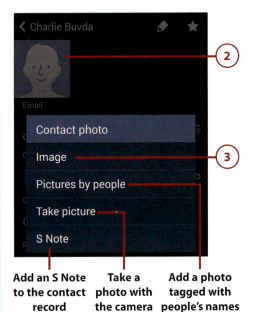

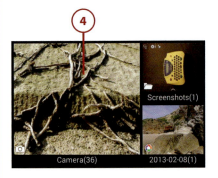

Add an S Note to the contact record

Take a photo with the camera

Add a photo tagged with people's names

5. Touch the photo you want to use.

6. Drag the cropping box to select the area of the photo you want to use for the contact photo.

7. Drag the outside of the cropping box to expand or contract it as needed.

8. Touch Save to save the cropped photo as the contact photo.

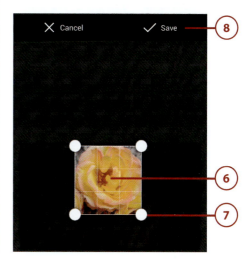

Adding and Managing Contacts

As you add contacts to your work email account or Google account, those contacts are synchronized to your Galaxy Note 3 automatically. When you reply to or forward emails on your Galaxy Note 3 to an email address that is not in your Contacts, those email addresses are automatically added to the contact list or merged into an existing contact with the same name. You can also add contacts to your Galaxy Note 3 directly.

Add a Contact from an Email

To manually add a contact from an email, first open the email client (either Email or Gmail) and then open a message. Please see Chapter 4, "Email," for more on how to work with email.

1. Touch the blank contact picture to the left of the sender's name.

2. Touch Create Contact to open the Save Contact To dialog.

3. Touch the account to which you want to save the contact.

4. Type the contact's name if Contacts has not picked it up from the email message.

5. Touch Save to save the contact.

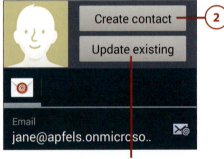

Add the email address to an existing contact instead

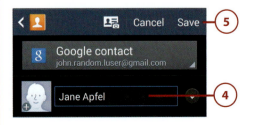

Add a Contact Manually

1. Touch the Contacts icon on the Home screen.

2. Touch to add a new contact.

3. Touch to select the account you want to add the new contact to. For example, you might add the new contact to your work email account instead of to your personal account.

4. Type the person's full name, including any middle name. Your Galaxy Note 3 automatically populates the first name, middle name, and last name fields.

5. Touch to choose a contact picture.

6. Drag to reach other fields.

7. Touch Save to save the new contact.

Add a Contact from a vCard

A vCard is a file that contains a virtual business card—which can include a contact's name, job title, email address, physical address, phone numbers, and so on. You can easily exchange vCards with other people by attaching them to email messages or instant messages. When you receive a vCard, you can import it into the Contacts app as a new contact by using the following steps.

1. Touch View under the attachment that has the .vcf extension.

Choosing the App for vCard Files

If your Galaxy Note 3 displays the Complete Action Using dialog when you touch View to open a vCard file, touch Contacts and then touch Always.

2. Touch to select the account to add the new contact to. For example, you might want to add the new contact to your work email account instead of to your personal account.

Touch Contacts

Touch Always

Add a Contact Using Near Field Communications

Your Galaxy Note 3 has Near Field Communications (NFC) functionality built in. NFC (discussed in Chapter 1, "Connecting to Bluetooth, Wi-Fi, and VPNs") enables you to exchange contact cards between NFC-enabled smartphones or to purchase items in a store by holding your Galaxy Note 3 near the NFC reader at the checkout counter. If you encounter someone who has an NFC-enabled smartphone, or she has an NFC tag that contains her business card, follow these steps to import that information.

1. Hold the other person's smartphone back to back with your Galaxy Note 3 and give the command for sharing via NFC, or hold the NFC tag close to the back cover of your Galaxy Note 3. Your Galaxy Note 3's screen dims and the phone plays a tone to indicate that it is reading the NFC information.

2. Touch to select which account you want to add the new contact to. For example, you might want to add the new contact to your work email account instead of to your personal account.

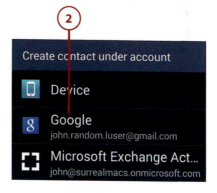

Manage Contacts Settings

To make the Contacts app display contacts the way you prefer, you can customize it. For example, you can choose the contact list display order and whether to display contacts using their first names first or last names first.

1. Touch the Contacts icon on the Home screen.

2. Touch the Menu button.

3. Touch Settings.

4. Touch List By to choose the sort order of the list of contacts in the Contacts app. You can sort the list by first name or last name.

5. Touch Display Contacts By to choose how each contact is displayed. You can display contacts with the first name first or the last name first.

6. Touch to save the settings and return to the Contacts app.

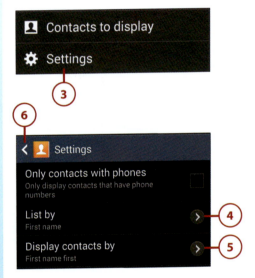

Create Contact Groups

You can create contact groups—such as Friends, Family, Inner Circle—and then divide your contacts among them. This can be useful if you don't want to search through all your contacts. For example, to find a family member, you can simply touch the Family group and see only family members.

1. From the Contacts main screen, touch the Groups icon to display the Groups screen.

2. Touch the Menu button.

3. Touch Create.

4. Enter a name for your new group.

5. Optionally, touch Group Ringtone to set a specific ringtone for the group. You can use the ringtone and vibration pattern to make calls from the group easy to distinguish.

6. Optionally, touch Message Alert to set a distinctive message alert tone for the group.

7. Optionally, touch Vibration Pattern to set a specific vibration pattern for the group.

8. Touch Add Member to add members to the group.

9. Touch the check boxes next to contacts' names to select each member of the group.

10. Touch Done.

11. Touch Save to save the group.

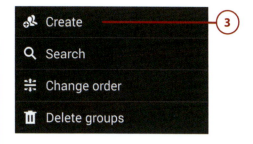

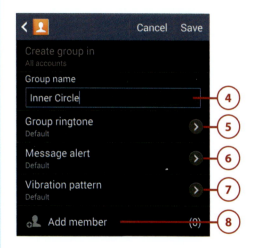

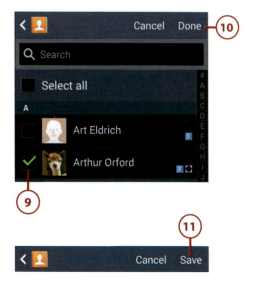

Change the Contacts in a Contacts Group

1. Touch the Groups tab on the Contacts main screen.

2. Touch the group to edit.

3. Touch to add a contact to the group.

4. Touch the Menu button.

5. Touch Remove Member.

6. Touch the contact or contacts you want to remove.

7. Touch Done to remove the contact and save the changes.

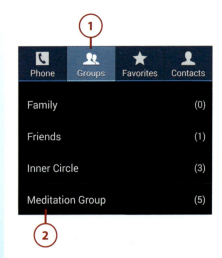

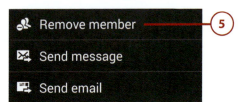

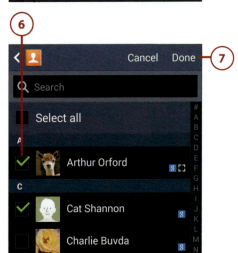

Choose Which Contacts to Display

You can choose to hide certain contact groups from the main contacts display. For example, you can choose to show only contacts from Twitter. You can also choose which contact groups in each account to include.

1. Touch the Contacts icon on the Home screen.

2. Touch the Menu button.

3. Touch Contacts to Display.

4. Touch to display all contacts from all accounts.

5. Touch an account to show only contacts in that account.

6. Touch to choose a customized selection.

7. Touch to customize which groups in each account are displayed.

8. Touch to expand an account to see subgroups of contacts.

9. Touch to select or deselect a subgroup of contacts.

10. Touch Done to save your settings.

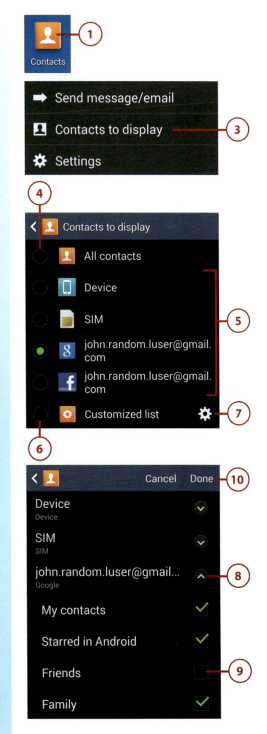

Link and Separate Contacts

As you add contacts to your Galaxy Note 3, they are automatically linked if the new contact name matches a name that's already stored. Sometimes you need to manually link contacts or separate them if your Galaxy Note 3 has joined them in error.

Link Contacts Manually

1. Touch the contact that you want to link a contact to.

2. Touch the Menu button.

3. Touch Link Contact to display the Link Contact screen. The Suggestions list shows contacts in which Contacts has found apparently suitable data, but you can choose a contact from the All Contacts list if necessary.

4. Touch the contact you want to link with.

5. Touch the contact's name to return to the Contacts screen.

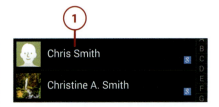

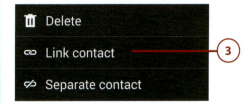

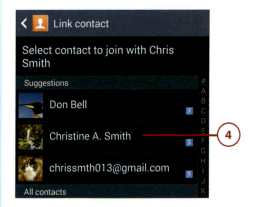

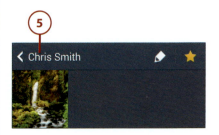

Separate Contacts

1. Touch the contact that you want to separate.

2. Touch the Menu button.

3. Touch Separate Contact to display the Separate Contact screen.

4. Touch the contact you want to separate.

5. Touch OK to separate the contacts.

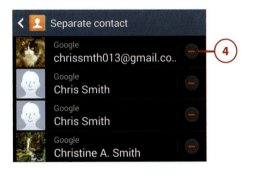

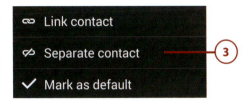

Adding a Contact to Your Home Screen

If you communicate with some contacts so much that you are constantly opening and closing the Contacts application, you can save time and effort by adding a shortcut to the contacts on the Home screen.

1. Touch the Apps icon on the Home screen.

2. Touch Widgets and then swipe right until you see the Contact widget.

3. Touch and hold the Contact widget.

4. While still holding the widget, position the widget on the Home screen and release your finger. The Select Contact Shortcut screen appears.

5. Touch the contact you want to add to the Home screen.

>>>Go Further

IMPORTING AND EXPORTING CONTACTS

You can import any contacts that are stored on your SIM or vCards that you have saved to your Galaxy Note 3's internal storage. You can also export your entire contact list to your Galaxy Note 3's SIM card or to a USB storage device. To access the import/export functions, touch the Menu button and touch Import/Export.

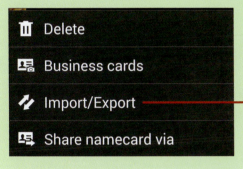

Touch to import or export contacts

Turn your current call
into a conference call

In this chapter, you find out how to make and take phone calls and send instant messages on your Galaxy Note 3. Topics include the following:

→ Making phone calls
→ Making conference calls
→ Sending and receiving text messages
→ Sending and receiving multimedia messages

8

Phone, SMS, and MMS

As a cellular phone, your Galaxy Note 3 includes powerful features that enable you to make phone calls swiftly and easily. Your Galaxy Note 3 can also send both text-only instant messages and multimedia instant messages by using the Messaging app.

Phone

With the Phone app, you can quickly make and receive calls across the cellular network. When you need to talk to more than one other person, you can turn your current call into a conference call.

Open and Navigate the Phone App

The Phone app contains four tabs that enable you to make calls in various ways and to track the calls you receive.

1. On the Home screen, touch Phone.

Opening the Phone App from the Lock Screen

By default your Note 3 does not show any app shortcut icons on the lock screen. You can change this by going to Settings, Device, Lock screen and turning on Shortcuts. Now the Lock screen will show the Phone app shortcut along with a few others. To access the phone from the Lock screen, swipe the phone icon upward and your Note 3 will unlock and go straight to the phone app.

2. Touch the keys to dial a number.

3. If the Phone app displays a suggested contact with a matching number, you can tap the contact if it is the one you want.

4. Touch to place the call.

Turn on shortcuts

Shortcuts — Set shortcuts on lock screen — ON

Personal message — Customize personal message — OFF

Touch to see all numbers for this contact

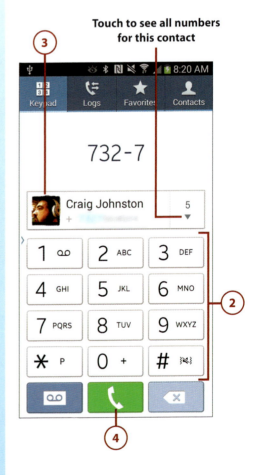

5. Touch Logs to see a list of the calls and messages you have placed and sent.

Making Your Logs Display the Information You Need

At first, the Phone app displays all your logs, but you can narrow the view to specific logs so you can more easily find the calls and messages you need. You learn to do this later in this chapter.

6. Touch Favorites to see lists of Favorites and Frequently Contacted contacts.

7. Touch Contacts to display your full contacts list in the Contacts app.

8. Touch Phone to return to the Phone app.

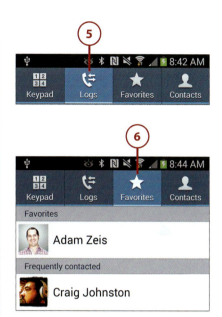

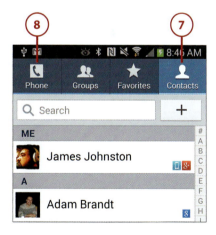

Receive a Call

When someone phones your Galaxy Note 3, you can accept the call, reject it, or reject it and send a text message.

Accept a Call

1. When the phone rings, look at the contact name (if it is available) or the phone number if it is not, and decide whether to take the call.

2. Touch and drag to accept the call.

3. Touch to switch to the speaker.

4. Touch to enable extra volume on the speaker.

5. Touch to switch to the headset.

6. Touch to mute the call. Touch again to turn off muting.

7. Touch to place the call on hold. Touch Unhold, which replaces the Hold button, when you are ready to restart the call.

8. Touch to end the call.

Touch to personalize call sound

Touch to enable/disable noise reduction

Reject a Call

If you do not want to accept the call, you can reject it so that it goes to your voicemail.

1. When the phone rings, touch and drag to reject the call.

The call goes to voicemail, and your Galaxy Note 3 displays the screen you were using before the call came in.

Reject a Call and Send a Message

Instead of simply declining a call and sending it to your voicemail, you can send a text message straight back to the caller. Your Galaxy Note 3 provides a selection of canned messages for general needs. You can also create your own messages or type custom messages for particular calls.

1. When the phone rings, touch and drag up to open the Reject Call with Message shade.

2. Touch to send one of the canned messages.

Touch to create and send a custom message

Creating Your Own Reject Messages

To create and save your own reject messages, open the Phone app and touch the Menu button. On the menu, touch Call Settings. On the Call Settings screen, touch Set Up Call Rejection Messages. On the Reject Messages screen, touch Create to create a new message, or touch an existing message to open it for editing.

Handle Missed Calls

If you miss a phone call, you can quickly locate it in the Phone app's logs so that you can return it.

1. Touch to see the missed call.

2. If the Logs tab is not displayed, touch to display it.

3. If you want to change the logs displayed, touch the Menu button.

4. Touch View.

5. Touch the button you want to filter by. For example, touch Missed Calls, or Dialed calls.

Missed call notification

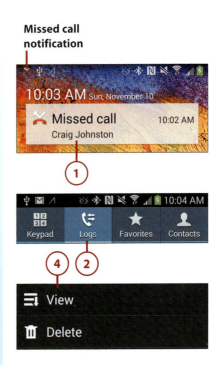

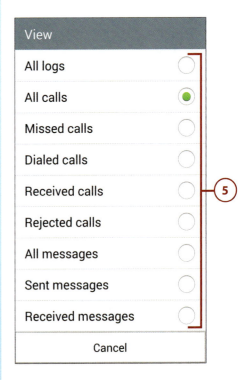

6. Touch a call to see its details.

7. Touch the Menu button for more options.

8. Touch to add the caller to the reject list. This makes your Note 3 automatically reject calls from this person.

9. Touch to send the caller's number to someone via text message (SMS).

10. Touch to delete one or more call log entries for this person.

11. Touch to copy the caller's number to the dialing screen.

12. Touch to send the caller a text message.

13. Touch to return the call.

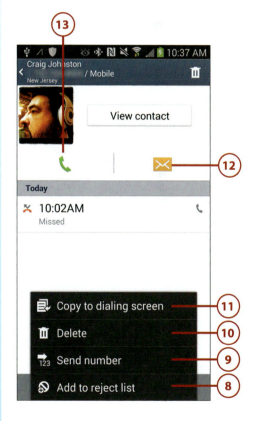

Place a Call

When you need to make a phone call, you can dial it manually using the keypad. But usually you can make a call more quickly by placing the call from a contact entry or by using your voice.

Dial with the Keypad

You can use the keypad to dial a call both when you need to call a number for which you do not have a contact and when you can remember part of the number for a contact.

1. Start typing the phone number. If you are typing to recall a number, type the part you remember.

2. If Phone suggests the correct number, touch to dial it.

3. Touch to dial the number you have typed if no matches were found.

Touch if there are more matches

Dial from a Contact Entry

If you know you have a contact entry for the person you want to dial, you can start from that contact entry.

1. In the Phone app, touch the Contacts tab to bring it to the front. Android switches from the Phone app to the Contacts app.

2. Touch the contact to display the contact's details.

Starting a Call from the Contacts App

Instead of launching the Phone app and then touching the Contacts tab to go to the Contacts app, you can start a call directly from the Contacts app. Touch Contacts on the Home screen or the Apps screen to launch the Contacts app, touch the contact to display his or her details, and then touch the Call button.

3. Touch the number you want to call.

Use the search bar to find contacts quickly

Dial Using Your Voice

Your Galaxy Note 3 also enables you to dial calls using your voice.

1. Double-press the Home button to launch S Voice.

2. Touch and release the microphone button and say, "Call," followed by the contact's name; if the contact has multiple phone numbers, say the type of number as well. For example, say, "Call Dana Smith mobile," or, "Call Maria Ramirez work."

3. Wait while S Voice dials the call. The Dialing screen appears.

Dial Using Your S Pen

Your Galaxy Note 3 also enables you to dial numbers using your S Pen.

1. Remove your S Pen.

2. Touch the Back button to cancel the Air Command window.

3. Hover your S Pen close to the screen and touch the writing icon.

4. Write the name of the person you want to call (or write numbers).

5. Touch a matched contact to call that person.

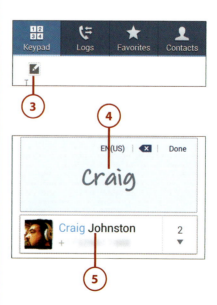

Control a Call

After accepting or establishing a phone call, you can control it from the Call screen.

1. Touch Hold to put the call on hold. When you do this, the person at the other end of the call normally receives an automatic announcement that you have put them on hold.

2. Touch Keypad to display the keypad (for typing more numbers after the call has connected).

3. Touch Mute to mute the call. Touch again to remove muting.

4. Touch Headset to switch the audio to the headset.

5. Touch Speaker to switch the audio to the speaker.

6. Touch to enable or disable extra volume.

7. Touch to enable or disable noise canceling.

8. Touch to end the call.

Using Other Apps During a Call

During a call, you can use most other apps freely, but you cannot play music or video. You can take photos with the Camera app, but you cannot shoot videos. To switch to another app, either use the Recent Apps list or press the Home button and use the Apps screen as usual. While you are using another app, your Galaxy Note 3 displays a green bar at the top of the screen to remind you that you are in a call. When you return to the Phone app, your Galaxy Note 3 displays a panel of options. Touch the Return to Call in Progress green phone button to go back to your call.

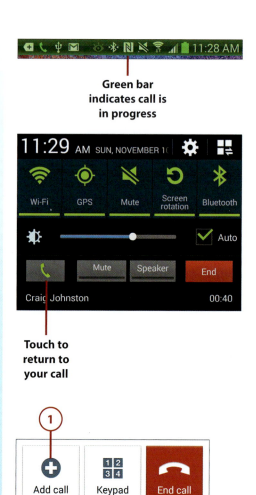

Green bar indicates call is in progress

Touch to return to your call

Make Conference Calls

You can quickly turn your current call into a conference call by adding further participants.

1. On the call screen, touch Add Call.

2. Dial the call in the most convenient way. For example, touch the Contacts tab, touch the contact in the list, and then touch the Call button on the contact's details screen.

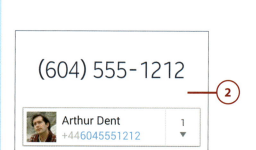

3. When your Galaxy Note 3 has established the new call, the original caller is on hold. Touch Merge to merge the calls.

4. When you are ready to finish the call, end it as you normally would.

Touch to manage the conference call

Managing Your Conference Call

During a conference call you can manage the callers. Touch the Menu button and touch Manage Conference Call. Touch End next to the caller you want to drop from the conference call. Touch Back to Call to return to the main dialpad screen.

Touch to end a specific call

Touch to return to your call

Configure the Phone App

To make the Phone app work your way, you can configure its settings.

1. Touch the Menu button.

2. Touch Call Settings.

3. Touch to set up Auto Reject mode and the numbers you want to automatically reject.

4. Touch to edit your canned reject messages.

What Does Auto Reject Mode Do?

Your Galaxy Note 3's Auto Reject mode can automatically reject either all calls or only the numbers on a list you provide. Automatically rejecting all calls can be useful for meetings and social occasions when you do not want to be disturbed. Automatically rejecting specific numbers enables you to avoid calls from people you do not want to talk to. You can turn Auto Reject mode on and off by moving the Auto Reject Mode switch.

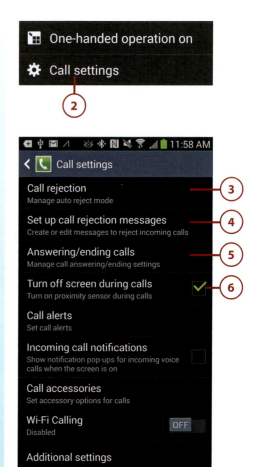

5. Touch to choose if you want to use the Home key or your voice to answer incoming calls. Also set the option to use the Power button to end calls.

6. Touch to enable or disable turning off the proximity sensor while on a call.

7. Touch to choose options for vibrations, cell status tones, and alerts during calls. You can choose whether your Galaxy Note 3 vibrates when someone answers your call and when they hang up. You can also choose which status tones and alerts to receive during calls and which to suppress.

8. Touch to choose whether you want a pop-up window to display when you receive an incoming call.

9. Touch to choose if you want calls automatically answered when you have the headset plugged in, and if you want to be able to make outgoing calls if your Note 3's screen is locked and you are using Bluetooth.

10. Touch to enable or disable Wi-Fi Calling.

11. Touch to see additional settings including how Caller ID is handled, call forwarding, call waiting, and Fixed Dialing Numbers (FDN).

12. Scroll down for more settings

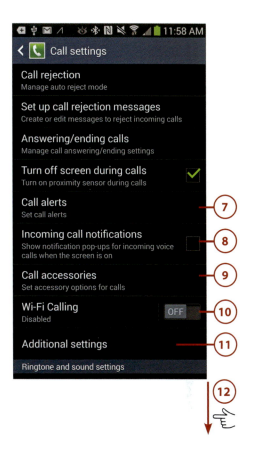

What Is Wi-Fi Calling?

Wi-Fi Calling (or its technical name Unlicensed Mobile Access [UMA]) is a technology that is provided by some carriers around the world, which enables your Galaxy Note 3 to roam between the cellular network and Wi-Fi networks. Typically when you are connected to a Wi-Fi network, any calls you make are free and of higher audio quality because of the faster speeds. As you move out of Wi-Fi coverage, your Note 3 hands the call off to the cellular network—and vice versa—allowing your call to continue without interruption. If you want to read more about UMA or Wi-Fi calling read this online article: http://crackberry.com/saving-call-charges-recession-your-blackberry. The article is on a BlackBerry blog, but the descriptions of the technology still apply.

13. Touch to choose the ringtone and vibration pattern for incoming calls, whether to play the ringtone and vibrate at the same time, and whether to play the keypad tones.

14. Choose to customize how the audio on phone calls sounds. You can choose among Soft Sound, Clear Sound, Adapt Sound, or choose Off to use standard audio.

15. Touch to enable or disable noise reduction by default while on a call.

16. Touch to make the Galaxy Note 3 ring more loudly when it detects it is in a pocket or a bag.

17. Touch to choose which voicemail service to use (if you have more than one option).

18. Touch to adjust voicemail settings (if options are available).

19. Touch to choose your ringtone for announcing voicemail.

20. Touch to choose vibration settings for voicemail.

21. Scroll down for more settings.

22. Touch to enable or disable TTY mode and choose which TTY mode to use.

23. Touch to enable or disable improving the sound quality when using a hearing aid.

24. Touch to save your changes and return to the main phone screen.

SMS and MMS

Short Message Service (SMS), also known as text messaging, has been around for a long time. Multimedia Message Service (MMS) is a newer form of text messaging that can contain pictures, audio, and video as well as text. Your Galaxy Note 3 can send and receive both SMS and MMS messages.

Get to Know the Messaging App

The Messaging app is what you use to send and receive text messages. This app has all the features you need to compose, send, receive, and manage these messages.

1. Touch the Messaging icon on the Home screen.

2. Touch to compose a new text message.

3. Touch the sender's picture to show the Quick Connect bar that allows you to contact the person using email, phone, and other methods.

4. Touch a message thread to open it.

5. Touch the Menu button to see more options.

6. Touch to search for a message.

7. Touch to delete a message thread.

8. Touch to open the Draft Messages folder to complete and send draft messages.

9. Touch to open the Locked Messages folder. Locked messages are messages that you have chosen to lock so they are not accidentally deleted.

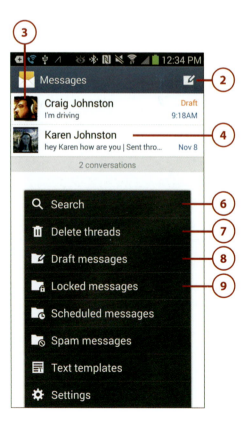

10. Touch to open the Scheduled Messages folder to see messages that are scheduled to be sent at a specific time.

11. Touch to open the Spam Messages folder.

12. Touch to manage your text template messages. Text templates are pre-composed text messages you can use, such as "Sorry, I missed your call."

13. Touch to open the Settings screen. See the next section for more on Settings.

How Do I Lock a Message?

You might want to lock a message so that it does not get accidentally deleted when you delete the message thread. To lock a message, touch and hold on the message and choose Lock. The lock symbol displays just below the locked message. To unlock the message, touch and hold on the message and choose Unlock.

Manage Settings for the Messaging App

You use the settings of the Messaging app to manage how the app handles your SMS and MMS messages. Before you actually start working with SMS and MMS, let's take a look at the settings.

1. Touch to enable or disable automatically deleting old messages when the limits you set in steps 2 and 3 are reached.

2. Touch to change the text message limit per thread (or conversation). The maximum number you can enter is 999. When the limit is reached, Messaging deletes messages within the thread or conversation using the first in, first out (FIFO) method.

3. Touch to change the multimedia message limit per thread (or conversation). The maximum number you can type is 999. When the limit is reached, messages within the thread or conversation are deleted using the FIFO method.

4. Touch to choose what kind of bubble style is used for text message display.

5. Touch to choose which background the app uses for messages.

6. Touch to use a split view when you turn your Galaxy Note 3 to landscape orientation.

7. Touch to enable changing text size by pressing the volume buttons.

8. Touch to turn on or off adding a signature to each mesasge you send. Remember that the text in the signature counts against the text message size.

9. Touch to edit your signature if you enabled it in step 8.

10. Touch the SMS/MMS tab.

11. Touch to enable or disable delivery reports. Although your Galaxy Note 3 supports this feature, it is not well supported by other phones, so you might not get delivery reports from some recipients.

12. Touch to manage the text messages stored on your Galaxy Note 3's SIM card.

13. Touch to change your message center number. This is the number at your carrier that the Galaxy Note 3 contacts to retrieve your messages.

14. Touch to choose the input method for composing SMS messages. Your choices are GSM alphabet, Unicode, or Automatic. Change the default setting only if you are sure you need to.

15. Scroll down for the rest of the settings.

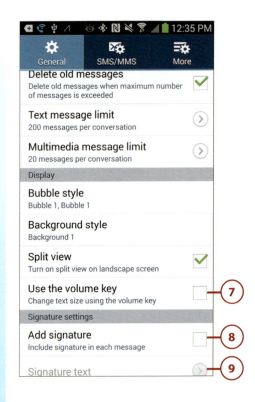

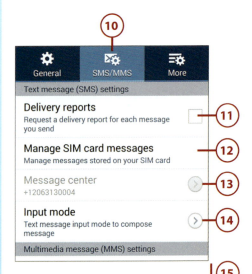

What Does the Manage SIM Card Messages Command Do?

Many old cell phones store text messages on the SIM card and not in the phone's memory. If you have just upgraded from an older phone, you might still have text messages on the SIM card that you would like to retrieve. Touch Manage SIM Card Messages on the Settings screen in the Messaging app to display the Manage SIM Card Messages screen. You can then copy the messages to your Galaxy Note 3's memory and copy the senders to your contacts in the Contacts app.

16. Touch to enable or disable the ability to send a single MMS to multiple recipients.

17. Touch to enable or disable automatically requesting a delivery report for each multimedia message you send.

18. Touch to enable or disable a read report for each multimedia message you send.

What's the Difference Between a Delivery Report and a Read Report?

A delivery report indicates that the message has reached the destination device. A read report indicates that the message has been opened for viewing. There is still no guarantee that whoever opened the message has actually read it, let alone understood it.

19. Touch to enable or disable automatically retrieving multimedia messages.

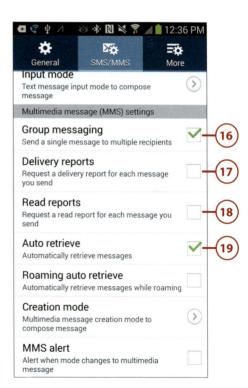

20. Touch to enable or disable auto-matically retrieving multimedia messages when roaming.

21. Touch to choose the Creation mode, which controls which con-tent you can include in multime-dia messages.

22. Touch to enable or disable a warning when you add content to an SMS message that makes it change to an MMS message.

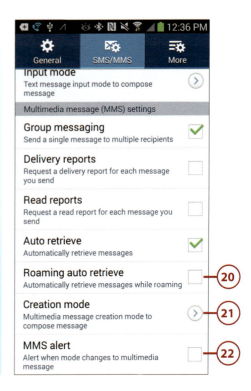

Don't Auto-Retrieve MMS While Roaming

Disable the automatic retrieval of multimedia messages when you travel to other countries because automatically retrieving these messages when you're roaming can result in a big bill from your provider. International carriers love to charge large amounts of money for people traveling to their countries and using their networks. The only time it is a good idea to leave this enabled is if your carrier offers an international SMS or MMS bundle where you pay a flat rate up front before leaving. When you have auto-retrieve disabled, you see a Download button next to a multimedia message. You have to touch it to manu-ally download the message.

What Is the Creation Mode for Multimedia Messages?

The Creation mode feature lets you control which content Messaging allows you to include in messages. Choose Restricted to have the Galaxy Note 3 pre-vent you from including content that the recipient might not be able to receive or view. Choose Warning to have the Galaxy Note 3 warn you about such con-tent but allow you to proceed. Choose Free to be able to include potentially problematic content without warning.

23. Touch the More tab.

24. Touch to enable or disable receiving messages "pushed" from the server. Push messages arrive at your Galaxy Note 3 shortly after they arrive at the server, which is usually faster than waiting until the Galaxy Note 3 checks for messages.

25. Touch to choose how to handle remote requests to load services. Your choices are Always, Prompt, and Never.

26. Touch to enable or disable receiving notifications when messages arrive.

27. Touch to select the ringtone that announces incoming messages. This is grayed out if your Note 3 is in Silent mode.

28. Touch to enable or disable vibration for message notifications. This is grayed out if your Note 3 is in Silent mode.

29. Touch to choose how often your Galaxy Note 3 repeats a message alert. Your choices are Once, Every 2 Minutes, or Every 10 Minutes.

30. Touch to enable or disable the display of a preview of each incoming message in the status bar.

31. Scroll down for the remaining settings.

It's Not All Good

What Setting Should I Choose for Service Loading?

Samsung's Service Loading feature has been used for attacks that remotely wipe smartphones without the owner's consent. Because of this danger, never choose Always as the Service Loading setting. Choose Prompt if you want your Galaxy Note 3 to let you decide about service loading requests. Choose Never if you prefer to suppress service loading requests.

32. Touch to manage which emergency alerts you want to receive. These alerts are sent out by your government or law enforcement (for example, AMBER alerts).

33. Touch to experience a preview of how emergency alerts will look and sound on your Note 3.

34. Touch to enable or disable the settings for detecting spam messages. Spam messages are unwanted commercial messages.

35. If you enable spam settings, touch to register a phone number as a sender of spam. Your Galaxy Note 3 then blocks this number.

36. If you enable spam settings, touch to build a list of phrases that identify messages as being spam.

37. Touch to enable or disable blocking of all senders who are not in your contacts.

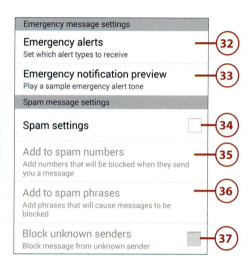

Compose Messages

When you compose a new message, you do not need to make a conscious decision whether it is an SMS message or an MMS message. As soon as you add a subject line or attach a file to your message, your Galaxy Note 3 automatically treats the message as an MMS message.

Here is how to compose and send messages.

1. Touch to compose a new message.

2. Start typing the recipient's phone number, or if the person is in your contacts, type the name. If Android finds a match, touch the mobile number.

3. Touch and start typing your message.

4. Touch to send your message.

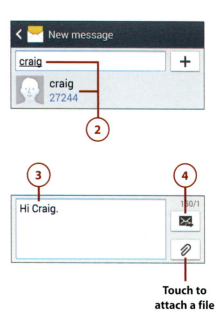

Touch to attach a file

Inserting Smiley Icons

To insert smiley icons (or emoticons), touch the Menu button and then touch Insert Smiley. In the Insert Smiley dialog, scroll down if needed, and then touch the smiley you want to insert.

Delay Sending the Message

You might decide that you want a text message to be sent at a later time automatically. To do this, before sending the message, touch the Menu button and choose Scheduling. Choose the date and time you want your message to be sent and touch Done. Then touch the Send button and your message will only send when you set it to.

MESSAGE LIMITS AND MESSAGES

>>>Go Further

Text messages can only be 160 characters long. To get around this limit, most modern phones simply break up text messages you type into 160-character chunks. Your Galaxy Note 3 displays a readout showing the number of characters remaining and the number of messages it will send: The readout starts at 160/1 when you begin a new message and runs down to 1/1, then starts at 145/2 (because there is some overhead on linking the messages). The phone receiving the message simply combines them into one message. This is important to know if your wireless plan has a text message limit. When you create one text message, your Galaxy Note 3 might actually break the message into two or more.

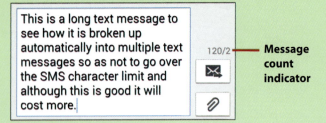

> This is a long text message to see how it is broken up automatically into multiple text messages so as not to go over the SMS character limit and although this is good it will cost more.

120/2 ——— **Message count indicator**

Attach Files to Messages

If you want to send a picture, audio file, or video along with your text message, all you need to do is attach the file. Attaching a file turns your SMS message into an MMS message.

1. Touch to attach a file.

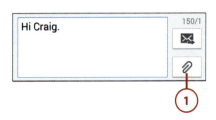

Hi Craig.

150/1

2. Touch to attach a picture already stored in your Gallery app.

3. Touch to take a picture and attach it.

4. Touch to attach a video already stored in your Gallery app.

5. Touch to capture a video and attach it.

6. Touch to attach an audio file that is already stored on your Galaxy Note 3.

7. Touch to record audio and attach it.

8. Touch to attach an S Note document.

9. Touch to attach a calendar item.

10. Touch to attach your location.

11. Touch to attach a contact record from the Contacts app.

It's Not All Good

Is It Worth Attaching Files?

Attaching files to text messages is not as useful as you might desire. Most carriers limit the attachment size to around 300KB. This means that you can only really attach about 60 seconds of very low-quality video; pictures with low resolution, high compression, or both; and very short audio files. The Messaging app automatically compresses larger picture files to make them small enough to send, but you will often find that it simply refuses to send video files because they are too large. Choosing the option of capturing pictures, capturing video, or recording audio when you choose to attach is the only way you can guarantee that the files are small enough. This is because when you do this, the camera and audio recorder apps are set to a mode that makes them record low-quality audio and take low-quality pictures.

Receive Messages

When you receive a new SMS or MMS message, you can read it, view its attachments, and even save those attachments to your Galaxy Note 3.

1. When a new SMS or MMS message arrives, your Galaxy Note 3 plays a ringtone and displays a notification in the status bar.

2. Pull down the notification shade to see newly arrived messages.

3. Touch a message alert to display the message in the Messages app.

4. Touch an attachment to open it for viewing.

5. Touch and hold a message to display the Message Options dialog. Skip to step 7 for more about the additional options.

6. Touch to write a reply to the message.

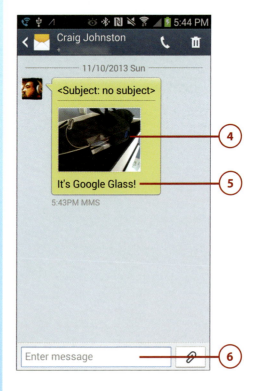

7. Touch to delete the message. This deletes just the message and not the entire thread.

8. Touch to view a slideshow of attached images.

9. Touch to copy the message text so you can paste it elsewhere.

10. Touch to forward the message and attachment to someone else.

11. Touch to lock the message against deletion.

12. Touch to save the attachment to your Galaxy Note 3.

13. Touch to share the message via social media or other methods.

14. Touch to view the message details, such as its size and the date and time it was sent.

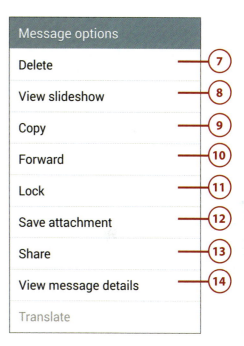

Message options

Delete — 7

View slideshow — 8

Copy — 9

Forward — 10

Lock — 11

Save attachment — 12

Share — 13

View message details — 14

Translate

Usable Content

If a text message contains links to websites, phone numbers, or email addresses, touching those links makes the Galaxy Note 3 take the appropriate action. For example, when you touch a phone number, your Galaxy Note 3 calls the number; when you touch a web link, the Galaxy Note 3 opens the page in Chrome or your other default browser.

Browse
through and
purchase music

Search for music

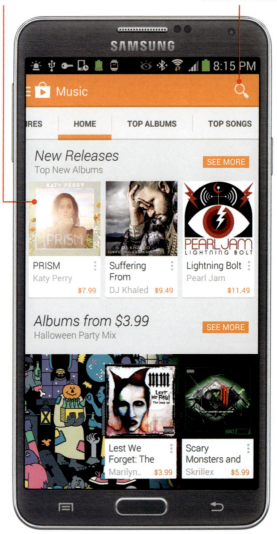

In this chapter, you discover your Galaxy Note 3's audio and video capabilities, including how your Galaxy Note 3 plays video and music, and how you can synchronize audio and video from your desktop or laptop computer or Google Music. This chapter also covers how to take pictures and videos. Topics include the following:

→ Using Google Music for music
→ Using the Gallery app for pictures and video
→ Shooting still photos and videos
→ Enjoying videos with the YouTube app

Audio, Video, Photos, and Movies

Your Galaxy Note 3 is a powerful multimedia smartphone with the ability to play back many different audio and video formats. The large screen enables you to turn your Galaxy Note 3 sideways to enjoy a video in its original 16:9 ratio. You can also use your Galaxy Note 3 to take photos and videos, watch videos, and even upload videos to YouTube right from your phone. Android version 4 fully embraces the cloud, which enables you to store your music collection on Google's servers so you can access it anywhere.

Enjoying Music with the Music Application

To get the most out of music on your Galaxy Note 3, you probably want to use the Play Music app, which enables you to listen to music stored on your phone as well as from your collection in the Google Music cloud.

INSTALL THE PLAY MUSIC APP IF NECESSARY

If your Galaxy Note 3 does not include the Play Music app, you need to install it. Touch Apps on the Home screen and look through the list of apps. The Play Music app may appear either directly on the Apps screen or in a Google folder that gathers apps such as Chrome, Gmail, and Google+ together with Play Magazines, Play Movies & TV, and Play Music.

If you don't find the Play Music app, touch the Apps icon on the Home screen, and then touch the Play Store icon to open the Play Store app. Touch Apps, touch the search icon, and type **play music**. Touch the Google Play Music search result, touch Install, and then touch Accept & Download. Your Galaxy Note 3 downloads the Play Music app and installs it.

Find Music

When you're certain the Play Music app is installed on your Galaxy Note 3, you can add some music. One way to add music is to purchase it from Google.

1. Touch the Play Music icon on the Apps screen or in the Google folder.

2. Touch the headphones icon in the upper-left corner to display the navigation panel.

3. Touch Shop to display the Play Store screen.

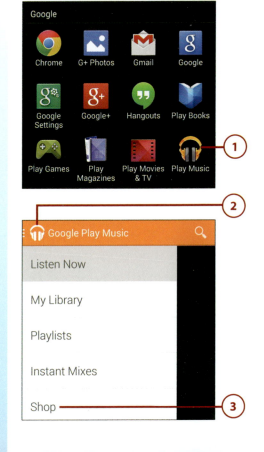

4. Touch to see new releases.

5. Swipe right to see a list of music genres.

6. Swipe left or touch Top Albums to see the Top Albums list. Swipe left again from the Top Albums list to see the Top Songs list.

7. Touch to search for music.

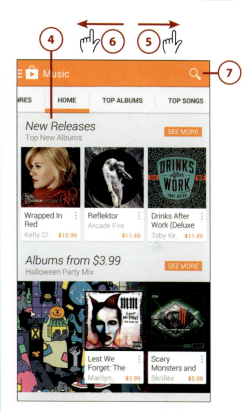

Purchase Music

After you find a song or album you want to purchase, use the following steps to make the purchase.

Free Music

Sometimes songs are offered for free. If a song is offered for free, you see the word Free instead of a price for the song. Even though the song is free, you still need to follow the steps outlined in this section; however, the price appears as 0.

1. Touch the price to the right of the song title or album.

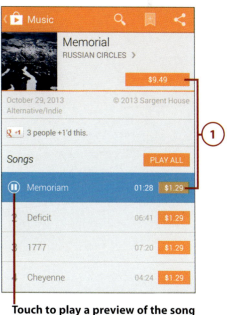

Touch to play a preview of the song before purchasing it

2. Touch Buy. Google Play processes your payment, and Play Music downloads the song. You can then play it.

Touch to change your payment method

It's Not All Good

Cloud and Data Usage

Although cloud storage (where your music is stored on Google computers as opposed to on your Galaxy Note 3) can be very beneficial, it does mean that anytime you listen to your music collection it is streamed over the network. If you are connected to Wi-Fi, this data streaming is free; however, if you are not connected to Wi-Fi, the data is streamed over the cellular network and counts against your data package. If you don't have a large or unlimited data package, you could incur large overage fees, so please be careful. Be extra careful about this when traveling abroad because international data roaming charges are very expensive. Another disadvantage of streaming from the cloud is that when you have no cellular or Wi-Fi coverage, or you have very slow or spotty coverage, you are unable to access and listen to your music collection, or the songs stutter because of the poor connection.

Add Your Existing Music to Google Music

You can upload up to 20,000 songs from Apple iTunes, Microsoft Windows Media Player, or music stored in folders on your computer to your Google Music cloud account by using the Google Music Manager app on your desktop computer. If you haven't already installed Google Music Manager, please follow the steps in the "Install Google Music Manager" section in the Prologue.

1. Click (right-click for Windows) the Google Music Manager icon. On the Mac, this icon appears in the menu bar at the top of the screen. On Windows, the icon appears in the taskbar at the bottom of the screen.

2. Choose Preferences on the Mac; choose Options on Windows.

3. Click Add Folder to add a folder of music to upload.

4. Click Remove Folder to remove the folder you have selected in the list box from your Google Play account.

5. Click Upload after you have made your selections.

6. Select this check box to allow Google Music Manager to auto-matically upload new songs added to the folders you have specified.

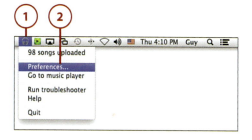

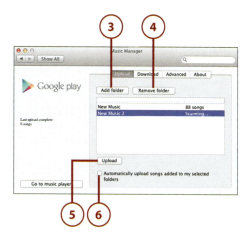

Automatic Upload

If you choose to have your music uploaded automatically in step 6, Google Music Manager continually monitors your Music folders to see if music has been added. If Google Music Manager finds new music, it automatically uploads it. After you install Google Music Manager, the app runs continuously, enabling it to detect music you add to iTunes, Windows Media Player, or your Music folders.

Can I Download Music to My Computer?

You can download your entire music collection from Google Music to your computer, or just download music you have purchased on your Galaxy Note 3. While in Google Music Manager Preferences, click Download.

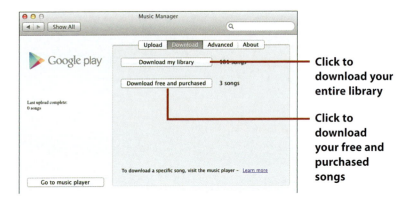

Click to download your entire library

Click to download your free and purchased songs

Use the Music Application

Now that you have synced some music to Google Music, and maybe bought some music online, it's time to take a look at how to use the Google Music app on your Galaxy Note 3.

Open and Navigate in the Music App

1. Touch the Play Music icon on the Apps screen or in the Google folder.

2. Touch the headphones icon in the upper-left corner to display the navigation panel. This panel enables you to switch among your different sources of music. You can also swipe right to display the navigation panel.

3. Touch Listen Now in the navigation panel to display the Listen Now screen, which contains music you have added recently. Listen Now also recommends music to you based on the music you have and your recent listening habits.

4. Touch My Library to display your music library. Your library contains both the music on your Galaxy Note 3 and the music in your Google account.

5. Touch Playlists to display the Playlists screen. The Play Music app automatically creates some playlists for you, and you can manually create as many other playlists as you want. Read more about playlists later in this chapter.

6. Touch Instant Mixes to display the Instant Mixes screen, which contains both instant mixes you create yourself and ones that Google Play recommends to you. An *instant mix* is a selection of songs based on—and supposedly related to—a particular starting song. For example, you can create an instant mix based on "Berzerk" or "Blurred Lines."

7. Touch Shop to switch to the Play Store app and go to the Music section of Google Play, where you can browse and buy music as explained earlier in this chapter.

Listen to Music in Your Library

1. Touch the headphones icon in the upper-left corner to display the navigation panel and then touch My Library to display your music library.

2. Touch to display a pop-up menu that enables you to switch between all your music (touch All Music) and only the music on your Galaxy Note 3 (touch On Device).

3. Touch to search for music using search terms.

4. Touch Genres to display the list of genres. You can then touch the genre by which you want to browse your library.

5. Touch Artists to display the list of artists so you can browse by artists.

6. Touch Albums to display the list of albums so you can browse by albums.

7. Touch Songs to display the list of songs. You can then easily locate a song by name in the alphabetical list.

8. Touch the Menu button on an item to display a pop-up menu of commands you can perform for that item. In this example, you can start an instant mix for this artist or shop the artist's music at the Play Store.

9. Touch the Play button or Pause button to control playback on the current song or most recent song played.

10. Touch an artist to display the albums and songs your library contains by that artist.

11. Touch the album you want to open. The album's songs appear.

12. Touch the song you want to start playing.

13. Touch Pause to pause playback. Touch the resulting Play button to start the music playing again.

14. Touch the album picture to display the Now Playing screen, which gives you full control of your music, as explained in the next section.

The My Library section shows the items in your music library

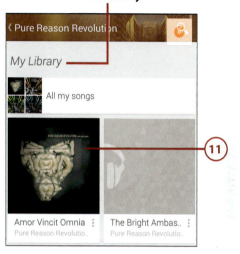

Indicates the song that is now playing

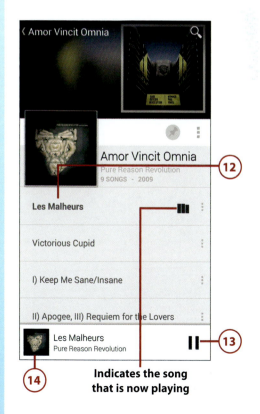

Control Playback

While playing music, you can control both how the music plays and the selection of music that plays.

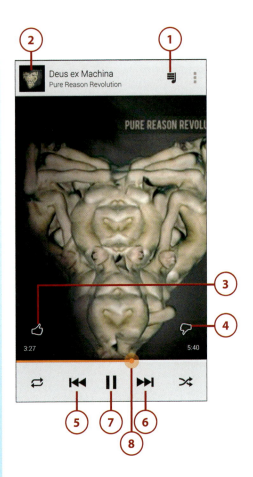

1. Touch to display the queue, which shows the songs that are lined up to play. You can then touch a song to start it playing.

2. Touch to return from the Now Playing screen to the previous screen.

3. Touch to indicate you like the song. The thumbs-up icon turns solid to indicate you have applied the rating. Touch again to remove the rating. The Google Music app also adds the song to the "Thumbs Up" playlist.

4. Touch to indicate you do not like the song. The thumbs-down icon turns solid to indicate you have applied the rating, and Play Music starts playing the next song.

5. Touch once to go back to the start of the current song. Touch again to skip back to the previous song in the album, playlist, or shuffle.

6. Touch to skip ahead to the next song in the album, playlist, or shuffle.

7. Touch to pause the song. The button turns into the Play button when a song is paused. Touch again to resume playing a paused song.

8. Touch and drag the Playhead to change the position in the song.

9. Touch to enable or disable song shuffling. When Shuffle is enabled, songs in the current playlist, album, or song list are randomly played.

10. Touch to enable repeating. Touch once to repeat all songs, touch again to repeat the current song only, and touch a third time to disable repeating.

11. Touch the Menu button to display the menu of actions you can take with the song.

12. Touch to start an instant mix based on the song.

13. Touch to add the song to a play-list. In the Add to Playlist dialog that opens, you can either touch New Playlist to start creating a new playlist or touch the name of an existing playlist to use that playlist.

14. Touch Go to Artist to display the artist the song is by.

15. Touch Go to Album to display the album the song is on.

16. Touch Clear Queue to clear the playback queue.

17. Touch Save Queue to save the playback queue. In the Add to Playlist dialog that opens, you can either touch New Playlist to create a new playlist containing the songs on the queue or touch the name of an existing playlist to add the songs to that playlist.

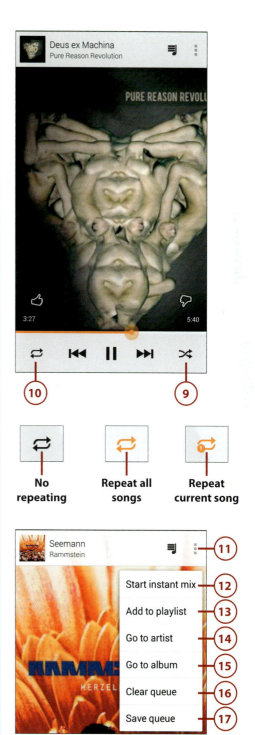

What Is an Instant Mix?

If you are playing a song and choose to create an instant mix as mentioned in step 12, the Google Music app creates a new playlist and adds songs to it that are similar to the one you are currently playing. The name of the playlist is the name of the current song plus the word mix. For example, if you are playing the song "Piquant" and choose to create an instant mix, the playlist is called "Piquant Mix."

Work and Listen to Music

You don't have to keep the Play Music app displayed while you are playing music. Instead, you can switch back to the Home screen and run any other app but still have the ability to control the music.

1. Pull down the Notification bar.

2. Touch to pause the song.

3. Touch to skip ahead to the next song in the list, album, or playlist.

4. Touch the song title or the album art to open the Google Music app for more control.

5. Touch to stop playing the song and remove the playback control from the Notification screen.

What If I Get a Call?

If someone calls you while you are listening to music, your Galaxy Note 3 pauses the music and displays the regular incoming call screen. After you hang up, the music continues playing.

Work with Playlists

Playlists can be a great way of listening to music, enabling you to group together related songs or simply those you want to hear in a particular sequence. On your Galaxy Note 3, you can create new playlists, add songs to existing playlists, rename playlists, and change the order of the songs they contain.

Create a New Playlist on Your Galaxy Note 3

1. Using the techniques described earlier in this chapter, navigate to a song you want to add to the new playlist.

2. Touch the song's Menu button to display the menu of actions you can take with the song.

3. Touch Add to Playlist. The Add to Playlist dialog opens.

4. Touch New Playlist. The Playlist Name dialog opens.

5. Type the name for the new playlist.

6. Touch OK.

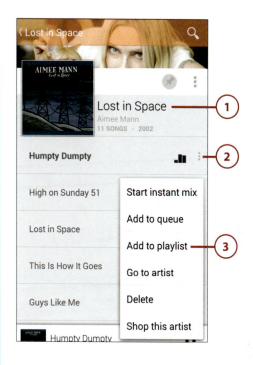

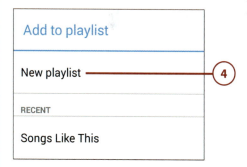

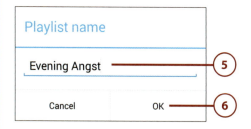

Add a Song to an Existing Playlist

1. Using the techniques described earlier in this chapter, navigate to a song you want to add to the new playlist. You can also use the song on the Now Playing screen, as in this example.

2. Touch the song's Menu button to open the menu of actions you can take with the song.

3. Touch Add to Playlist. The Add to Playlist dialog opens.

4. Touch the playlist you want to add the song to.

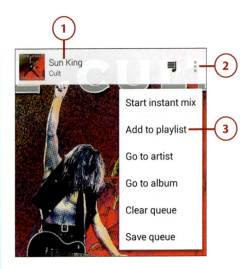

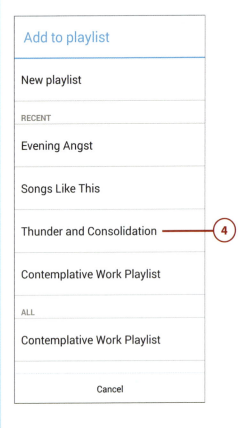

Delete a Playlist

When you no longer need a playlist, you can delete it in moments.
Deleting the playlist doesn't delete
its songs—only the list is deleted.

1. Touch the icon in the upper-left
   corner of the screen to display the
   navigation panel, and then touch
   Playlists to display the Playlists
   screen.

2. Touch the Menu button for the
   playlist you want to delete.

3. Touch Delete. A confirmation dialog opens.

4. Touch OK.

Renaming a Playlist

At this writing, the Play Music
app doesn't provide a command
for renaming a playlist. To work
around this, create a new, empty
playlist with the new name. Then
touch the Menu button for the
playlist you want to rename,
touch Add to Playlist to display
the Add to Playlist dialog, and
then touch your new playlist to
place the existing playlist's contents in the new playlist. You can
now delete the old playlist and
use the new playlist instead.

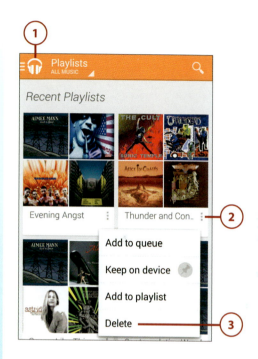

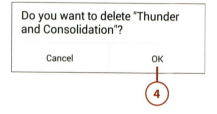

Rearrange the Songs in a Playlist

You can keep a playlist fresh by adding songs to it as explained earlier in this chapter, but you can also delete songs from the playlist and rearrange the songs it contains.

1. On the Playlists screen, touch the playlist to display its songs.

2. Touch and hold the three-line handle to the left of the song you want to move. Drag the song up or down until it is in the right place and then release it.

3. To remove a song, swipe it to the left or to the right. You can also touch its menu button and then touch Remove from Playlist.

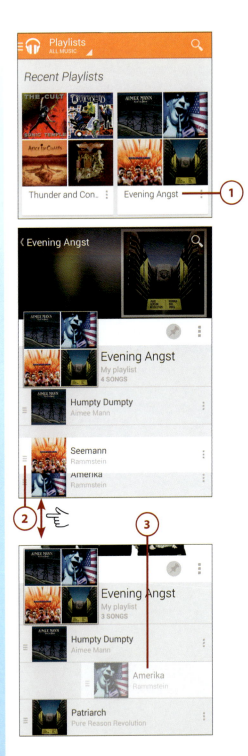

Listen to Music with No Wireless Coverage

If you use Google Music and store your music online, your Galaxy Note 3 streams the music over the cellular or Wi-Fi network when you play the music. If you know you are going to be without a signal but still want to listen to your music, you need to store it on your Galaxy Note 3.

1. Using the techniques discussed earlier in this chapter, go to the music you want to store on your Galaxy Note 3.

2. Touch the gray pushpin, which indicates that the music is not stored on your Galaxy Note 3.

3. The Play Music app downloads and stores the music. As it does so, the pushpin displays a progress indicator. When the music is available, the pushpin appears on an orange background.

>>>Go Further

SYNCHRONIZE MUSIC AND OTHER MEDIA USING A USB CABLE

If you don't use Google Music, or Google Music is not available in your country, you can synchronize music and other media using a USB cable or Wi-Fi. You can use Kies, the program that Samsung provides for managing its phones and tablets, or another app such as doubleTwist (http://www.doubletwist.com). Alternatively, you can connect your Galaxy Note 3 via USB and access its file system using Windows Explorer or Android File Transfer (http://www.android.com/filetransfer/) on the Mac.

>>>Go Further

ENJOY MUSIC ON YOUR GALAXY NOTE 3 USING OTHER APPS

As you have seen so far in this chapter, Google's Play Music app is easy to use and enables you to access the music you store in your Google account. But you will probably also want to explore the other apps most Galaxy Note 3 models include for enjoying music.

The Music Hub app enables you to upload your music collection to Samsung's online service and play it back from there. You can also buy music from the millions of songs the Music Hub sells. Music Hub is a subscription service.

The Music app is an easy-to-use app for playing back music. Music includes features such as the SoundAlive equalizer, which provides both basic and advanced features for making the audio sound the way you like it.

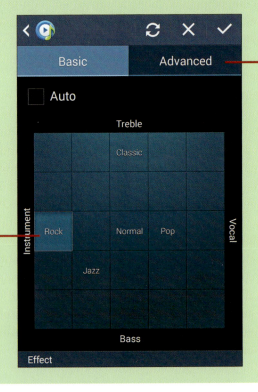

On the Advanced tab in the Music app, you can use a conventional graphic equalizer

On the Basic tab, you can apply equalizations by music type or frequency category

Playing and Sharing Videos

The Gallery app enables you to view pictures and video; you can also share pictures and video with people on Facebook, or via MMS, Bluetooth, YouTube, and email. This section explains how you can view and share videos.

Understanding the Two Ways to Access Videos

Your Galaxy Note 3 enables you to access videos in two main ways: through the Gallery app or through the Videos app. This section shows you how to use the Gallery app, which enables you to review your photos and videos at the same time and choose which to use or view. From the Gallery app, you can open the video for viewing in either the Photos app, as explained here, or in the Videos app.

This section explains how to view and share videos. Later in this chapter, you learn how to take pictures and share them.

1. Touch the Gallery icon on the Apps screen to launch the Gallery app.

2. Touch the navigation pop-up menu in the upper-left corner.

3. Touch the category you want to see. Your choices are Albums, All, Time, Locations, People, and Favorites. This example uses Albums.

4. Touch an album to open it, revealing the pictures and videos it contains.

5. Touch a video to open it for playback. Videos have a little Play icon on them.

6. Touch the Play icon to start the video playing.

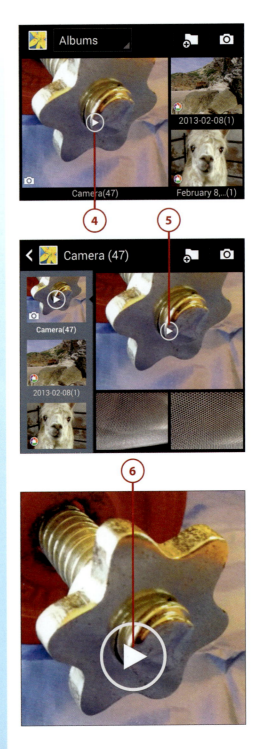

Choosing the App to Use for Playing Videos

The first time you tap the Play icon for a video in the Gallery app, your Galaxy Note 3 displays the Complete Action Using dialog to let you choose between the available video players. Normally, these are the Photos app and the Video Player app, but you might have installed other video-capable apps on your Galaxy Note 3.

Touch the app you want to use. Then touch Always if you want to always use that app. Touch Just Once if you want your Galaxy Note 3 to prompt you again in the future.

Complete action using

Photos   Video Player

Always   Just once

Touch Always to always use this app   **Touch the app to open the video in it**   **Touch Just Once to use the app only this time**

7. Touch the screen while the video is playing to reveal the video controls. If you do not use the controls, they disappear after a few seconds.

8. Touch to pause or unpause the video.

9. Drag the slider to scrub quickly forward and backward.

10. Touch to skip to the end of the video.

11. Touch to return to the beginning of the video.

12. Touch to switch between viewing the video full screen and viewing it as best fits the Galaxy Note 3's screen.

13. Touch to display the video in a pop-up window. You can then switch to another screen and continue to watch the video as you work or play.

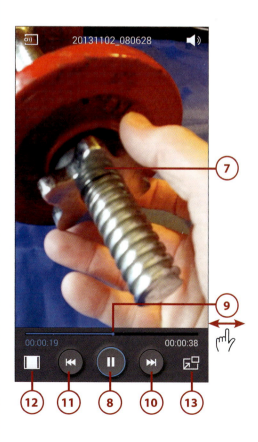

Changing the Orientation for a Video

When watching a video shot in landscape orientation, rotate your Galaxy Note 3 from portrait orientation to landscape orientation so you can enjoy the video full screen.

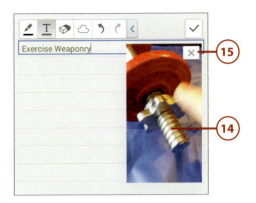

14. Touch to pause or restart the video. When you touch, an X appears in the upper-right corner.

15. Touch the X to close the pop-up video window.

Share Videos

From the Gallery app, you can share small videos with other people.

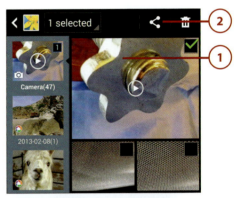

1. Touch and hold the video you want to share. After a moment, a green check mark appears on the video.

2. Touch to open the Share Via dialog.

3. Scroll if necessary to display other methods of sharing.

4. Touch a method for sharing the video.

Sharing Only Small Videos

It is best to share only small videos from your Galaxy Note 3. Even when using email, try to share videos no larger than 10MB, which is only two or three minutes of high-quality video. Otherwise, your videos will be too large to transfer successfully.

Bluetooth Sharing Might Fail

Many phones do not accept incoming Bluetooth files, but devices like computers do. Even on computers, the recipient must configure her Bluetooth configuration to accept incoming files.

Share a Video on YouTube

YouTube gives you a quick, easy, and effective way to share your videos with the whole wired world.

If you have not previously set up your YouTube account on your Galaxy Note 3, you are prompted to do so before you can upload your video.

1. Enter the title of your video.

2. Enter a description of your video.

3. Select whether to make your video public for everyone to see or whether to keep it private.

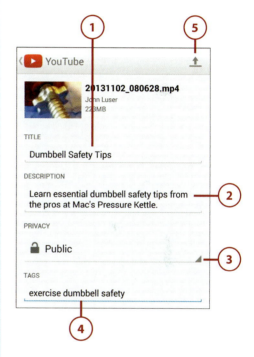

Sharing a YouTube Video Only with Specific People

As well as the Public setting and the Private setting, the Privacy pop-up list provides an Unlisted setting. Choose Unlisted when you need to share the video with some people but not with everyone. The video then does not appear in the public view of your YouTube account, but you can send the URL for the video to anyone you want to view it.

4. Enter any tags for your video. Tags are keywords that help people find videos by searching.

5. Touch Upload.

>>>Go Further

LIMITING YOUR YOUTUBE UPLOADS TO WI-FI NETWORKS

When you go to upload a video to YouTube, your Galaxy Note 3 may display the Upload dialog box, prompting you to choose between uploading only when on Wi-Fi networks and uploading on any network. Normally, it is best to touch Only When on Wi-Fi and then touch OK, because uploading even relatively small video files over the cellular network can quickly become expensive.

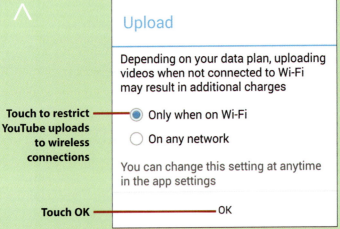

Touch to restrict YouTube uploads to wireless connections

Upload

Depending on your data plan, uploading videos when not connected to Wi-Fi may result in additional charges

⦿ Only when on Wi-Fi

◯ On any network

You can change this setting at anytime in the app settings

Touch OK — OK

If you need to change this setting later, open the YouTube app, touch the Menu button, and then touch Settings. Touch General to display the General screen, touch Uploads to display the Uploads dialog, and then touch Only When on Wi-Fi.

Share Video on Facebook

After you have set up a Facebook account on your Galaxy Note 3, you can upload videos to your account.

1. Enter a description of your video.

2. Touch if you want to add the location to the video.

3. Touch to set the audience for the video.

4. Touch Public, Friends, Only Me, or a specific list, as needed.

5. Touch Post to post the video.

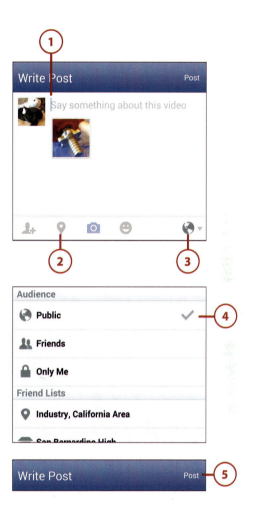

Delete Videos

1. Touch and hold the video you want to delete. After a moment, a green check mark appears on the video.

2. Touch to delete the video.

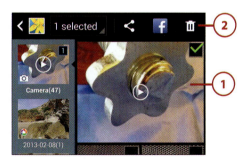

3. Touch OK.

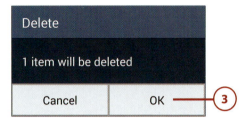

Delete

1 item will be deleted

Cancel	OK

— 3

Taking Photos and Videos with the Camera App

The Camera app enables you to take still photos and record videos. You can either shoot photos and videos with the default settings or choose among the many options the Galaxy Note 3 offers.

Take Photos

1. Touch to launch the Camera app. The Camera app opens and displays the input from the rear camera (the main camera) at first.

2. Touch to switch from the rear camera to the front camera so you can take photos of yourself. The front camera is lower resolution than the rear camera, but it works well for capturing candid self-portraits. When you switch to the front camera, the Camera app changes to the Beauty Face mode automatically on the assumption that you want to take a photo of yourself (and that you want to look good).

3. Look at the Mode readout at the top of the screen to see which mode the Camera app is using. For regular shots, you'll want the Auto mode. You learn about the other modes—and how and when to use them—later in this chapter.

4. Touch to switch to Dual Camera mode. The Camera app displays a stamp-like frame on the screen showing the input from the front camera overlaid on the input from the rear camera. Tap the frame to resize it or reposition it.

5. Touch to take a photo.

Taking a Burst of Photos

Instead of taking a single shot, the Camera app can take a burst of photos. This feature is great when you do not have time to compose your photo perfectly or your subject is moving. To take a burst of photos, touch and hold the shutter release.

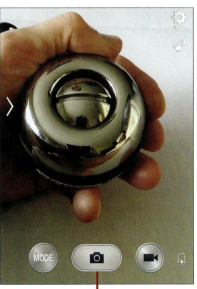

Touch and hold to take a burst of photos

Zoom In and Out

Your Galaxy Note 3's Camera app includes a powerful digital zoom that enables you to close in on the objects you want to photograph.

1. Open the Camera app and point the lens so that your subject occupies the center of the screen.

2. Place two fingers (or a finger and a thumb) on the screen. A zoom indicator appears in the middle of the screen, with a readout showing the zoom factor. A factor of x1.0 represents no zoom.

3. Move your fingers apart to zoom in. The readout shows the zoom factor you've reached.

4. Touch to take the photo.

When you need to zoom back out, place two fingers (or a finger and a thumb) on the screen and pinch them together.

The readout shows the zoom factor.

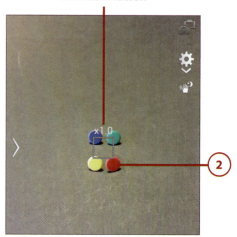

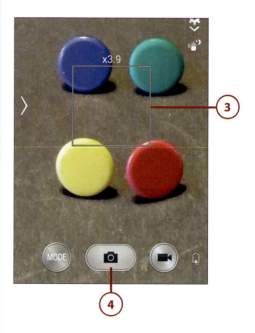

It's Not All Good

Digital Zoom Can Make Photos Grainy

In digital cameras, there are two main types of zoom: optical zoom and digital zoom. Optical zoom implements the zoom by moving the lens (or sometimes changing the lens used), which retains full quality even if you zoom in as far as the camera can. By contrast, digital zoom works by enlarging the pixels (the dots that make up the picture) of the part of the picture that you want to zoom in on.

Larger pixels can make the photos grainy, especially if you zoom in to extremes. So if you have the choice between moving your Galaxy Note 3 closer to your subject and using digital zoom, it's best to move closer because your photos will be higher quality. But when moving closer isn't an option, digital zoom is still pretty good as long as you don't push it too far.

>>>Go Further

CHOOSE WHERE TO FOCUS

When you take a photo, the Camera app focuses on the center of the screen by default, because that's where the subject is most likely to be. Much of the time this works well, but at other times you may need to focus manually.

To focus manually, touch the point on the screen where you want the focus to be. The Camera app displays a white rounded rectangle where you touch, and then plays a chirping noise and displays a green rectangle momentarily to indicate it has refocused.

If the focus is correct, touch the Shutter button to take the photo. If the focus still isn't right, touch again to refocus.

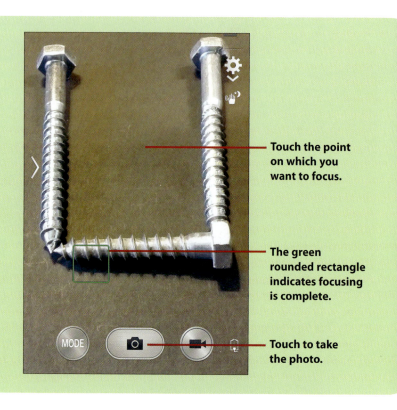

Touch the point on which you want to focus.

The green rounded rectangle indicates focusing is complete.

Touch to take the photo.

Apply Effects to Photos

To make your photos more glamorous, more artistic, or simply more fun, you can apply effects to them. The Camera app includes effects such as Cartoon, Faded Color, Fish Eye, Grayscale, Moody, Oil Pastel, Rugged, Sepia, Tint, Turquoise, Vignette, and Vintage.

1. Touch the > button on the left side of the screen to display the Effects panel.

2. Touch the effect you want to apply. (Touch the No Effect picture at the top of the panel if you need to restore normality.)

3. Touch outside the Effects panel to close the panel.

4. Touch to take the photo.

Touch No Effect when you want to restore normality

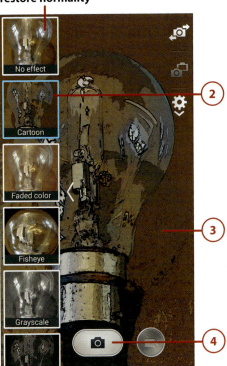

Change Key Camera Settings

You can get good photos by using your Galaxy Note 3 as a point-and-shoot camera, as described in the previous section. But you can get better photos by changing settings to harness the full power of the Camera app.

1. Touch to display the column of settings icons.

2. Touch to cycle the flash setting among Off, On, and Auto Flash.

Making the Most of the Flash

Choose the Off setting for the flash when you need to take photos where the flash would be disruptive. Choose the On setting when you need to light the foreground of a shot even though the rest of the scene is amply lit—for example, to light your subject's face in front of a bright background. Choose the Auto setting for general use.

3. Touch to toggle the Smart Stabilization feature on or off. Usually, this feature is helpful when you are taking photos holding the Galaxy Note 3, but you may want to turn it off if you use a tripod or other steadying device.

4. Touch to turn Voice Control on for taking photos. You can then say "Cheese," "Smile," "Shoot," or "Capture" to take photos. (The Camera app responds in the same way to each command. Your subjects may not.)

5. Touch to choose the recording mode for video, which is covered later in the chapter.

6. Touch to display the Share dialog, in which you can choose Off (the default), Share Shot, Buddy Photo Share, ChatON Photo Share, or Remote Viewfinder. See the "Use the Camera App's Sharing Features" sidebar for details.

7. Touch to hide the column of settings icons.

Touch to open the Settings dialog

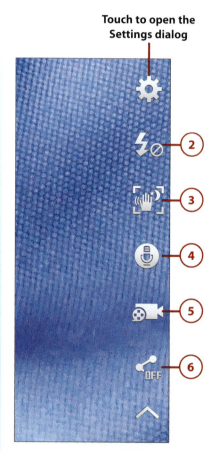

Touch the means of sharing you want to use

USE THE CAMERA APP'S SHARING FEATURES

Your Galaxy Note 3's Camera app comes with enough sharing features to confuse even experienced Android users. Here's what you need to know to make sense of Share Shot, Buddy Photo Share, ChatON Photo Share, and Remote Viewfinder.

Share Shot is a feature for sharing photos with other Samsung phones via a Wi-Fi Direct network. After you turn on Share Shot, your Galaxy Note 3 immediately shares photos you take to participating phones. This feature is good when you need to share every photo you take in a particular session, but it puts the onus on you to keep up the quality.

Buddy Photo Share enables you to share photos with your buddies based on the faces you identify in them. For example, if you tag a face as being Chris Smith, you can then tap the Email button next to the tag to send that photo to Chris Smith.

ChatON Photo Share lets you share photos easily with your friends on the ChatON service, Samsung's global mobile communications service. If you use ChatON, this feature is well worth exploring.

Remote Viewfinder is perhaps the most fun and useful of the sharing features for most people. By touching Remote Viewfinder in the Share dialog, you can turn your Galaxy Note 3 into a remote camera for another compatible Samsung device. So you can set up your Galaxy Note 3 on a tripod or stand and use it (for example) as a baby monitor or to take photos of unsuspecting people or animals from another Samsung device. Or you can set up that other Samsung device as the remote camera and use your Galaxy Note 3 as the viewfinder. (On the other device, open the Camera app, touch Settings, touch Share, touch Remote Viewfinder in the Share dialog, and then follow the instructions that appear.)

Choose Advanced Camera Settings

The column of settings icons on the right of the screen lets you control the key settings in the Camera app. But when you need to take complete control of the Camera app, you can open the Settings dialog and work with the full range of settings it offers.

1. Touch the Settings icon to display the Settings column.

2. Touch the Settings icon to display the Settings dialog.

3. Touch to display the settings for still photos.

4. Touch Photo Size to choose the photo size. Normally, it's best to use either the 4128×3096 pixel resolution (which gives a 4:3 aspect ratio) or the 4128×2322 pixel resolution (which gives a widescreen 16:9 aspect ratio).

5. Touch Burst Shot to enable or disable the Burst Shot feature. Usually, it's best to keep it on unless you find yourself shooting bursts unintentionally.

6. Touch Tap to Take Pics to enable or disable the Tap to Take Pics feature. When this is on, you can take a photo by touching (tapping) the screen instead of touching the Shutter button.

7. Touch Face Detection to enable or disable the Face Detection feature. This feature attempts to locate faces in the photos you take. You can then tag the faces to identify the people they belong to.

8. Touch Metering to choose the light-metering method. See the nearby Note for details.

9. Scroll down to reach the other settings.

Adjusting the Light Metering for Your Photos

By default, your Galaxy Note 3 uses center-weighted light metering, giving most importance to the light conditions in the center of the photo. Open the Metering dialog and choose Spot instead to base the light metering on the spot you touch in the frame. Choose Matrix to base the metering from samples across the entire frame.

10. Touch ISO to set the ISO rating, which specifies the digital equivalent of film sensitivity. The default setting is Auto, but you can set ISO 100, ISO 200, ISO 400, or ISO 800 manually.

11. Touch Smart Stabilization to use the stabilization feature. This feature helps you avoid taking blurry photos because you're not holding your Galaxy Note 3 steady.

12. If you've set the Mode to Rich Tone (HDR), you can touch Save As and then choose Rich Tone Only to save only the tone-adjusted photo or Rich Tone and Original to save both the tone-adjusted photo and the original photos used to create it. (More on Rich Tone in a moment.)

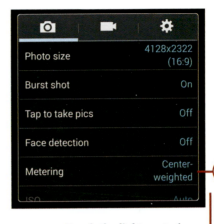

Photo size	4128x2322 (16:9)
Burst shot	On
Tap to take pics	Off
Face detection	Off
Metering	Center-weighted
ISO	Auto

Touch the light-metering method you want to use

Metering

- Center-weighted
- Matrix
- Spot

Tap to take pics	Off
Face detection	On
Metering	Matrix
ISO	200
Smart stabilization	Off
Save as	Rich tone only

Why Are Some Settings Unavailable?

Some of the Camera app's settings depend on each other, so choosing one setting might make another setting unavailable. For example, the ISO setting is available only if you set the Smart Stabilization feature to Off. Similarly, the Save As feature is available only when you have set the Mode to Rich Tone (HDR).

13. Touch to display the settings for shooting video.

14. Touch Video Size to set the video size. For most purposes, 1920×1080 pixel resolution is the best bet because it creates full high-definition video. If you need top quality, choose 3840×2160 pixel resolution.

15. Touch Video Stabilization to enable or disable video stabilization. Normally, using stabilization is a good idea unless you are using a tripod or another device to hold your Galaxy Note 3 still.

16. Touch Audio Zoom to enable or disable audio zoom. You would usually use audio zoom when the audio source is distant from you.

17. Touch to display the general settings for the Camera app.

18. Touch Location Tag to enable or disable adding the GPS location to photos and videos you take. Adding the location enables you to sort the photos and videos by location but may raise privacy issues.

19. Touch Review to enable or disable displaying each photo for review immediately after you take it. Usually, it's better to shoot photos freely and review them later, especially if your subjects are live and restless and the moments are unrepeatable.

20. Touch Volume Key to choose which function to assign the Volume key when the Camera app is active. Your choices are The Zoom Key, The Camera Key (in other words, the Shutter button), and The Record Key (for starting to shoot video).

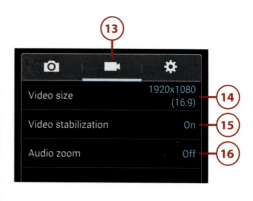

21. Touch Timer to open the Timer dialog, in which you can touch 2 Sec, 5 Sec, or 10 Sec to set a delay for taking photos (such as group portraits including the photographer). Touch Off to turn the Timer off.

22. Touch White Balance to change the white balance among Auto, Daylight, Cloudy, Incandescent, and Fluorescent.

23. Scroll down to reach the next settings.

24. Touch Exposure Value to increase or decrease the exposure—for example, increase the exposure when filming against a bright background.

25. Touch Guidelines to turn on a grid of lines that help you compose your shots and orient the camera.

26. Touch Flash to change the flash setting among Off, On, and Auto.

27. Touch Voice Control to enable or disable the Voice Control feature. As mentioned earlier, you can say words such as "Cheese!" to take a photo using your voice.

28. Touch Contextual Filename to include GPS information in the filenames. This feature works only when Location Tag is enabled, so if you enable Contextual Filename when Location Tag is disabled, the Camera app prompts you to enable Location Tag.

29. Scroll down to reach the last few settings.

30. Touch Save as Flipped to change pictures or videos taken on the front camera to mirror images before saving them.

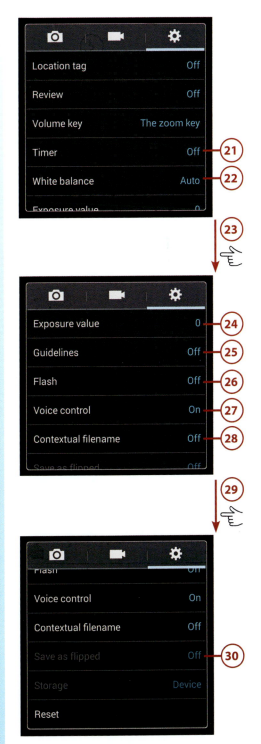

31. Touch Storage to choose between storing the photos on your Galaxy Note 3 (choose Device) and on an SD card you've inserted (choose SD Card).

32. Touch Reset if you want to reset the Camera app's settings to their defaults.

33. Touch outside the Settings dialog to close the dialog.

USING THE SHOOTING MODE SETTINGS

Your Galaxy Note 3's Camera app gives you a wide choice of shooting modes. By choosing the right mode for the type of photos you are taking, you improve your chances of getting high-quality pictures.

To choose the shooting mode, touch Mode on the main Camera screen. You can then scroll through the modes on the carousel and touch the one you want to apply. Alternatively, touch the button in the upper-left corner of the screen to display the Modes screen, which presents all the modes as a list of icons; you can then tap the mode you want to use.

Touch to display the Modes screen

Touch the mode to enable it

Touch a mode to bring it to the front of the carousel

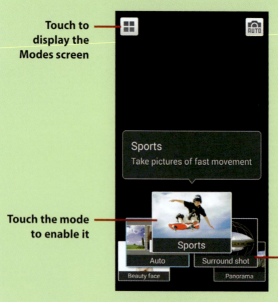

Some of the shooting modes are straightforward: Touch Auto to have the Camera app handle as many decisions as possible, leaving you free to shoot; choose Panorama when you need to stitch together a sequence of photos into a panorama photo; or choose Golf to capture a golf swing as a sequence of pictures you can replay either forward or backward to admire the swing, critique it, or both.

Other shooting modes have less obvious names but can be equally useful. Choose Rich Tone to capture several photos at once and merge them into a single photo that has greater intensity and contrast; this feature is also known as High Dynamic Range, or HDR. Choose Best Photo to have the Camera app take a rapid burst of eight photos and walk you through choosing the best-looking one. Choose Best Face to take five shots at a slightly slower pace and then choose the best shot or most amusing expression. Choose Beauty Face to automatically enhance facial features when taking a photograph of a person.

View the Photos You Take

After taking photos, you can quickly view the photos you have taken, mark them as favorites, share them with other people, or simply delete them.

1. In the Camera app, touch the thumbnail to view the last photo you took.

Zooming In and Out on Your Photos

When viewing a photo, you can zoom in by placing two fingers on the screen and pinching outward or by double-tapping on the area you want to expand. Pinch inward or double-tap again to zoom back out.

2. Touch to display the onscreen controls and the row of thumbnails. They disappear after a few seconds of not being used.

3. Touch to edit the photo. You can rotate it, crop it, apply a color filter, apply an effect, or take other actions.

4. Touch a thumbnail to display its photo; scroll the thumbnails first if necessary. You can also swipe left from the photo displayed; after that, you can swipe either left or right.

5. Touch to open the Select Device dialog, in which you can tap the device to which you want to send the photo.

6. Touch to share the photo. In the Share Via dialog, touch the means of sharing, and then provide any information needed—for example, the recipient for a photo you share via email.

7. Touch to share the photo on Facebook. On the Write Post screen that appears, type the text you want to add, and then touch Post.

8. Touch to delete the photo and then touch OK in the confirmation dialog.

9. Touch to return to the previous screen. You can then touch the Camera icon to return to the Camera app.

Record Videos with the Camera App

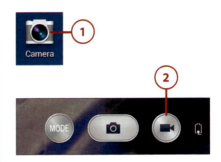

Recording videos with the Camera app is even easier than taking still photos because there are fewer options to choose.

1. Touch to launch the Camera app.

2. Touch to switch to the video camera and start recording video.

3. If necessary, place two fingers (or a finger and a thumb) on the screen and pinch apart to zoom in. Pinch together to zoom back out.

4. Touch to pause recording.

5. Touch to stop recording.

Using Automatic and Manual Focusing

While the Camera app is recording video, it automatically adjusts the focus for the object in the center of the screen. If you need to focus on another part of the screen, touch it.

Using Other Features When Recording Video

When recording video, you can use other features such as Dual Camera mode and Effects. Just touch the appropriate icons and choose settings, as described earlier in this chapter.

The size readout shows the file size of the video

The time readout shows the time elapsed

The REC indicator shows that video is recording

Choose the Recording Mode for Video

The Camera app can capture special-purpose video as well as normal video. To control which type of video the Camera app captures, you set the recording mode.

1. Touch to display the Recording Mode dialog.

2. Touch Normal to return to Normal mode. Normal mode is suitable for general-purpose shooting.

3. Touch Limit for MMS to shoot low-resolution video suitable for sending via instant messaging (which cannot transmit large files).

4. Touch Slow Motion to shoot at a high frame rate that will play back in slow motion. You would normally use slow motion as a special effect—for example, to create a dreamlike effect.

5. Touch Fast Motion to shoot at a high frame rate that will play back in fast motion. You would normally use fast motion as a special effect—for example, for comedy.

6. Touch Smooth Motion to shoot at a high frame rate that will play back at normal speed. You would normally use smooth motion for shooting sports, animals, and moving objects.

7. Touch outside the Recording Mode dialog to close the dialog.

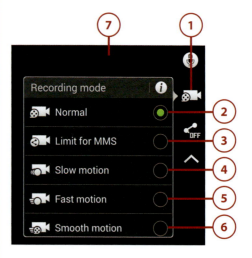

Enjoying Videos with the YouTube App

Your Galaxy Note 3 comes with a YouTube app that enables you to find and watch videos, rate them, add them to your favorites, and share links with other people. The app even enables you to upload your own videos to YouTube.

Meet the YouTube Main Screen

1. Touch the YouTube icon to launch the YouTube app.

2. Touch to search YouTube using keywords.

3. Touch Uploads to see the list of videos you've uploaded.

4. Touch History to display the History screen, which enables you to return to videos you watched earlier.

5. Touch Favorites to display the list of videos you've marked as your favorites. Marking a video as a favorite enables you to return to it easily even after it has disappeared from your History list.

6. Touch Playlists to display the Playlists screen, which lists any playlists you have created.

7. Touch Watch Later to display the Watch Later screen, which contains any videos you have marked for watching later.

8. Touch What to Watch to display the What to Watch screen, which contains recommendations for you.

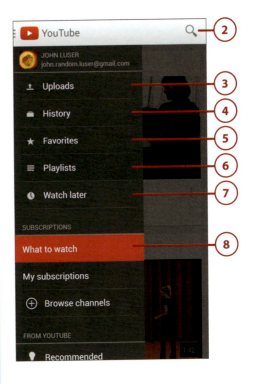

9. Touch My Subscriptions to display the Videos screen, which shows updates from the channels you have added.

10. Touch Browse Channels to display the Browse Channels screen, which contains channels such as Recommended for You, Most Subscribed, Most Viewed, and Local.

11. Swipe left if you want to close the Account pane without navigating to another screen from it.

12. Touch a channel to display its screen. You can then touch a video to display more information about it and play it.

Touch a + sign
to subscribe to a
channel

Play a Video

While playing a YouTube video, you can rate the video, read comments about it, or share it with other people.

1. Touch the video to display the onscreen controls for a few seconds.

2. Touch to start or pause the video.

3. Touch to switch the video to full screen in Landscape mode.

4. Drag to scrub forward or backward through the video.

5. Touch to display the Add To dialog, from which you can add the video to your Watch Later list, your Favorites list, or a playlist.

6. Touch to share the video's link (its URL) via apps such as Gmail, Facebook, or Twitter.

7. Touch to see information about the video, including who uploaded it, the video title, description, and how many times it has been viewed.

8. Touch to see the YouTube channel of the person who uploaded the video.

9. Touch to like the video.

10. Touch to dislike the video.

11. Touch to subscribe to this channel.

12. Touch to flag the video as inappropriate—for example, for hateful or abusive content, or because it infringes your rights.

13. Touch to display choices for the video, such as watching it with closed captioning (CC) or in high definition (HD).

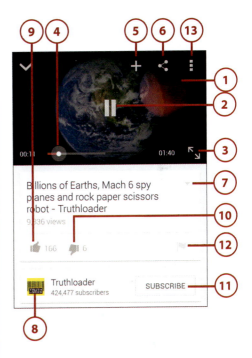

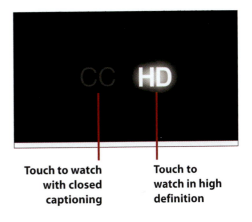

Touch to watch with closed captioning

Touch to watch in high definition

Change YouTube Settings

To get more out of YouTube, you might want to change your settings. Your options include choosing whether to watch high-quality videos on cellular connections, clearing your YouTube search history, and enabling the preloading of items on your subscriptions list or your Watch Later list.

1. From within the YouTube app, touch the Menu button.

2. Touch Settings.

3. Touch General.

4. Touch High Quality on Mobile to enable or disable always starting videos in High Quality mode. The video might take longer to start playing, and it uses more data in High Quality mode.

5. Touch Caption Font Size to set the size of the font used when a video has captions.

6. Touch Uploads to choose when your Galaxy Note 3 uploads videos to YouTube. Your choices are Only When on Wi-Fi or On Any Network.

7. Touch Content Localization to choose a specify country or region that you want to prioritize—for example, the country you live in.

8. Touch Improve YouTube to enable or disable sending anonymous usage data to YouTube to help improve the service.

9. Touch New Video Notifications to enable or disable receiving notifications of new videos that YouTube claims may match your interests.

10. Touch to return to the main Settings screen.

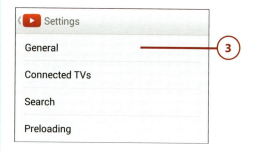
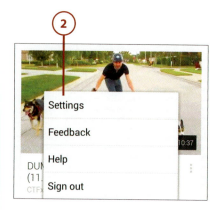
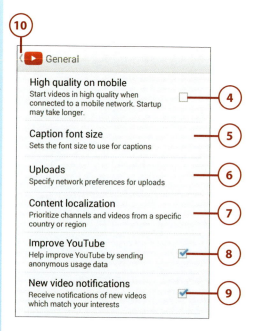

11. Touch Connected TVs.

12. Touch to pair your Galaxy Note 3 with a TV so you can broadcast to the TV.

13. Touch to edit your list of paired TVs. You can rename a TV for clarity or remove a TV you no longer want to use.

14. Touch to return to the main Settings screen.

15. Touch Search.

16. Touch to clear your YouTube search history. Touch OK in the Clear Search History? dialog that opens.

17. Touch to enable the Never Remember History feature, which prevents YouTube from ever storing your search history.

18. Touch to set the types of videos that are displayed when you search. Your choices are Don't Filter and Strict. If you set this setting to Don't Filter, no videos are filtered out based on content.

19. Touch to return to the main Settings screen.

20. Touch Preloading.

21. Touch to enable or disable preloading of videos to which you have subscribed. Preloading videos enables you to start watching them sooner on slow networks, but storing the files takes up space on your Galaxy Note 3.

22. Touch to enable or disable preloading of videos you have added to your Watch Later list.

23. Touch to return to the main Settings screen.

24. Touch the Back button or the YouTube button to return to the YouTube app.

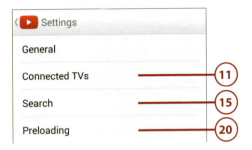

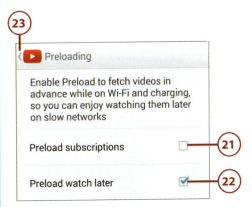

Upload a Video to YouTube from the YouTube App

After you create your own channel, you can easily upload your videos to YouTube straight from the YouTube app.

1. On the YouTube navigation panel, touch Uploads to display your Uploads screen.

2. Touch to start uploading a video.

3. In the Choose Video to Upload dialog, touch the source of the video. For example, touch Gallery.

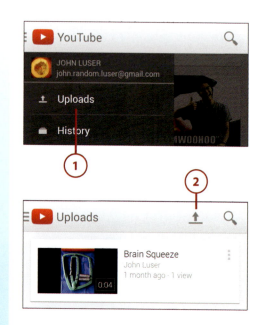

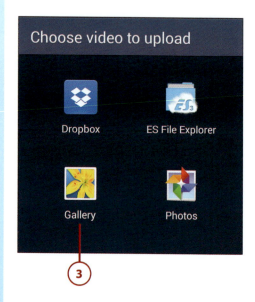

4. Touch the video you want to upload.

5. On the Upload Video screen, enter the information for the video, as discussed earlier in this chapter, and then touch Upload.

Browse quickly
through thumbnails
of magazine pages

In this chapter, you discover your Galaxy Note 3's capabilities for carrying and displaying books and magazines. Topics include the following:

→ Reading books with the Play Books app
→ Installing and using Amazon's Kindle app
→ Finding free e-books online
→ Reading magazines with the Play Magazines app

Books and Magazines

With its large, bright screen, your Galaxy Note 3 is great for reading books and magazines. You can load an entire library and newsstand onto your Galaxy Note 3, take the device with you anywhere, and read to your heart's content.

Reading Books with Play Books and Kindle

Books are perfect media for your Galaxy Note 3 because their file sizes are mostly small but they deliver long-lasting entertainment. Your Note 3 likely comes with one or more apps for reading books, but you will probably want to supplement them with other apps, such as the free Kindle app from Amazon.

Open the Play Books App and Meet Your Library

Google's Play Books app provides straightforward reading capabilities and ties in to the Books area of Google's Play Store, from which you can buy many books and download others for free.

1. On the Apps screen, touch Play Books. If you don't find the Play Books icon on the Apps screen, touch the Google folder and then touch Play Books.

2. Touch My Library in the navigation panel to display the books in your library. Normally, this panel opens automatically, but you can also open it manually by touching the button in the upper-left corner of the Play Books screen.

Touch to display the navigation panel

3. Touch to open the pop-up menu.

Where to Get Books

Depending on where you bought your Galaxy Note 3, your library might include several public-domain books as samples—plus any books you have already added to your library on your Note 3 or another Android device. If your library is empty, you can get books from the Play Store.

4. Touch to choose which list of books to view. Your choices are All Books, Uploads, Purchases, and Samples. Uploads are books you have uploaded to your Google account. You find out how to upload books later in this chapter.

Downloading a Book to Your Galaxy Note 3

A white pushpin on a blue circle indicates the book is stored on your Galaxy Note 3, so you can read it offline. To download a book to your Galaxy Note 3, touch the book's Menu button (the button showing three vertical dots) and then touch Keep on Device on the pop-up menu.

5. Touch to search your library for books by keyword. Searching is useful when you have built up a large library. When your library contains only a few books, it is usually easier to browse through them.

Touch Keep on Device   **Touch the book's menu button**

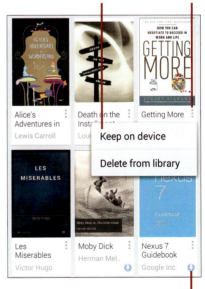

A pushpin indicates the book is stored on your Galaxy Note 3

6. Touch the Menu button.

7. Touch Sort to display the Sort By dialog.

8. Touch the way you want to sort: Recently Read, Title, or Author. The Play Books app displays the books in that sort order.

9. Touch a book to open it. If the book is not stored on your Galaxy Note 3, Play Books downloads the book and then opens it.

Sort

Refresh

Settings

Help

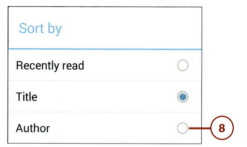

Sort by

Recently read ○

Title ⊙

Author ○

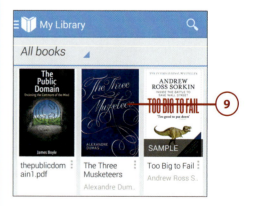

Get Books from the Play Store

The Books area of the Play Store offers a fair number of e-books for free and a much larger number of e-books for sale. You can access the Books area of the Play Store easily from the Play Books app.

1. Touch the button in the upper-left corner of the Play Books app to display the navigation panel.

2. Touch Shop to display the Books area of the Play Store. The Play Books Home screen appears first.

3. Touch to search for books.

4. Touch to see the list of top-selling books.

5. Touch to see books that have been newly added to the Play Store.

6. Touch a featured book or a recommended book to see its details.

7. Touch a featured category to see the list of books it contains.

8. Touch to display the list of categories. You can also swipe right once from the Home screen to display the list of categories.

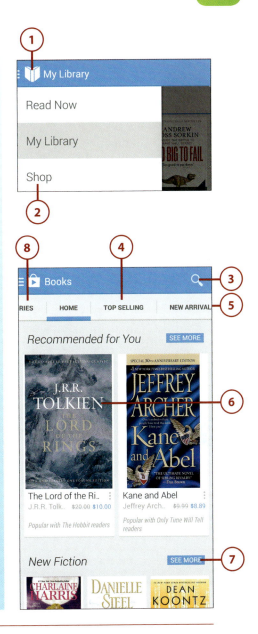

Navigate Quickly Among Tabs by Swiping

The Books area of the Play Store contains various tabs, including Categories, Home, Top Selling, New Arrivals in Fiction, New Arrivals in Nonfiction, and Top Free. You can navigate among these tabs by tapping their names on the tab bar, but it is usually quicker to swipe left or right one or more times to change tabs.

9. Touch the category you want to display. The Featured list for the category appears first.

10. Swipe up to see more of the list.

11. Touch the New Arrivals tab or swipe left to see the New Arrivals list for the category.

12. Touch a book to display its details.

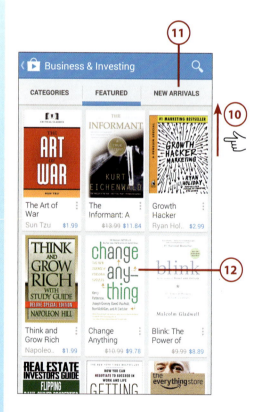

13. Touch to add the book to your wish list.

14. Touch Rate & Review to rate or review the book. You would normally do this after reading the book, but many raters and reviewers skip the reading step.

15. Touch to expand the description.

16. Swipe up to read the reviews, to see the Users Also Viewed list of books that may interest you if this one does, and to read the About the Author blurb.

17. Touch Free Sample to download a free sample of the book. Reading the sample can be a great way to decide whether to spend the money on the book. Android downloads the book and displays its first page in the Google Books app.

18. Touch the price button to buy the book, and then follow through the payment process on the next screen. If the book is free, touch the Open button. Android downloads the book and displays its first page in the Play Books app.

Buying Books from the Play Store

To buy a book from the Play Store, you must either add a credit card to your Google account or redeem a voucher. When you begin to buy a book, the Play Store app prompts you to add a credit card and walks you through the steps for adding it.

Share a Book with Other People

When you find a book you simply must tell someone about, you can do so easily from the Play Store app. Touch the Share button in the upper-left corner of the screen to display the Share dialog, touch the means of sharing you want to use, and then complete the sharing in the app that Android opens.

Finding Free E-Books Online

Apart from buying e-books online at Google's Play Store or other stores such as Amazon (www.amazon.com) and Barnes & Noble (www.barnesandnoble.com), you can find many books for free. Most online stores offer some free e-books, especially out-of-copyright classics, so it is worth browsing the Free lists. Other good sources of free e-books include ManyBooks.net (www.manybooks.net) and Project Gutenberg (www.gutenberg.org).

Touch the Share button to share the book

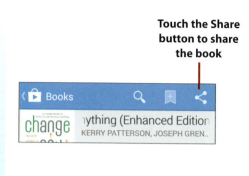

Touch the means of sharing you want to use

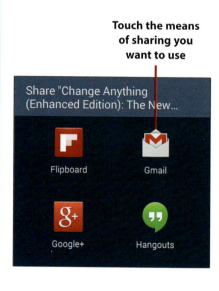

Read Books with the Play Books App

1. In the navigation panel of the Play Books app, touch Read Now to display your Read Now screen. This screen shows the books you have been reading recently plus books you have recently bought (or downloaded for free) or uploaded to your Google account. Further down the screen is a Recommended for You section that suggests books you might be interested in based on the books you have.

2. Touch the book you want to open. The cover or default page appears if this is the first time you have opened the book. Otherwise, the page at which you last left the book appears.

A gray pin means the book has not been downloaded yet

A white pin means your Galaxy Note 3 has downloaded the book

3. Touch the middle of the screen to display the navigation controls at the top and bottom of the screen. The controls remain onscreen for a few seconds and then disappear if you do not use them. You can make them disappear more quickly by touching the screen again.

4. Touch to search within the book for specific text.

5. Touch to display the Contents screen. From here, you can touch Chapters to display a list of the book's chapters and major headings, and then touch the place you want to display; or touch Bookmarks to display a list of the bookmarks you have created in the book, and then touch the bookmark you want to go to.

6. Drag to move quickly through the book.

7. Touch the right side of the screen or drag left to turn the page forward. Dragging lets you turn the page partway to peek ahead.

8. Touch the left side of the screen or drag right to turn the page back.

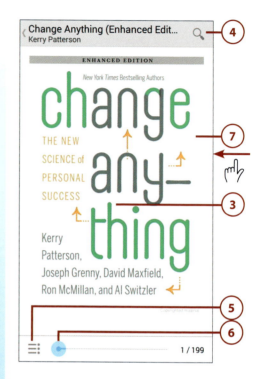

Choose Options for the Play Books App

You can configure the Play Books app to make it work your way. Options include switching between flowing text and the original pages of the book, adding bookmarks, and having your Galaxy Note 3 read aloud to you.

1. With the Play Books app open and active, touch the Menu button.

2. Touch Buy to buy the book in the Play Store. This command appears only when you are reading a sample of a book.

3. Touch About This Book to display the book's page in the Play Store.

4. Touch Share to share the book's URL on the Play Store via Facebook, Gmail, Twitter, or another means of sharing.

5. Touch Add Bookmark to add a bookmark to the current page. To remove the bookmark, go to the page, touch the Menu button, and then touch Remove Bookmark.

6. Touch Help to display the Help dialog, from which you can access various help resources, such as Help Center, Contact Us, or Report a Problem.

7. Touch Display Options to open the Display Options panel.

8. Touch to choose among the Day theme, the Night theme, and the Sepia theme. The Day theme uses black text on a white background; the Night theme uses white text on a black background; and the Sepia theme uses black text on a sepia background.

9. Touch to change the typeface used.

10. Touch to change the text alignment. The choices are Default, Left, and Justify.

11. Touch to enable or disable automatic brightness.

12. Drag to adjust the brightness manually.

13. Touch to decrease the font size.

14. Touch to increase the font size.

15. Touch to decrease the spacing between lines.

16. Touch to increase the spacing between lines.

17. Touch the book page to close the Display Options panel.

18. Touch the Menu button.

19. Touch Settings to display the Settings screen.

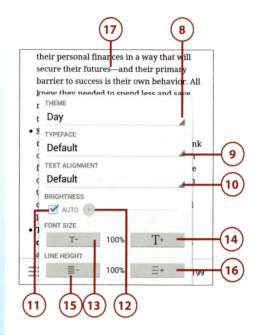

20. Touch Account if you need to change the Google account you are using for the Play Books app.

21. Touch Auto-Rotate Screen if you want to specify how to control rotation. In the Auto-Rotate Screen dialog that opens, touch Use System Setting, Lock in Portrait, or Lock in Landscape, as appropriate.

22. Touch to enable or disable restricting the Play Books app to downloading over Wi-Fi. Enable this restriction if your cellular plan gives you only a miserly data allowance.

23. Touch to enable using the volume key on the side of the Galaxy Note 3 to turn the pages in the Play Books app. This setting can be helpful if you normally hold your phone with your fingers over the volume key.

24. Touch to enable or disable the 3-D effect for turning pages. Disable this effect if you don't like it.

25. Touch to enable or disable the Galaxy Note 3's capability to read text aloud for you. You need to turn on the TalkBack feature in Accessibility settings to get reading aloud to work; see Chapter 2, "Customizing Your Samsung Galaxy Note 3," for details.

26. Touch to leave the Settings screen and return to the screen you were previously using in the Play Books app.

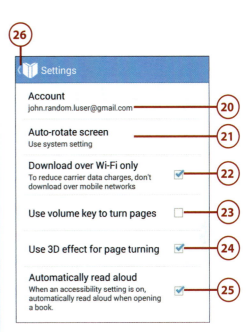

Delete a Book from Your Play Books Library

When you no longer want a particular book in your library, you can delete it directly using the Play Books app. Note that deleting the book removes it from your Google Play library entirely, not just from your Galaxy Note 3 (or whichever other device you're using).

1. In the My Library view in Play Books app, touch the Menu button that appears on the book's listing.

2. Touch Delete from Library. The Delete from Library confirmation dialog opens.

3. Touch Delete.

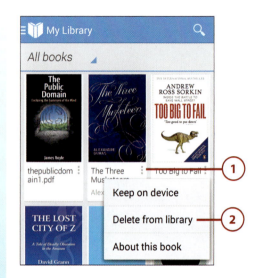

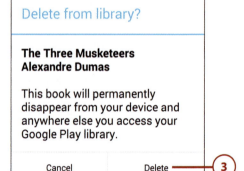

>>>Go Further

UPLOAD YOUR DOCUMENTS TO GOOGLE PLAY BOOKS

The Play Books app is great for reading books you buy or get for free from the Play Store, but you can also use it to read your own PDF files and e-books in formats such as the widely used ePub format. To do so, you use your computer to upload the files to your Google account, from which the Play Books app can then access them.

To upload the files, open your computer's web browser and go to play.google.com. Click the Sign In button, and then sign in with your Google account. Click Books in the navigation panel on the left, and then click My Books to display the screen containing your books. Now click the Upload Files button, and then follow the instructions onscreen to select the file or files.

Touch the pop-up button and then touch Uploads to display only your uploaded files

Touch a file to open it for reading in Play Books

Touch Menu and Refresh to get the latest list of books

After you upload a file, Google processes it to make it compatible with the Play Books app. The books appear in your library, but you might find it easier to access them on the Uploads screen; to display this screen, touch the pop-up menu in the upper-left corner of the My Library screen, and then touch Uploads. If the books do not appear, touch the Menu button and then touch Refresh to force Play Books to refresh the list. You can then touch a book to download it and read it.

Install the Kindle App

Google's Play Store has a good selection of books, but if you want to buy or download books from Amazon's vast bookstore, you need to use the Kindle app instead. If you already own any Kindle books, installing the Kindle app gives you most of the benefits of owning a Kindle reader without having to buy or haul around an extra device.

Installing the Kindle App

If the Kindle app is not already installed on your Galaxy Note 3, you need to install it from the Play Store. Touch Play Store on the Apps screen, touch Apps on the Google Play screen, touch the Search icon, and type **kindle**. Touch the Kindle result and then touch Install.

Touch to search **Touch to install**

Sign In and Navigate the Kindle App

1. On the Apps screen, touch the Amazon Kindle icon. The first time you run the Kindle app, it displays the Start Reading screen.

2. Touch the Sign In button to sign in to your existing account. The Sign In to Start Reading screen appears.

Touch to start creating a new Amazon account

3. Type your email address.

Creating an Amazon Account

To buy books or download free books from Amazon, you must have an Amazon account. If you do not have one, touch the Create an Account button on the Start Reading screen and then follow through the screens to create an account.

4. Type your Amazon password.

5. Touch Sign In. The Kindle app signs you into your account and then displays its Home screen. The books in your Kindle library appear on a carousel.

6. Touch to refresh the display of books. You would do this if you have just bought a book using your computer or a different device and the book hasn't yet appeared on the Kindle app on your Galaxy Note 3.

7. Touch to go to the Kindle Store to browse or buy books.

8. Touch to display the navigation panel.

Books in your Kindle library

Books that Amazon recommends for you

9. Touch Search Kindle to search your Kindle library for the terms you type.

10. Touch Home to display the Kindle Home screen.

11. Touch All Items to display the All Items screen. This screen shows all the items in your Kindle library, whether they are on your Galaxy Note 3 or not.

12. Touch On Device to see the list of books and other items stored on your Note 3.

13. Touch Books to see the list of books, rather than documents, newspapers, and magazines.

14. Touch Docs to display the documents stored in your Kindle account. These are documents you have sent via email to your Send to Kindle email address, a Kindle-only address that Amazon provides with Kindle accounts.

15. Touch Newsstand to display your Newsstand items.

16. Touch Kindle Store to go to the Kindle Store.

17. Touch Settings to display the Settings screen for configuring the Kindle app.

18. Touch Info to display information about Kindle and the Kindle app.

19. Touch Send Feedback to send feedback to Amazon.

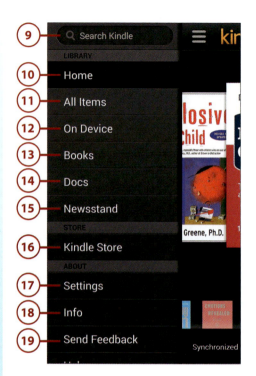

Read a Book with the Kindle App

1. In the Kindle app, touch the book you want to open. This example uses the On Device screen, but you can also start from another screen, such as the Home screen or the All Items screen.

Reaching the On Device Screen from a Book

If you currently have a book open in the Kindle app, touch the Back button to go back to the main screens and then touch On Device. Alternatively, touch the Menu button, touch Home to display the Kindle Home screen, and then touch On Device.

Touch Kindle to return to the main screens

Touch the screen to display the controls

2. Touch the middle of the screen to display the title and location bar. Touch again to hide these items.

3. Drag the slider to change the location in the book.

4. Touch the right side of the screen to display the next page. You can also display the next page by dragging or swiping left.

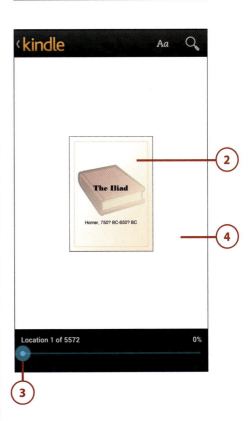

5. Touch the left side of the screen, or drag or swipe right, to move back a page.

6. Touch the Menu button to display the menu.

7. Touch Share Progress to display the Share Progress dialog, in which you can pick a way to share your reading progress. For example, you can post a link to Facebook or send an email message saying you're 50% through the book.

8. Touch Add a Bookmark to bookmark the current page. Adding a bookmark gives you an easy way to return to a particular page by using the View My Notes & Marks command on the menu.

9. Touch Sync to Furthest Page Read to go to the furthest page you've read in this book on any of your Kindle devices. Normally, you'll want to do this after reading on another device.

10. Touch View My Notes & Marks to view the list of notes and bookmarks you have added to the current book. From there, you can touch one of your bookmarks or notes to go to its page.

11. Touch Shop in Kindle Store to go shopping for Kindle books.

12. Touch Go To to display the Go To dialog.

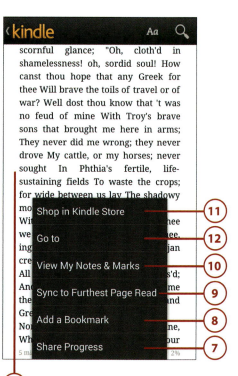

13.   Touch to display the cover.

14.   Touch to display the table of contents. This command is unavailable if the book has no table of contents.

15.   Touch to go to the beginning of the text, after the cover.

16.   Touch to go to a page by number. If the book does not have page numbers, this command is unavailable.

17.   Touch to go to a location. The locations are numbered divisions of the text. You can see the number of the current location by touching the middle of the screen and looking at the Location slider. But unless you know the number of the location to which you want to go, this command is of little use.

Choose View Options for the Kindle App

To make your books easy to read, you can choose view options for them.

1.   With a book open in the Kindle app, touch the screen to display the controls.

2.   Touch to display the View Options panel.

3.   Touch to decrease the font size.

4.   Touch to increase the font size.

5.   Touch to adjust the space between lines.

6.   Touch to adjust the margin width.

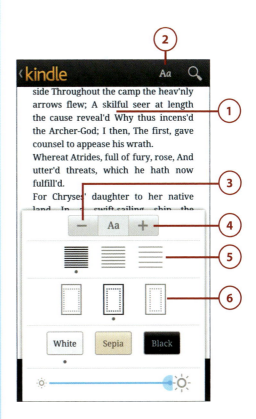

7. Touch to choose the color scheme: White, Sepia, or Black.

8. Drag to adjust the brightness.

9. Touch the document to close the View Options panel.

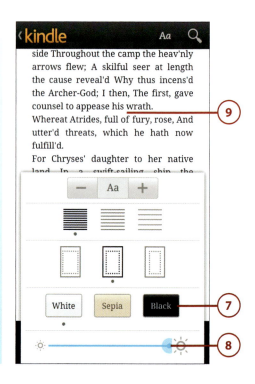

EXPLORE OTHER BOOK READERS

Between them, the Play Books app and the Kindle app give you access to a phenomenal range of books. But there are many other book readers you might want to explore to give yourself access to other bookstores and other books. In particular, the Aldiko app, the Kobo app, and the Nook app are worth trying. You can get each of these apps from the Play Store for free. The Nook app ties into Barnes & Noble's online bookstore.

Reading Magazines with Play Magazines

Your Galaxy Note 3 includes Google's Play Magazines app, which gives you access to a wide range of magazines.

Exploring Other Magazine Apps

If the Play Magazines app does not deliver the content you need, or does not otherwise suit you, explore other magazine apps such as PressReader and Zinio. You can download both these apps for free from the Apps section of the Play Store.

Open the Play Magazines App and Choose Your Magazines

1. On the Apps screen or in the Google folder, touch Play Magazines. The app may open in either Read Now view, showing magazines you have read and ones you have added recently, or in My Library view, showing your entire magazine library.

2. Touch the button in the upper-left corner to open the navigation panel.

3. Touch Shop to display the Magazines section of the Play Store.

4. Touch to see the list of top-selling magazines. You can also swipe left once from the Home screen.

5. Touch to see the list of newly released magazines. You can also swipe left twice from the Home screen or once from the Top Selling screen.

6. Touch a featured magazine or a recommended magazine to see its details.

7. Touch a featured category to see the list of magazines it contains.

8. Touch to display the list of categories. You can also swipe right to display the list of categories.

9. Touch the category you want to display.

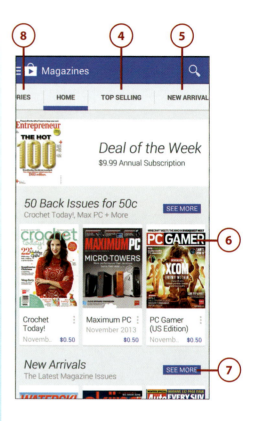

10. Swipe up to see more of the list.

11. Touch New Arrivals or swipe left to see the New Arrivals list for the category.

12. Touch a magazine to display its details.

13. Touch to add the magazine to your wish list.

14. Touch Rate & Review to rate or review the magazine.

15. Swipe up to read the reviews and to see the Similar Magazines list, which might contain magazines that interest you. At the bottom of the screen, you also find the Back Issues list.

16. Touch Subscribe to start a 14-day trial subscription to the magazine, followed by a paid subscription if you do not cancel it. You can choose between a yearly subscription and a monthly subscription. Android downloads the magazine and displays its first page in the Google Magazines app.

17. Touch the price button to buy the magazine, and then follow through the payment process on the next screen. If the magazine is free, touch the Open button. Android downloads the magazine and displays its first page in Google Magazines.

Read a Magazine with the Play Magazines App

1. On either the Read Now screen or the My Library screen in the Play Magazines app, touch the magazine you want to open. The cover appears if this is the first time you have opened the magazine. Otherwise, the page at which you last left the magazine appears.

2. Touch the middle of the screen to display the navigation controls at the top and bottom of the screen. The controls remain onscreen for a few seconds and then disappear if you do not use them. You can make them disappear more quickly by touching the screen again.

3. Touch to display a text-only version of the magazine. The text-only version can be much easier to read on your Galaxy Note 3's screen, but only some magazines have a text-only version.

4. Drag the thumbnails to scroll through the pages.

5. Touch to display the next page.

6. Touch a page's thumbnail to display that page.

7. Touch to display a table of contents.

8. Touch an article to display the page that contains it.

9. Double-tap or pinch outward with two fingers to zoom the page as needed.

10. Swipe left to display the next page or swipe right to display the previous page.

"During 2012, big brands successfully embraced cuttin...

"Life punishes those who delay." Gorbachev's legendary sentence...

.net/advisory panel

Molly Holzschlag A well-known web standards advocate, Molly is...

/contributors

We've scoured the web to find the best writers, designers and net...

Choose Options for the Play Magazines App

The Play Magazines app has several settings you can choose to control when it downloads magazines and when it notifies you about new issues. You can also change the account you use to pay for Play Magazines.

1. From the Read Now screen or the My Library screen in the Play Magazines app, touch the Menu button.

2. Touch Settings.

3. Touch to change the account used for Play Magazines.

4. Touch to enable or disable automatic downloading of all your magazine purchases and subscriptions.

5. Touch to enable or disable limiting magazine downloads to when your Galaxy Note 3 has a Wi-Fi connection. Because magazine files can be relatively large, checking this box is a good idea if your cellular data plan is limited.

6. Touch to allow Play Magazines to show you notifications about new issues or to prevent it from doing so.

7. Touch to return to the previous screen.

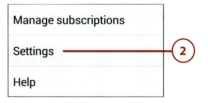

Browse for apps

Search for apps

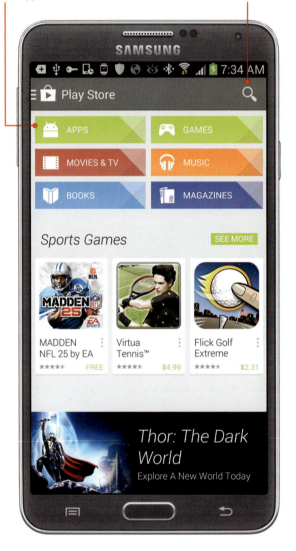

In this chapter, you find out how to purchase and use Android apps on your Galaxy Note 3. Topics include the following:

→ Finding apps with Google Play
→ Purchasing apps
→ Keeping apps up to date

Working with Android Apps

Your Galaxy Note 3 comes with enough apps to make it a worthy smartphone. However, wouldn't it be great to play games, work on business or school documents, or keep a grocery list? Well, finding these types of apps is what the Google Play Store is for. Read on to learn about finding, purchasing, and maintaining apps.

Configuring Google Wallet

Before you start buying apps in the Play Store app, you must first sign up for a Google Wallet account. If you plan to only download free apps, you do not need a Google Wallet account.

1. From a desktop computer or your Galaxy Note 3, open the web browser and go to http://wallet.google.com.

2. Sign in using the Google account that you will be using to synchronize email to your Galaxy Note 3. See Chapter 4, "Email," or Chapter 7, "Contacts," for information about adding a Google account to your Galaxy Note 3.

3. Choose your location. If your country is not listed, you have to use free apps until it's added to the list.

4. Enter your name.

5. Enter your ZIP Code.

6. Enter your credit card number. This can also be a debit card that includes a Visa or MasterCard logo, also known as a check card, so that the funds actually are withdrawn from your checking account.

7. Select the month and year of the card's expiration date.

8. Enter the card's CVC number, which is also known as the security code. This is a three- or four-digit number that's printed on the back of your card.

9. Check this box if your billing address is the same as your name and home location. Otherwise, uncheck this box and enter your billing address and phone number when prompted.

10. Uncheck this box unless you want to receive Google Wallet special offers, invitations, and other marketing messages.

11. Click Accept and Create when you finish filling in the form.

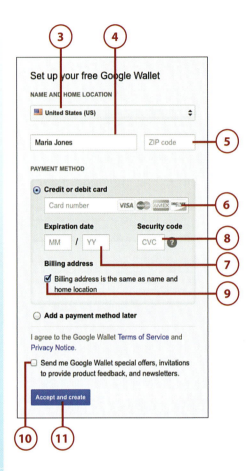

Navigating Google Play

Android is the operating system that runs your Galaxy Note 3, so any apps that are made for your Note 3 need to run on Android. The Google Play Store is a place where you can search for and buy Android apps.

1. On the Home screen, touch Apps to display the Apps screen.

2. Touch the Play Store app icon to launch the Play Store app.

3. Touch to browse all Android apps.

4. Touch to browse all Android games.

5. Touch to search Google Play.

6. Touch to display the navigation panel.

7. Touch Store Home to display the Home page of the Play Store.

8. Touch My Apps to display the list of apps you have already purchased or acquired for free.

9. Touch My Wishlist to display your wishlist. This is a list to which you can add items you want to buy or you want others to buy for you.

10. Touch Redeem to redeem a gift card or promotional code.

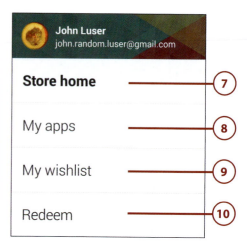

Download Free Apps

You don't have to spend money to get quality apps. Some of the best apps are actually free. Other free apps are feature-light versions that give you a chance to test-drive the app without paying and decide whether you want to upgrade to the full version.

1. Touch the app you want to download. The screen for the app appears.

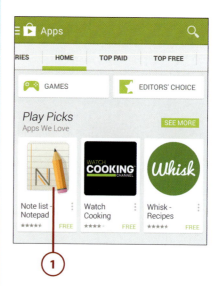

2. Scroll down to read the app features, reviews by other people who installed it, and information on the person or company who wrote the app.

3. Scroll left and right to see the app screenshots.

4. Touch Install to download and install the app.

5. Touch to accept the app permissions and proceed with the download.

Beware of Permissions

Each time you download a free app or purchase an app from Google Play, you are prompted to accept the app permissions. App permissions are permissions the app wants to have to use features and functions on your Galaxy Note 3, such as access to the wireless network or access to your phone log.

Pay close attention to the kinds of permissions each app is requesting and make sure they are appropriate for the type of functionality that the app provides. For example, an app that tests network speed will likely ask for permission to access your wireless network, but if it also asks to access your list of contacts, it might mean that the app is malware and just wants to steal your contacts.

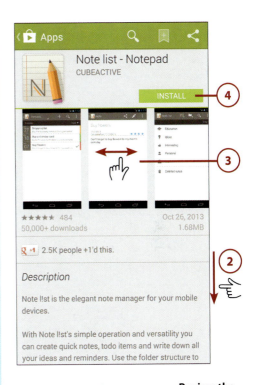

Review the permissions to your phone the app is requesting

Touch to see the full list of permissions

6. After your Galaxy Note 3 downloads and installs the app, the
Open button appears in the Play
Store app. Tap Open to open the
app.

OPEN A NEWLY INSTALLED APP IN OTHER WAYS

>>>Go Further

If you keep the Play Store app open while downloading an app, the Open
button on the app's screen provides a handy way to open the app and put
it through its paces. But if the app is large or your Internet connection is
slow, you probably won't want to hang about in the Play Store app until
the download completes.

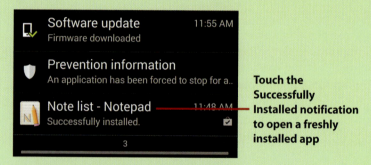

Touch the
Successfully
Installed notification
to open a freshly
installed app

When the installation finishes, a notification briefly appears telling you that
the app has been installed successfully. You can then launch the app by opening the notifications panel and touching the Successfully Installed notification
for the app. Alternatively, go to the Apps screen, touch the Downloaded button to the right of the Widgets button, and then touch the app's icon on the
Downloaded Applications screen.

Touch to display
the Downloaded
Applications screen

Buy Apps

If an app is not free, the price appears next to the app icon. If you want to buy the app, remember that you need to already have a Google Wallet account. See the "Configuring Google Wallet" section earlier in the chapter for more information.

1. Touch the app you want to buy.

What If the Currency Is Different?

When you browse apps in Google Play, you might see apps that have prices in foreign currencies, such as in euros. When you purchase an app, the currency is simply converted into your local currency using the exchange rate at the time of purchase.

2. Scroll down to read the app's features, reviews by other people who have used it, and information on the person or company who created the app.

3. Scroll left and right to see the app screenshots.

4. Touch the price to download and install the app.

5. Review the app permissions and make sure you can accept them. Some apps, such as the one shown here, do not require any permissions, but most require at least some. Then touch Accept (if the app requires permissions) or Continue (if it requires none) to proceed with the purchase.

6. Touch Buy to purchase the app. You will receive an email from Google Play after you purchase an app. The email serves as your invoice.

Getting a Refund on an App

If you realize you've bought the wrong app, or otherwise regret a purchase, you can return it within 15 minutes and get a full refund. To do this, open the Play Store app, go to the My Apps screen, touch the app to display its screen, and then touch Refund. If the Refund button doesn't appear, you're too late.

Review the permissions the app requires, if any

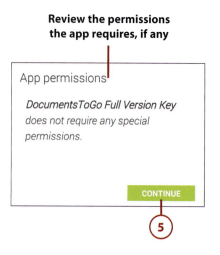

Touch Refund to get a refund on an app you've just bought

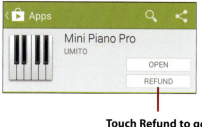

Manage Apps

You can use the My Apps section of Google Play to update apps, delete them, or install apps that you have previously purchased.

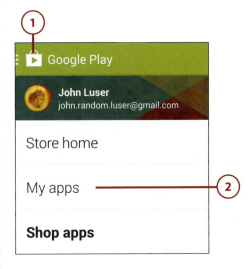

1. Touch to display the navigation panel.

2. Touch My Apps.

3. Touch All to see all apps that you have installed on your Galaxy Note 3.

4. Look for the Installed indicator to see whether the app is currently installed.

5. Touch an app marked with Free to install a free app again. The Free readout shows a free app that you previously installed, but that is no longer installed.

6. Touch the X button to remove an app from the list of apps.

7. Touch an app marked as Purchased to reinstall an app that you previously purchased and installed, but that is no longer installed. Because you have already purchased the app, you do not need to pay for it again.

Allowing an App to Be Automatically Updated

When the developer of an app you have installed updates it to fix bugs or add new functionality, you are normally notified in the Notification bar and Notification panel so that you can manually update the app. Google Play enables you to choose to have the app automatically updated without your intervention. To do this, open the My Apps screen and touch the app you want to update automatically. On the app's screen, touch the Menu button, and then check the Auto-Update box. Be aware that if these updates occur while you are on a cellular data connection, your data usage for the month will be affected.

Uninstalling an App

To uninstall an app, touch the app's button on the My Apps screen, and then touch Uninstall on the app's screen. Uninstalling the app removes both the app itself and its data from your Galaxy Note 3. Although the app no longer resides on your Note 3, you can reinstall it as described in step 7 because the app remains tied to your Google account.

Touch to uninstall the app

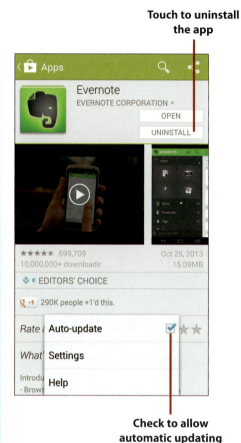

Check to allow automatic updating

Manage Google Play Settings

1. In the Play Store app, touch the Menu button.

2. Touch Settings.

3. Touch to enable or disable notifications of app or game updates.

4. Touch to enable or disable automatic updating for apps. In the Auto-Update Apps dialog that opens, touch the setting you want. Your choices are Do Not Auto-Update Apps, Auto-Update Apps at Any Time, and Auto-Update Apps over Wi-Fi Only. Because apps can be large, choosing Auto-Update Apps over Wi-Fi Only is usually the best choice unless you want to disable automatic updating.

5. Touch to allow or prevent an app icon from appearing on your Home screen for each app that you install.

6. Touch to clear the Google Play search history. There's no double-check or confirmation beyond a quick blink of the button.

7. If you want to filter content in apps, make sure the Password check box is checked. If it's not checked, touch to check it.

8. Touch Content Filtering to display the Allow Apps Rated For dialog, in which you can adjust or set your content filtering for apps.

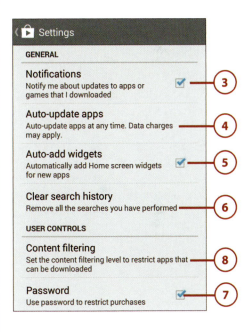

9. Touch the check box for the highest level of maturity you want to allow: Everyone, Low Maturity, Medium Maturity, High Maturity, or Show All Apps. Android checks any check boxes above the one you touch and unchecks any check boxes further down the list. For example, if you touch the Medium Maturity check box, Android selects the Everyone check box and the Low Maturity check box, and deselects the High Maturity check box and the Show All Apps check box.

10. Touch OK to close the Allow Apps Rated For dialog. The Content PIN dialog opens.

11. Touch to set a four-digit PIN that must be typed in before changing the Google Play User Control settings (Content Filtering, PIN for purchases, and Set PIN).

12. Touch OK. The Content PIN dialog closes, and the Confirm Content PIN dialog opens.

13. Type the PIN again, and then touch OK again. Android returns you to the Play Store app (not to the Settings screen).

Why Lock the User Settings?

Imagine if you buy a Galaxy Note 3 for your child but want to make sure that he doesn't get to any undesirable content. First, you set the content filtering to restrict the content visible in Google Play. Next, you set the PIN so he can't change that setting. A similar idea goes for limiting purchases.

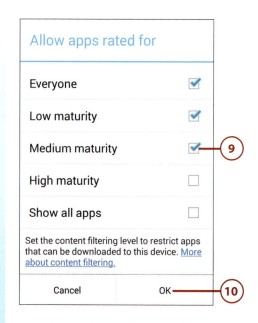

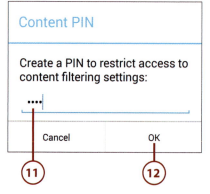

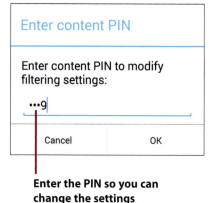

Enter the PIN so you can change the settings

Accidentally Uninstall an App?

What if you accidentally uninstall an app or you uninstalled an app in the past but now decide you'd like to use it again? To get the app back, go to the My Apps view in Google Play. Scroll to that app and touch it. Touch Install to reinstall it.

Keeping Apps Up to Date

Developers who write Android apps often update their apps to fix bugs or to add new features. With a few quick touches, you can easily update the apps you have installed.

1. On the Home screen, touch Apps to display the Apps screen.

2. Touch the Play Store app icon to launch the Play Store app.

3. Touch to display the navigation panel.

4. Touch My Apps to display the My Apps screen.

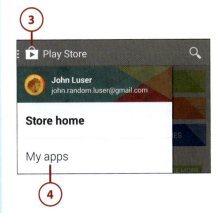

5. Touch Installed to display the Installed screen.

6. Touch Update to update an app.

Starting an Update from the Notification Panel

When your Galaxy Note 3 detects an update available for one of the apps you have installed, it displays the update notification in the Notification bar. You can open the My Apps screen in Google Play quickly by pulling down the Notifications panel and touching the notification.

Touch Update All to apply all available updates in one move

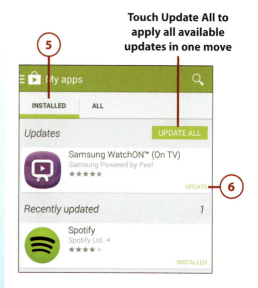

Touch an update notification to go straight to the My Apps screen

Touch to play a sound
on your Galaxy Gear and
illuminate its screen

In this chapter, you discover how to set up your Samsung Galaxy Gear smart watch and use it with your Samsung Galaxy Note 3.

→ Setting up your Galaxy Gear
→ Choosing settings and installing apps
→ Navigating the Galaxy Gear's interface
→ Using the Galaxy Gear's apps

12

Using Your Samsung Galaxy Note 3 with the Samsung Galaxy Gear

To get the most out of your Galaxy Note 3, you can link it to a Galaxy Gear smart watch. Samsung designed the Galaxy Gear as a companion product for the Galaxy Note 3 and other high-end phones in its range. The Galaxy Gear enables you to display essential information, make phone calls, and take photos without taking your Galaxy Note 3 out of your pocket.

Setting Up Your Samsung Galaxy Gear

To set up the Samsung Galaxy Gear, you need to use your Galaxy Note 3.

Setting Up Your Samsung Galaxy Gear with Another Phone

Normally, you'll want to use your Galaxy Note 3 to set up your Galaxy Gear. But you can use another Samsung phone or tablet if necessary. At this writing, only the Galaxy Note 3 and the Galaxy Note 10.1 tablet work with the Galaxy Gear, but Samsung will doubtless add other models soon.

1. Unpack the Galaxy Gear and identify its components: the Galaxy Gear itself, a charging dock, and a charger.

2. Turn the Galaxy Gear on by pressing and holding its button for a moment. The button is on the right side of the Galaxy Gear.

3. Touch the charging dock to the back of your Galaxy Note 3. The Installation dialog appears on the Galaxy Note 3's screen.

4. Touch OK. The Gear Manager screen appears, telling you that you need to download and install the Gear Manager app.

Your Galaxy Note 3 May Already Have the Gear Manager App

If the Gear Manager app is already installed on your Galaxy Note 3, the Gear Manager app opens automatically. Skip to step 6.

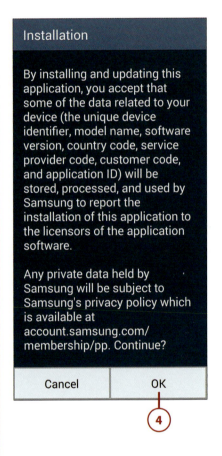

Installation

By installing and updating this application, you accept that some of the data related to your device (the unique device identifier, model name, software version, country code, service provider code, customer code, and application ID) will be stored, processed, and used by Samsung to report the installation of this application to the licensors of the application software.

Any private data held by Samsung will be subject to Samsung's privacy policy which is available at account.samsung.com/membership/pp. Continue?

Cancel   OK

5. Touch Install. Your Galaxy Note 3 installs the Gear Manager app and then launches it.

6. Gear Manager tries to connect to the Galaxy Gear automatically. If it succeeds, go to step 9. If not, touch Connect Manually and continue with the following steps to establish the connection manually.

7. Touch OK in the Notice dialog that opens. The Connect to Gear screen then appears.

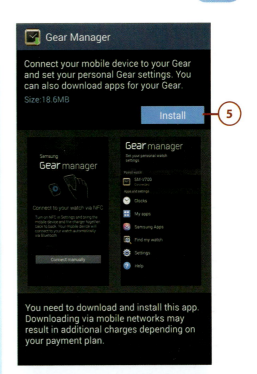

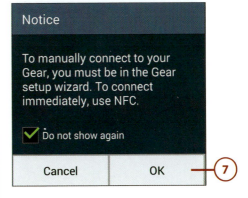

8. Touch the Galaxy Gear in the Available Devices list. Your Galaxy Note 3 connects to the Galaxy Gear. The End User License Agreement screen appears.

9. Touch to select the check boxes if you want to proceed.

10. Touch Yes or No Thanks to control whether Gear Manager shares its error logs with Samsung.

11. Touch Finish. The Information Provision Agreement screen appears, warning you that Voice Memo uses voice-recognition services that involve your voice information being stored on a server in the United States.

12. Touch Agree if you want to use Voice Memo (not shown). The Gear Manager screen then appears, and you can configure the Galaxy Gear as explained in the next section.

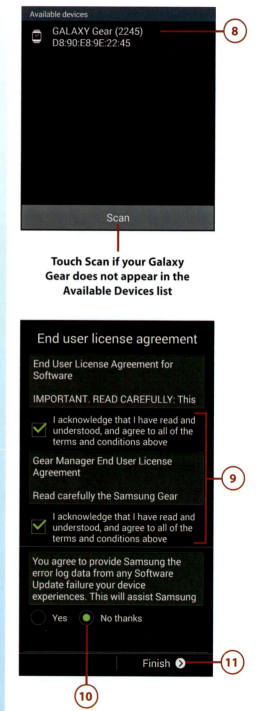

Touch Scan if your Galaxy Gear does not appear in the Available Devices list

Choosing Settings for Your Galaxy Gear

After pairing your Galaxy Gear with your Galaxy Note 3, you'll probably want to spend some time customizing the Galaxy Gear. You can use the Gear Manager app on your Galaxy Note 3 to configure overall settings for the Galaxy Gear, as explained in this section. To configure other settings, such as the display color and the ringtones, you use the Settings app on the Galaxy Gear itself, as discussed in the following section.

Choose Settings in the Gear Manager App

The Gear Manager app gives you access to features and settings for configuring and managing your Galaxy Gear. From the Gear Manager screen, you can control pairing, set clocks, install apps, locate your Galaxy Gear when it goes missing, and choose settings for everything from automatic locking to emergency notifications.

Control Paired Gear Settings

The Paired Gear screen lets you control which Galaxy Gear is paired with your Galaxy Note 3. You can connect and disconnect the Galaxy Gear, connect a new Galaxy Gear, and check for software updates.

1. On the Gear Manager screen, touch the Galaxy Gear listed in the Paired Gear category. This button shows the name currently assigned to the Galaxy Gear. The Paired Gear screen appears.

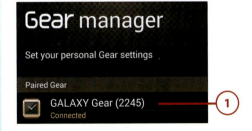

2. Touch Rename if you want to rename your Galaxy Gear. Type the new name in the Device Name dialog, and then touch OK. For example, you might name your Galaxy Gear "Jane's Gear" or a similar descriptive name.

3. Touch Disconnect if you want to disconnect the Galaxy Gear that's currently connected, and then touch Disconnect in the Disconnect dialog that opens. The message "Bluetooth disconnected" appears briefly on the Galaxy Gear's screen. Touch the resulting Connect button to connect to the paired Galaxy Gear. The message "Bluetooth connected" appears briefly on the Galaxy Gear's screen.

4. Touch Connect New Gear if you want to connect to another Galaxy Gear. The Connect to Gear screen appears, and you can pick up from step 8 in the list in the previous section.

5. Touch Software Update if you want to check for software updates or change the settings for software updates. The Software Update screen appears.

6. Touch Update to check for updates now.

7. Touch to enable or disable checking for updates automatically.

8. Touch to enable or disable restricting the downloading of updates to Wi-Fi. Unless you have a generous data allowance, restricting downloads to Wi-Fi is wise.

9. Touch to return to the Paired Gear screen.

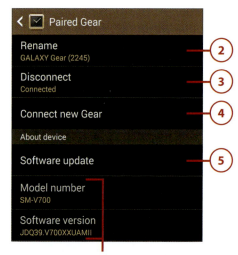

You may need to know the model number and software version for troubleshooting.

Choose Clocks Settings

By using the Clocks screen in Gear Manager, you can choose which of various preset clocks your Galaxy Gear displays on screen. You can customize the clocks to contain the items you find most useful.

1. On the Gear Manager screen, touch Clocks to display the Clocks screen.

2. Touch the clock you want to use: Analog Clock 1, Analog Clock 2, Analog Clock 3, Digital Clock, Dual Clock (a digital clock with two time zones), Event Clock (a digital clock that shows your next calendar event), Pedometer Clock (a digital clock that shows the current count of steps), Shortcut Clock (a digital clock that shows three shortcuts), or Weather Clock (a digital clock that shows the current weather summary). The clock you touch moves to the Idle section at the top of the list.

3. Touch the Settings icon to display the configuration screen for the clock. The options on this screen vary depending on the clock. For example, the three analog clocks have a single option, letting you choose only whether to show the date, whereas the Shortcut Clock has a handful of options.

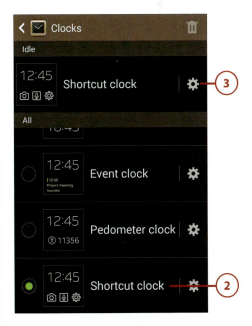

4. Use the controls to set options for the clock. For example, touch Show Date to enable or disable the display of the date.

5. Touch to return to the Clocks screen.

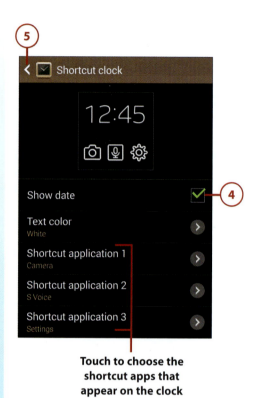

Touch to choose the shortcut apps that appear on the clock

Set Up the My Apps Feature

To control which third-party apps the Galaxy Gear contains, you use the My Apps feature in Gear Manager. You can also install Samsung apps, as described later in this chapter.

1. In Gear Manager, touch My Apps to display the My Apps screen.

Understanding the Three Tabs of the My Apps Screen

The My Apps screen has three tabs. The Favorites tab enables you to choose whether to display the Logs app and the Contacts app and change the order of the apps listed in the All Favorites list. The Installed Apps tab lists all the apps installed on the Galaxy Gear and lets you configure some apps and remove apps you no longer want. The Featured tab presents a list of other apps you may want to install so as to get more out of your Galaxy Gear.

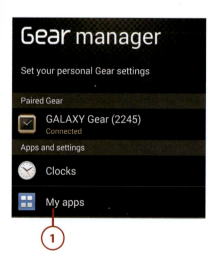

2. Touch Favorites to display the Favorites tab.

3. Touch the Logs check box to enable or disable the display of Logs.

4. Touch the Contacts check box to enable or disable the display of Contacts.

5. Touch a Settings button to display the Settings screen for an app.

6. Choose settings for the app. The settings available vary depending on what the app is and what it does. For example, for the S Voice app, you can enable or disable the Voice Control feature for incoming calls and for the Camera app.

7. Touch the button in the upper-left corner to return to the Favorites tab.

>>>Go Further

ADDING, REORDERING, AND REMOVING FAVORITE APPS

From the Favorites tab of the My Apps screen, you can also add apps, remove apps, and change the order of the apps on the list.

Touch to add an app

Touch to change the order of the apps

Touch to remove an app

To add an app, touch the Add (+) button, touch the check box for the appropriate app on the Add screen, and then touch Done.

Touch Done

Touch the check box to add an app

To change the order of apps, touch Reorder, then drag apps up or down the Reorder screen. Touch Done when you finish.

Touch Done

Drag apps up or down as needed

To remove an app, touch Remove, touch the check box for the appropriate app on the Remove screen, and then touch Done.

— **Touch Done**

— **Touch the check box to remove an app**

8. Touch Installed Apps to display the Installed Apps tab.

9. Touch the Settings button for the app you want to configure. You can then choose settings for the app as discussed in step 6.

10. Touch Featured to display the Featured tab.

11. Touch an app you want to install, and then follow the instructions for installing it.

Install Samsung Apps on the Galaxy Gear

To get more out of your Galaxy Gear, you can install Samsung Apps on it by using Gear Manager. Samsung Apps are apps provided by Samsung rather than third-party developers.

You Need a Samsung Account to Use Samsung Apps

To download and install Samsung Apps, you must create a Samsung account. You can set up the free account while you're browsing for Samsung Apps. In addition to enabling you to get Samsung Apps, a Samsung account gives you access to a range of services including ChatON Global Messenger, Samsung Music, Samsung Books, and Samsung Learning.

1. In Gear Manager, touch Samsung Apps. The Select Category screen appears.

2. Touch the category of apps you want to see.

3. Touch an app to see its details.

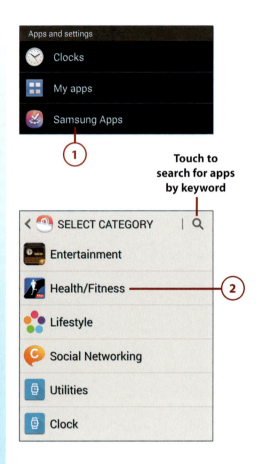

Touch to search for apps by keyword

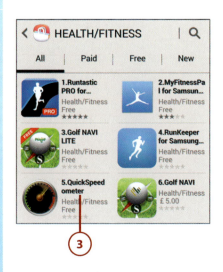

4. Touch the Free button or the price button to get the app.

Keeping Your Samsung Apps Up to Date

If, when you touch Samsung Apps in Gear Manager, the Update screen appears, you should apply the updates before you work with the Samsung apps. Touch the Update button and wait while your Galaxy Note 3 downloads and installs the latest versions of the Samsung apps. The Samsung Apps screen then appears, and you can work with the apps.

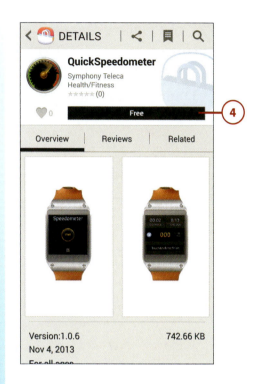

**Touch
Update**

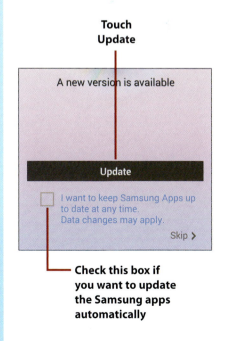

**Check this box if
you want to update
the Samsung apps
automatically**

Locate Your Galaxy Gear If You Misplace It

If you misplace your Galaxy Gear, you can use the Find My Gear feature in Gear Manager to locate it.

1. In Gear Manager, touch Find My Gear to display the Find My Gear screen.

2. Touch Start to play a sound on the Galaxy Gear and turn its screen on if it is off. You can now locate the Galaxy Gear by tracking the sound or (if it is dark) looking for the glow of the screen.

3. Touch Stop to stop playing the sound.

Configure Settings for the Galaxy Gear

To make your Galaxy Gear work your way, you can configure a variety of settings on it. These settings include configuring the Galaxy Gear to automatically unlock your Galaxy Note 3, controlling which notifications you receive on the Galaxy Gear, and turning on or off the gesture used to wake the Galaxy Gear.

1. On the Gear Manager screen, touch Settings to display the Settings screen.

2. Set the Auto Lock switch to On if you want to use your Galaxy Gear to unlock your Galaxy Note 3. This capability is often helpful. When you set the switch to On, the Auto-Lock screen appears automatically; if the switch is already set to On, you can display the Auto-Lock screen by touching anywhere on the Auto Lock button except the switch.

3. Read the information about auto-lock: When your Galaxy Note 3 can't detect the Galaxy Gear, the Galaxy Note 3 uses pattern lock. When your Galaxy Note 3 can detect the Galaxy Gear, the phone uses swipe lock.

4. Touch Continue. The screen called Draw Pattern to Unlock Screen appears.

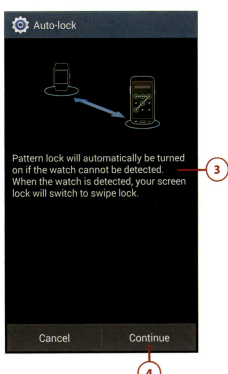

5. Draw the pattern you will use for unlocking.

6. Touch Continue. The Draw Pattern Again to Confirm screen appears.

7. Draw the pattern again.

8. Touch Confirm. Your Galaxy Note 3 stores the pattern, and the Settings screen appears again.

9. Make sure the Notification switch is set to On if you want to receive notifications on your Galaxy Gear.

10. Touch the Notification button (anywhere but the Notification switch) to display the Notification screen.

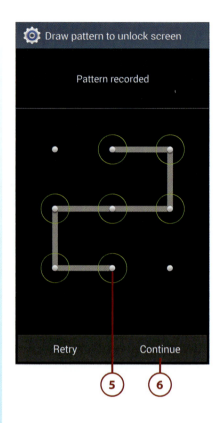

11. Touch to enable or disable alarms for each app in the list.

12. Touch to return to the Settings screen.

13. Touch Double Pressing Power Key if you want to change the action the Galaxy Gear takes when you press the power button twice in quick succession. The default action is S Voice. In the Double Pressing Power Key dialog that opens, you can choose other actions, including Camera, Contacts, Dialer, Find My Device, Pedometer, Stopwatch, Timer, and Voice Memo.

14. Touch Safety Assistance to display the Safety Assistance screen.

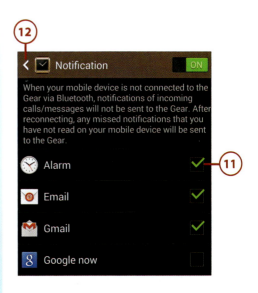

Understanding the Safety Assistance Features

Your Galaxy Gear includes a Safety Assistance feature designed to help you summon assistance when an emergency strikes. You set up Safety Assistance ahead of time by turning the feature on, creating an emergency message and choosing how often to send it, and specifying emergency contacts who will receive the message. Then, in an emergency, you press the Galaxy Gear's power button three times. The Galaxy Gear takes a photo of whatever is in front of the lens and sends it with your emergency message and your GPS location to the emergency contacts.

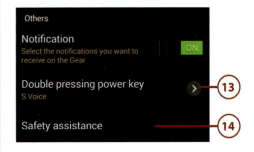

15. Set the Safety Assistance switch to On. Another Safety Assistance screen appears, showing a detailed explanation and disclaimers. Touch each check box to select it, and then touch OK to agree to the conditions. The previous Safety Assistance screen appears again.

16. Touch Edit Emergency Message to display the Edit Emergency Message screen, type your emergency message, and then touch Save.

17. Touch Message Interval to display the Message Interval dialog, and then touch Once, Every 10 Minutes, or Every 20 Minutes, as needed. Sending multiple emergency messages may run up data charges, but if you are genuinely in trouble, it will be worth the extra expense.

18. Touch Emergency Contacts to display the Emergency Contacts screen. Here, you can set up your Emergency Contacts group by tapping Add Contact and then selecting the check box for each contact you want to add.

19. Touch to return to the Settings screen.

20. Set the Smart Relay switch to On if you want to be able to view content from your Galaxy Gear on your Galaxy Note 3 by picking up the Galaxy Note 3 when you receive a notification.

Turn On Motions to Make Smart Relay Work

For the Smart Relay function to work, you must set the Motions switch in the Settings app to On. Touch Settings on the Apps screen to open the Settings app, touch Controls to display the Controls screen, and then set the Motions switch to On.

21. Set the Wake-Up Gesture switch to On if you want to be able to wake up the Galaxy Gear by raising the wrist that's wearing the watch. This feature is usually helpful, but it uses a bit more battery power because the Galaxy Gear has to keep monitoring the accelerometer. You might find you need to make an exaggerated movement to trigger the wake-up gesture.

22. Touch to return to the Gear Manager screen.

Choose Settings in the Settings App on the Galaxy Gear

The Galaxy Gear has its own Settings app that enables you to configure the way the Gear runs and behaves.

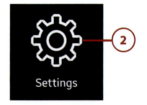

If the Settings icon appears on the Home screen, touch it

Open the Settings App

1. From the Galaxy Gear's Home screen, swipe left or right until the Settings icon appears.

2. Touch the Settings icon to open the Settings app.

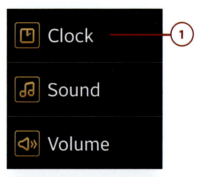

Settings

Choose Clock Settings

1. Touch Clock to display the Clock screen.

2. Touch Clock Type to set the clock type. You can then swipe left or right to cycle through the clock types discussed earlier in this chapter. When you reach the clock you want, swipe down to go back to the Clock screen.

3. Touch Date and Time to display the Date and Time screen.

4. Touch Auto Sync to enable or disable syncing the date and time with your Galaxy Note 3. Enabling Auto Sync on your Galaxy Gear and having your Galaxy Note 3 sync with an Internet time server is usually the best way to have your Galaxy Gear set to the right time.

5. Touch Set Date if Auto Sync is disabled, and you need to set the date.

6. Touch Set Time if Auto Sync is disabled, and you need to set the time.

7. Swipe down to go back to the Clocks screen.

8. Touch Hourly Alert to enable or disable the hourly alert.

9. Swipe down to go back to the main Settings screen.

Choose Sound Settings

1. Touch Sound to display the Sound screen.

2. Touch Sound Mode to choose among the three sound modes: Sound, Vibrate, or Mute.

3. Touch the Touch Sounds button to enable or disable playing a sound when you touch the screen.

4. Touch Ringtones to display the Ringtones screen.

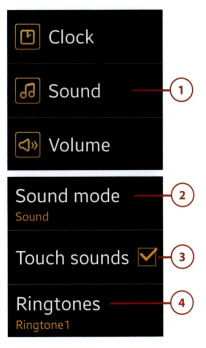

5. Touch the ringtone you want to hear. The Galaxy Gear plays the ringtone.

6. Touch OK to return to the Sound screen.

7. Swipe up to display the next group of Sound settings.

8. Touch Notifications to choose the notification sound to play.

9. Touch Vibration to set the vibration strength. Your choices are Strong, Medium, or Weak.

10. Touch Preferred Arm to set your preferred arm. This setting controls which microphone the Galaxy Gear uses—the right microphone if you choose Left Arm or the left microphone if you choose Right Arm. Left Arm is the default.

11. Swipe down to return to the main Settings screen.

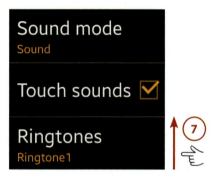

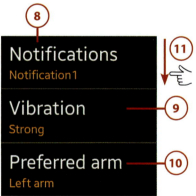

Choose Volume Settings

1. Touch Volume to display the Volume screen.

2. Touch Multimedia to display the Multimedia screen.

3. Touch + to increase the volume or – to decrease it.

4. Touch OK to return to the Multimedia screen.

5. Touch Ringtones to set the volume for ringtones.

6. Touch Notifications to set the volume for notifications.

7. Touch System to set the volume for system sounds.

8. Swipe down to return to the main Settings screen.

Choose Display Settings

1. Touch Display to show the Display screen.

2. Touch Brightness to set the screen brightness.

3. Touch Screen Timeout to set the period of inactivity before the screen goes off. Your choices are 30 seconds, 1 Minute, or 5 Minutes. Keeping the screen on for longer can be useful, but it goes through the battery power faster.

4. Touch Home BG Color to set the color of the background for the Galaxy Gear. Swipe left or right through the color options, and then swipe down to keep the current one.

5. Swipe down to reach the other Display options.

6. Touch Font Size to choose the font size for the display. Your choices are Small, Normal (the default), or Large.

7. Touch Battery Percentage to enable or disable the display of the battery percentage on the Home screen. Seeing the battery percentage can help you track power consumption—but the readout takes up valuable screen real estate.

8. Swipe down to return to the main Settings screen.

Viewing the Battery Status

If you don't display the battery percentage on the Home screen, you can view the battery's status by touching Battery on the Settings screen. Swipe down to return to the main Settings screen.

View the battery's exact charging status by touching Battery on the Settings screen

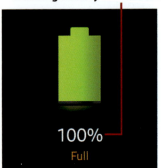

Control Bluetooth and Visibility

Your Galaxy Gear communicates with your Galaxy Note 3 via Bluetooth, so normally you'll want to keep Bluetooth enabled to keep both devices happy. But if you separate them, you can disable Bluetooth on the Galaxy Gear to conserve battery power. You can also control whether the Galaxy Gear is visible via Bluetooth. Normally, you would do this only when the Galaxy Gear isn't able to communicate with the Galaxy Note 3.

1. Touch Bluetooth to display the Bluetooth screen.

2. Touch Bluetooth to enable or disable Bluetooth.

3. If Visibility is available, touch to enable visibility. Visibility is only available when your Galaxy Gear is disconnected from your Galaxy Note 3.

4. Swipe down to return to the main Settings screen.

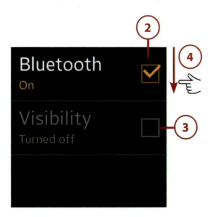

Set a Privacy Lock

To prevent anyone else using your Galaxy Gear, you can set a privacy lock pattern.

1. Touch Privacy Lock to display the Privacy Lock screen.

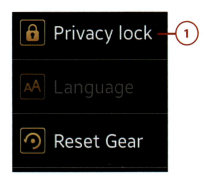

2. Touch Privacy Lock to display the next screen.

3. Touch Pattern.

4. Draw your pattern on the screen.

5. Touch Next.

6. Repeat the pattern on the screen that appears. The Privacy Lock screen then reappears, including the See Pattern check box.

7. Swipe down to return to the main Settings screen.

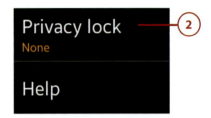

Privacy lock ②
None

Help

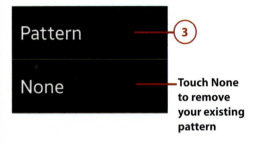

Pattern ③

None ——— **Touch None to remove your existing pattern**

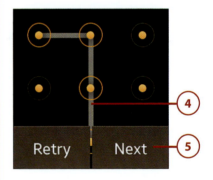

Retry | Next ——— ⑤
④

Privacy lock ⑦
Pattern

See pattern ☑ —— **Touch to enable the display of the pattern as you draw it**

Help

Reset Your Galaxy Gear

If your Galaxy Gear stops respond-ing to your Galaxy Note 3, you might need to reset it. Before resetting the Galaxy Gear, make sure that Bluetooth is enabled, as discussed a little earlier in this chapter.

1. Touch Reset Gear on the main Settings screen.

2. Touch Reset to reset the Galaxy Gear.

3. After the Galaxy Gear restarts, fol-low the instructions onscreen for connecting it to your Galaxy Note 3 again.

Navigating the Galaxy Gear's Interface

You can control your Galaxy Gear by using either gestures or the S Voice app. Normally, you will want to use a combination of gestures and S Voice to control the Galaxy Gear, depending on what exactly you're doing and where you're doing it.

Controlling the Galaxy Gear Using Gestures

If you followed through the previous section, you've already learned the main gestures for navigating the Galaxy Gear's interface—but here's a quick recap:

• Raise your wrist (or your arm) or press the Power button to wake the Galaxy Gear.

• Touch to select an option.

• Swipe left or right to navigate through options.

- Scroll up or down to reveal other options that don't fit on the screen.

- Swipe down from the top of the screen to go up one menu level in the user interface.

Armed with this knowledge, you can quickly navigate through the interface. For example, here's how to go to the Apps screen and launch the Stopwatch app.

1. From the Home screen, swipe several times to display the Apps icon. The Galaxy Gear cycles through the icons, so you can swipe either way to go around the circle.

2. Touch Apps to display the Apps screen.

3. If necessary, swipe left or right one or more times until the screen with the Stopwatch icon appears.

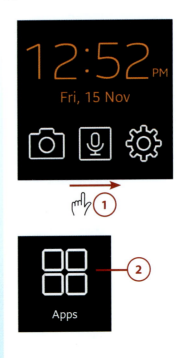

4. Touch Stopwatch to open the Stopwatch app.

5. Use the Stopwatch app.

6. Swipe down the screen to return to the Apps screen.

7. Swipe left or right until the Home screen appears.

Controlling the Galaxy Gear Using S Voice

Instead of navigating by touch, you can control your Galaxy Gear using the S Voice app. This is especially useful when you are in a situation where you cannot use the touchscreen reliably.

1. From the Home screen, swipe left twice to display the S Voice icon.

2. Touch S Voice to display the S Voice screen.

3. When the microphone icon shows a blue circle around it and a beep sounds, give your command. For example, say "Call Chris Smith" to place a phone call or say "Open Camera" to open the Camera app.

Speak your command when the blue circle appears

Using the Galaxy Gear's Apps

Now that you have configured your Galaxy Gear and learned how to navigate its interface, you will find its apps easy to use. You can launch an app in any of these ways:

- Touch its icon on the Home screen (if it appears there).

- Swipe left or right from the Home screen until the app's icon appears, and then touch the icon. If the app is on the Apps screen, swipe until the Apps icon appears, touch the Apps icon, and then touch the app's icon.

- Tell S Voice to open the app by saying "Open" and the app's name.

Make and Receive Phone Calls

You can make phone calls easily using your Galaxy Gear to control your Galaxy Note 3. And you can receive incoming calls even more easily.

Make Phone Calls

To make phone calls with the Galaxy Gear, choose the contact from the Contacts app and pick the correct number.

1. Swipe right from the Home screen to display the Contacts icon.

2. Touch Contacts to display the Contacts screen.

3. Touch the contact you want to call.

4. Touch the number to use. The Galaxy Gear makes the call via your Galaxy Note 3.

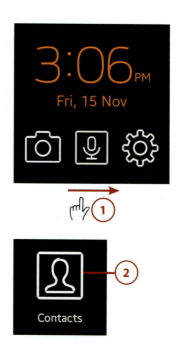

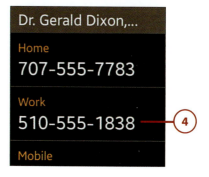

Dial Quickly with the Dialer

If you need to simply dial a call, swipe up from the Home screen to display the Dialer screen. You can then dial the number and touch the green Call icon to place the call.

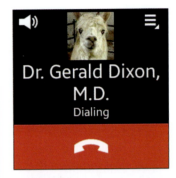

Dial the number

Touch to place the call

Receive a Phone Call

When someone calls you, the Galaxy Gear displays details of the call. Touch the button to accept the call or reject it.

Accept the call

Reject the call

Take Photos and Videos

The Galaxy Gear's Camera app is great for capturing quick shots of what's happening without having to take out your Galaxy Note 3. It can also be useful for taking photos discreetly. For technical reasons, we can't show you screens of the Camera app, but you'll find it straightforward enough to use.

1. Open the Camera app by tapping its icon.

2. Tap the icon in the upper-left corner of the screen to switch between still photos (a camera icon appears) and taking videos of up to 15 seconds (a camcorder icon appears).

3. Aim the lens on the wrist strap at your subject. What the lens is seeing appears on the screen.

4. Touch the screen to take a photo or start the video recording (depending on which camera you've selected).

5. Touch the screen again to stop the video recording. Alternatively, let the recording run to its maximum 15 seconds, at which point the Galaxy Gear stops recording automatically.

CHOOSE SETTINGS FOR THE CAMERA APP

To choose settings for the Camera app, open the app and then touch the icon in the upper-right corner. The Options screen appears for the camera you're using.

These are the options for the still camera:

- **Focus mode.** Touch this button to choose between Auto and Macro. Use Macro for ultra-close shots. Use Auto for everything else.

- **Photo size.** Touch this button to choose between the square 1392×1392-pixel size and the 4:3-aspect ratio 1280×960-pixel size. All other things being equal, use the square size because it's higher resolution; you can crop your photos later.

- **Sound & Shot.** Touch this button to choose whether to record up to 9 seconds of audio after you take the photo.

- **Signature.** Touch this button to choose whether to add the Galaxy Gear's signature (text saying GALAXY Gear) to the lower-right corner of each photo you take.

The video camera has only one option, Video Size. Touch this to choose between 1280×720-pixel resolution (a 16:9 aspect ratio) and 640×640-pixel resolution (1:1). For most purposes, the higher resolution is the better choice.

See your battery
usage trends

In this chapter, you discover how to maintain your Galaxy Note 3 and solve problems. Topics include the following:

→ Updating Android
→ Optimizing battery life
→ Identifying battery-hungry apps
→ Caring for your Galaxy Note 3

Maintaining Your Galaxy Note 3 and Solving Problems

Every so often, Google releases new versions of Android that include bug fixes and new features. In this chapter, you find out how to upgrade your Galaxy Note 3 to a new version of Android and how to tackle common problem-solving issues and general maintenance of your Galaxy Note 3.

Updating Android

New releases of Android are always exciting because they add new features, fix bugs, and tweak the user interface. Here is how to update your Galaxy Note 3.

Updating Information

Updates to Android are not on a set schedule. The update messages appear as you turn on your Galaxy Note 3, and they remain in the Notification bar until you install the update. If you touch Install Later, your Note 3 reminds you at short intervals—30 minutes, 1 hour, or 3 hours—that there's an update. When to install the update is up to you. You might prefer to wait to see if each new update contains any bugs that need to be worked out rather than applying each update immediately.

1. Pull down the Notification bar to open the Notification shade.

Manually Checking for Updates

If you think there should be an update for your Galaxy Note 3 but have not yet received the onscreen notification, you can check manually by touching Settings, General, About Device, and Software Update. On the Software Update screen, touch Update to check for an update.

2. Touch Software Update to display the Software Update screen.

Touch to check manually for an update.

3. Touch Install.

4. Touch OK in the next Software Update dialog, which tells you that the device will be rebooted. Your Galaxy Note 3 restarts, installs the update, and then displays the Lock screen.

5. Unlock the Galaxy Note 3 as usual. For example, swipe the screen and then type your passcode. A Software Update dialog opens, confirming that the device has been updated successfully.

6. Touch OK to close the dialog. You can then resume using your Galaxy Note 3 normally.

Delaying an Update

If you do not want to install the software update immediately, touch Later on the Software Update screen. In the Reminder Interval dialog that appears, touch 30 Minutes, 1 Hour, or 3 Hours, as appropriate.

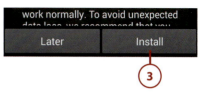

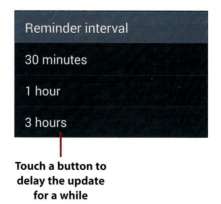

Touch a button to delay the update for a while

Optimizing the Battery

The battery in your Galaxy Note 3 is a lithium-ion battery that provides good battery life as long as you take care of it. You can change the way you use your Galaxy Note 3 to prolong the battery life so that the battery lasts long enough for you to use the phone all day.

Carrying a Spare Battery

One of the great things about the Galaxy Note 3 is how easily you can remove the back and change the battery. Given this feature, you might prefer to buy and carry a spare battery instead of scrimping on display brightness and phone usage. When your current battery runs out, you can power off the Note 3, pop in the spare battery, and restart it in less than a minute.

Take Care of the Battery

There are specific steps you can take to take care of the battery in your Galaxy Note 3 and make it last longer.

Follow these steps to care for your Galaxy Note 3's battery:

1. Try to avoid discharging the battery completely. Fully discharging the battery too frequently harms the battery. Instead, try to keep it at least partially charged at all times (except as described in the next step).

2. To avoid a false battery level indication on your Galaxy Note 3, let the battery fully discharge about every 30 charges. Lithium-ion batteries do not have "memory" like older battery technologies, but fully discharging the battery once in a while helps keep the battery meter working correctly.

3. Avoid letting your Galaxy Note 3 get overheated because this can damage the battery and make it lose charge quickly. Do not leave your Note 3 in a hot car or out in the sun anywhere, including on the beach.

4. Consider having multiple chargers. For example, you could have one at home, one at work, and one in your car. This enables you to always keep your phone charged.

Monitor Battery Use

Android enables you to see exactly what apps and system processes are using the battery on your Galaxy Note 3. Armed with this information, you can alter your usage patterns to extend the Galaxy Note 3's runtime on the battery.

1. On the Apps screen, touch Settings.

2. Touch the General tab.

3. Touch Battery to display the Battery screen.

4. Touch to manually refresh the display.

5. Touch an app or Android service to see more details about it, including how much time it has been active, how much processor (CPU) time it has used, and—if the app has used data—how much data it has sent and received.

6. Touch the battery charge and usage diagram to display the History Details screen, which contains more details on the power consumption.

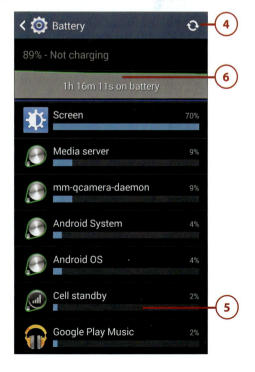

7. Look at the Mobile Network Signal readout to see when the mobile network signal was being used during the battery graph's time span.

8. Look at the GPS On readout to determine when the GPS radio was being used during the battery graph's time span.

9. Look at the Wi-Fi readout to see when the Wi-Fi radio was being used during the battery graph's time span.

10. Look at the Awake readout to learn when your Galaxy Note 3 was awake during the battery graph's time span.

11. Look at the Screen On readout to check when your Galaxy Note 3's screen was on during the battery graph's time span.

12. Look at the Charging readout to find out when your Galaxy Note 3 was charging (if at all) during the battery graph's time span.

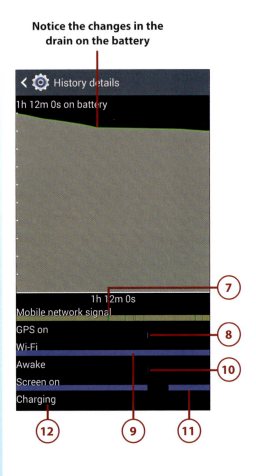

Notice the changes in the drain on the battery

How Can Seeing Battery Drain Help?

If you look at the way your battery has been draining, you can see when the battery was draining the fastest, and you should be able to remember what apps you were using at that time or what you were doing on your Galaxy Note 3. Based on that, you can change your usage habits—for example, you can plan to charge your Galaxy Note 3 after a session of phone calls. You can uninstall any apps that appear to be power hogs, or you can simply avoid using them when running on the battery.

Choose Power-Saving Options

Your Galaxy Note 3 includes a feature called Power Saving Mode that enables you to reduce the amount of power it consumes. After choosing which of three power-saving options to use, you can turn Power Saving on and off by using its switch on the Settings screen.

1. Touch Settings on the Apps screen.

2. Touch the General tab.

3. Touch the main part of the Power Saving button—anywhere apart from the switch—to display the Power Saving Mode screen.

4. Move the Power Saving Mode switch to On to make the settings available.

5. Check CPU Power Saving to enable throttling back the processor when the Galaxy Note 3 is running on battery power.

6. Check Screen Power Saving to enable reducing the screen's brightness on the battery.

7. Check Turn Off Haptic Feedback to enable turning off vibration when you touch the screen.

8. Touch Learn About Power Saving to see tips on saving power.

9. Touch to return to the Settings screen, where you can turn Power Saving Mode on and off by moving the Power Saving Mode switch. This switch has the same effect as the switch on the Power Saving Mode screen; it is simply easier to access.

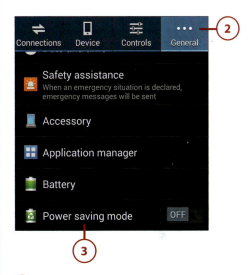

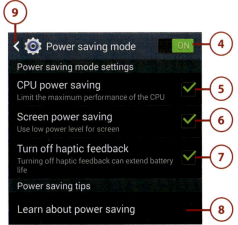

Turning Power Saving Mode On and Off Quickly

When you need to squeeze the most runtime out of your Galaxy Note 3's battery, you'll probably want to turn Power Saving Mode on and off at a moment's notice. To do so, pull down from the top of the screen to display the Notifications panel, touch the Quick Settings button, and then touch the Power Saving icon.

Touch the Power Saving icon to turn Power Saving Mode on or off

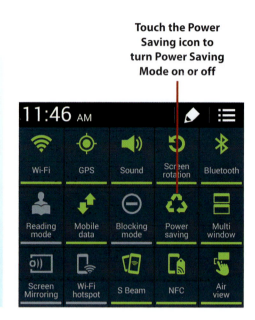

Apps and Memory

Each app you run on your Galaxy Note 3 has to share the phone's memory. Although Android usually does a good job of managing this memory, sometimes you have to step in to close an app that has grown too large.

1. On the Apps screen, touch Settings to open the Settings app.

2. Touch the General tab.

3. Touch Application Manager to display the Application Manager screen.

4. Swipe left one or more times as needed to display the Running tab. This tab lists the apps that are currently running.

5. The graph shows how much memory is being used by running apps and cached processes, and how much is free.

6. Touch an app to see more information about it.

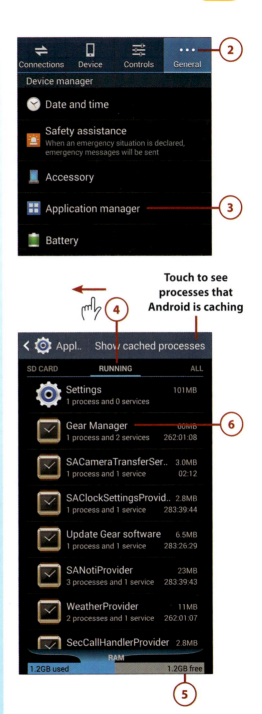

Touch to see processes that Android is caching

7. Touch Stop if you believe the app is misbehaving.

8. Touch to report an app to Google. You might want to do this if it is misbehaving, using up too many resources, or you suspect it of stealing data. Some apps disable the Report button to prevent reporting, as in the example.

9. Look at this readout to see the processes that are being used by this app.

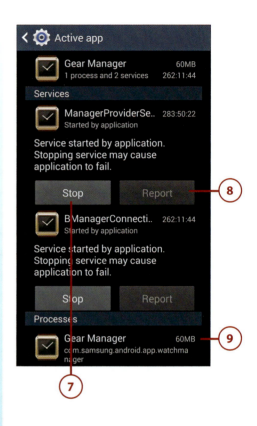

When Should You Manually Stop an App?

After you have been using your Galaxy Note 3 for a while, you'll become familiar with how long it takes to do certain tasks, such as typing, navigating menus, and so on. If you notice your phone becoming slow or not behaving the way you think it should, the culprit could be a new app you recently installed. Because Android never quits an app on its own, that new app continues running in the background, which might cause your Galaxy Note 3 to slow down. When this happens, it is useful to manually stop an app. If stopping one or more apps doesn't help, try restarting your Galaxy Note 3.

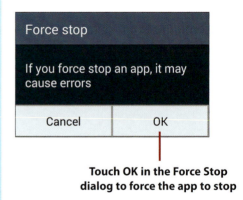

Touch OK in the Force Stop dialog to force the app to stop

Reining in Your Data Usage

If you are worried that you might exceed your data plan in a month, you can set a usage limit on your Galaxy Note 3. You can even prevent apps from using data while they are running in the background rather than in the foreground.

1. On the Apps screen, touch Settings to open the Settings app.

2. Touch Connections to display the Connections screen.

3. Touch Data Usage to display the Data Usage screen.

4. Make sure Mobile Data is checked to enable data transfer over your Galaxy Note 3's cellular connection.

5. Touch to enable or disable mobile data limits. When this is enabled, your Galaxy Note 3 automatically cuts off all mobile data usage when the limit you set in step 7 is reached.

6. Touch to set the monthly billing cycle your cellular carrier uses for your Galaxy Note 3's account.

7. Touch the red handle and drag the red line up or down to select the mobile data limit you want to impose. This might or might not match your cellular data plan limit.

8. Touch the orange handle and drag the orange line up and down to set a data usage warning threshold. When you reach or pass this threshold, you see a warning in the Notification bar.

9. Scroll down if necessary, and touch an app to see more details about its data usage and to control how it uses data in the background.

Set Background Data Limits

When you touch an app to see its data usage, you can also limit its usage when it is in the background. An app is in the background when you have launched the app but you are not currently using it. An app in the background still takes up memory and might still be transferring data.

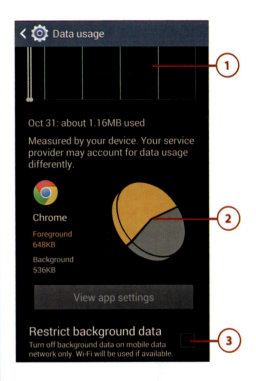

1. Look at the Data Usage chart to see the data usage for this app specifically.

2. Look at the pie chart to see the breakdown of data usage in the foreground and background.

3. Touch to restrict the app from using data while it is in the background.

Caring for the Galaxy Note 3's Exterior

Because you need to touch your Galaxy Note 3's screen to use it, it picks up oils and other residue from your hands. You also might get dirt on other parts of the phone. Here is how to clean your Galaxy Note 3 and how to avoid damaging its micro-USB port.

1. Wipe the screen with a microfiber cloth. You can purchase these in most electronic stores, or you can use the one that came with your sunglasses.

2. To clean dirt off other parts of your phone, wipe it with a damp cloth. Never use soap or chemicals on your Galaxy Note 3 as they can damage it.

3. When inserting the connector on the USB cable, try not to force it in the wrong way. If you damage the pins inside your Galaxy Note 3, you will need to take the battery out and use an external charger to charge it.

Protecting Your Galaxy Note 3's Exterior

Another way to care for your Galaxy Note 3's exterior is to protect it with a case. Many different types of cases are available from both brick-and-mortar stores and online stores. To protect the screen, you can apply a screen protector. When choosing a screen protector, make sure it is thin enough for the S Pen to work effectively.

Getting Help with Your Galaxy Note 3

There are many resources on the Internet where you can get help with your Galaxy Note 3.

1. Visit Samsung's official Galaxy Note 3 and Galaxy Gear site at http://www.samsung.com/global/microsite/galaxynote3-gear/.

2. Visit Google's official Android website at www.android.com.

3. Check out Android blogs such as these:

   - Android Central at www.androidcentral.com/

   - Android Guys at www.androidguys.com/

   - Androinica at http://androinica.com/

Index

N

O

My Samsung
Galaxy Note 3

Craig James Johnston
Guy Hart-Davis

que

FREE
Online Edition

Your purchase of **My Samsung Galaxy Note® 3** includes access to a free online edition for 45 days through the **Safari Books Online** subscription service. Nearly every Que book is available online through **Safari Books Online**, along with thousands of books and videos from publishers such as Addison-Wesley Professional, Cisco Press, Exam Cram, IBM Press, O'Reilly Media, Prentice Hall, Sams, and VMware Press.

Safari Books Online is a digital library providing searchable, on-demand access to thousands of technology, digital media, and professional development books and videos from leading publishers. With one monthly or yearly subscription price, you get unlimited access to learning tools and information on topics including mobile app and software development, tips and tricks on using your favorite gadgets, networking, project management, graphic design, and much more.

Activate your FREE Online Edition at
informit.com/safarifree

STEP 1:   Enter the coupon code: SPZBIWH.

STEP 2:   New Safari users, complete the brief registration form.
Safari subscribers, just log in.

If you have difficulty registering on Safari or accessing the online edition,
please e-mail customer-service@safaribooksonline.com